MAKING SENSE OF LITERACY SCHOLARSHIP

This book is a roadmap to the key decisions, processes, and procedures to use when synthesizing qualitative literacy research. Covering the major types of syntheses – including the dissertation literature review, traditional literature review, integrative literature review, meta-synthesis, and meta-ethnography – Compton-Lilly, Rogers, and Lewis Ellison offer techniques and frameworks to use when making sense of a large body of scholarship.

Addressing the standard and untraditional forms a research synthesis can take, the authors provide clear and practical examples of synthesis designs and techniques, and consider how epistemological, ontological, and ethical questions arise when designing and adapting a research synthesis. The extensive appendices feature sample literature reviews, guidance on communication with editors of journals, useful charts, and more.

The authors' critical reflection and analysis demonstrates how a research synthesis is not simply a means to an end, but rather reflects each scholar's interests, target audience, and message. This book is crucial reading for undergraduate and graduate students, as well as early career and more experienced researchers in literacy education.

Catherine Compton-Lilly is the John C. Hungerpiller Professor in the College of Education at the University of South Carolina, USA.

Rebecca Rogers is the E. Desmond Lee Endowed Professor in Tutorial Education and a Curators' Distinguished Research Professor in the College of Education at University of Missouri–St. Louis, USA.

Tisha Lewis Ellison is Associate Professor of Language and Literacy Education at University of Georgia, USA.

MAKING SENSE OF LITERACY SCHOLARSHIP

Approaches to Synthesizing Literacy Research

Catherine Compton-Lilly, Rebecca Rogers, and Tisha Lewis Ellison

NEW YORK AND LONDON

First published 2021
by Routledge
52 Vanderbilt Avenue, New York, NY 10017

and by Routledge
2 Park Square, Milton Park, Abingdon, Oxon, OX14 4RN

Routledge is an imprint of the Taylor & Francis Group, an informa business

© 2021 Catherine Compton-Lilly, Rebecca Rogers, and Tisha Lewis Ellison

The right of Catherine Compton-Lilly, Rebecca Rogers, and Tisha Lewis Ellison to be identified as authors of this work has been asserted by them in accordance with sections 77 and 78 of the Copyright, Designs and Patents Act 1988.

All rights reserved. No part of this book may be reprinted or reproduced or utilised in any form or by any electronic, mechanical, or other means, now known or hereafter invented, including photocopying and recording, or in any information storage or retrieval system, without permission in writing from the publishers.

Trademark notice: Product or corporate names may be trademarks or registered trademarks, and are used only for identification and explanation without intent to infringe.

Library of Congress Cataloging-in-Publication Data
Names: Compton-Lilly, Catherine, author. | Rogers, Rebecca (Rebecca L.), 1959- author. | Ellison, Tisha Lewis, author.
Title: Making sense of literacy scholarship : approaches to synthesizing literacy research / Catherine Compton-Lilly, Rebecca Rogers, Tisha Lewis Ellison.
Identifiers: LCCN 2021001543 (print) | LCCN 2021001544 (ebook) | ISBN 9780367645663 (hardback) | ISBN 9780367634001 (paperback) | ISBN 9781003125211 (ebook)
Subjects: LCSH: Literacy--Research--Methodology. | Language arts--Research--Methodology. | Qualitative research--Methodology.
Classification: LCC LC149 .C664 2021 (print) | LCC LC149 (ebook) | DDC 372.6--dc23
LC record available at https://lccn.loc.gov/2021001543
LC ebook record available at https://lccn.loc.gov/2021001544

ISBN: 978-0-367-64566-3 (hbk)
ISBN: 978-0-367-63400-1 (pbk)
ISBN: 978-1-003-12521-1 (ebk)

Typeset in Bembo

by SPi Global, India

We dedicate this book to the many children, youth, parents, and teachers who have given their time and knowledge as research participants in the primary studies we have reviewed. Your contributions help the field of education more deeply understand the complexities of literacy practices, in and out of schools. While many of you have pseudonyms in the studies we have reviewed, we want you to know that we see you and value your insights.

We also dedicate this book to our past, present, and future graduate students. We hope this book provides an intellectual foundation for designing research synthesis filled with intellectual risk-taking and a commitment to epistemological justice.

Personally, we each would like to thank people and communities who continue to support and inspire us.

Cathy Compton-Lilly sends love and appreciation to Carly and Todd, as well as her amazing team of colleagues at the University of South Carolina and the Friday afternoon Covid-19 painting group.

Rebecca Rogers dedicates this book to her loving family and especially, her daughter, Sofia Mancini and her niece, Olivia Spang. Their creative, collaborative energy is inspiring. She sends a special thank you to her parents, Thomas and Anolla Rogers, and her amazing partner Michael Mancini for the collective efforts to create space and time for writing this book during Covid-19.

Tisha Lewis Ellison dedicates this book to her parents, Thomas Lewis and (in loving memory of her mother) Lucille Upchurch Lewis, who were enduring sources of strength. They guided and impacted her spiritual, academic, and personal journeys, contributing to who she is today. Tisha also dedicates this work to the loving memory of her grandmother, Cherry Upchurch, whose conversations inspired her to study family literacy. Finally, she thanks her husband, Lee Ellison, for his love and support, and for being her accountability partner.

CONTENTS

Foreword	*ix*
Acknowledgements	*xii*
Authors	*xiii*

	Introduction: Reviewing Bodies of Literacy Scholarship: Practices, Possibilities, and Potentials	1
1	Surveying the Landscape of Published Qualitative Research Syntheses in Literacy Studies	15
2	Reflecting on and Redefining Approaches to Writing Dissertation Literature Reviews	51
3	Traditional Literature Reviews and Follow Up Reviews	75
4	Integrative Critical Literature Reviews	94
5	Meta-Ethnographies	121
6	A Metasynthesis of Scholarship by Black, Indigenous People of Color	144
7	Conclusions	176

viii Contents

Appendix A: Common Qualitative Research Synthesis Designs	*201*
Appendix B: Final Analytic Review Template for the Meta-Ethnography (ART)	*205*
Appendix C: Databases Used by University Scholars for Educational Research	*208*
Appendix D: Code Book from 2005 Literature Review	*227*
Appendix E: Code Book from 2016 Literature Review	*229*
Appendix F: Coding Chart for Spreadsheet	*232*
Appendix G: Sample Response Letter to Editors and Reviewers	*236*
Appendix H: Final Analytic Review Template for the Integrative Critical Review (ART)	*238*
Appendix I: Inter-Rater Reliability Check	*240*
Appendix J: Response Letter to Editors for Our Critical Integrative Literature Review	*243*
Appendix K: Response Letter to Editors for Our Meta-Ethnography	*246*
Appendix L: Analytic Review Template (ART) for our Metasynthesis of Family Literacy Scholarship Conducted by BIPOC Scholars	*251*
Appendix M: Descriptive Table for BIPOC – List #1	*257*
Index	*264*

FOREWORD

Since Gene Glass (1976) coined the term "meta-analysis," there has been a proliferation of articles and books by reputed publishers on methods of synthesizing quantitative research. These methods were so dominant in the last century that the term "research synthesis" was often used exclusively to refer to quantitative research synthesis. For instance, any mention of qualitative research synthesis methods was noticeably absent in the first edition of *The Handbook of Research Synthesis* (Cooper & Hedges, 1994). Likewise, the *American Educational Research Association's* (AERA's) publication, *Handbook of Complementary Methods in Education Research* (Green et al., 2012), included only two chapters related to research synthesis, both of which exclusively discussed quantitative research synthesis methods with no mention of qualitative research synthesis.

I deliberately use the term "research synthesis" with a methodologically inclusive connotation to contest the dominant discourse which privileges quantitative research over qualitative research in some circles. Since the late 1990s, there has been a rapid growth in publications that have problematized the impoverished conception of evidence-based education which excluded insights from qualitative research traditions (Suri & Clarke, 2009). Value of interpretive and critical syntheses of research is also explicitly recognized in the second edition of *The Handbook of Research Synthesis and meta-analysis* (Cooper, Hedges, & Valentine, 2009).

Despite Noblit and Hare's (1988) revolutionary publication on meta-ethnography, it was only in 1998 when educational research community seriously started engaging with interpretive and critical approaches to reviewing research. Within this context, I conceptualized the "Methodologically Inclusive Research Synthesis" (MIRS) framework to foster critically informed choices in production and use of research syntheses. The MIRS framework is "a coherent

x Foreword

conceptualization of research synthesis methods expressed through the identification of critical decisions and thorough discussion of varied options associated with each decision in the process of a rigorous research synthesis" (Suri, 2014, p. 4). It is a mindset, an attitude to research synthesis, rather than a prescriptive research synthesis method. *Towards Methodologically Inclusive Research Syntheses: Expanding Possibilities* (Suri, 2014) is my conception of the MIRS framework as a purposefully inclusive and reflexive approach to synthesizing research. I deliberately refrained from writing a "conclusion" chapter to emphasize that my conception of the MIRS framework was and would continue "to be situated, partial, temporal and tentative" (p. 163). Instead, my book ends with an *Epilogue* urging readers to use the MIRS framework as a departure point to "open spaces, raise questions, explore possibilities and contest taken-for-granted practices" (p. 164) in research syntheses. I encouraged research synthesists to review research in the same field for different, albeit equally worthwhile purposes, using epistemological and methodological choices that were consistent with the synthesis purpose.

In this book, *Making Sense of Literacy Scholarship: Approaches to Synthesizing Literacy Research*, Catherine Compton-Lilly, Rebecca Rogers, and Tisha Lewis Ellison exemplify this approach and make two significant contributions. First, this book is a useful and much needed practical resource for commencing as well as seasoned educational researchers on how to conduct five types of rigorous research reviews: dissertation literature reviews, traditional literature reviews and follow up reviews, critical integrative reviews, meta-ethnography, and meta-synthesis. The authors contribute to the praxis of synthesizing qualitative educational research by sharing a reflexive account of key learnings from their own individual and collaborative experiences spanning over 15 years. Second, the book is also a valuable resource for researchers with varying degrees of interest in literacy scholarship. The authors provide an insightful analysis of how literacy scholarship has evolved over a span of more than a century.

Informed by a review of research synthesis methods, publications from multiple disciplines, and methodological orientations, I have identified the following three guiding principles for quality research synthesis (Suri & Clarke, 2009):

    (i) Purposefully informed selective inclusivity

    (ii) Reflexivity and informed subjectivity

    (iii) Audience appropriate transparency.

This book is a practical illustration of how enactment of these guiding principles in five teleologically distinct reviews of literacy education involved different methodological choices related to what primary research was reviewed and how it was reviewed. The authors explicitly discuss how their individual and collective understandings of the field of literacy education informed these choices, which in turn, were also influencing the authors' positioning within the field of literacy education. This book has a broad reach and is a useful resource for novice as well as experienced educational researchers. The authors have shared the benefits as well as messiness inherent in synthesizing research with an open, rigorous, and reflexive approach. They provide useful practical guidelines for synthesizing research while maintaining a questioning gaze throughout the process. Particularly refreshing is an honest account of how the authors abandoned certain methodological choices based on their cost-benefit analysis of the associated resources required versus affordance for deepening understanding.

The authors are taking the field of qualitative research synthesis methods toward exciting new directions by sharing their reflexive accounts of methodological choices and processes they pursued, processes they aborted, and the detours they took in the process of carrying out five teleologically distinct research reviews in literacy education. They urge readers to move beyond the naïve assumption that a research synthesis can provide conclusive generalizations. They emphasize how insights gained through any review are inevitably situated, temporal, and partial. They remind us that attending to what is said in any study, and in any research synthesis, is as important as attending to what is not said. Reviewing research in any field remains, and should remain, an unfinished scholarly endeavor inviting deeper understandings.

Harsh Suri
Deakin University, Australia

References

Cooper, H. M., & Hedges, L. V. (1994). Research synthesis as a scientific enterprise. In H. M. Cooper & L. V. Hedges (Eds.), *The handbook of research synthesis* (pp. 3–14). New York: Sage.

Cooper, H. M., Hedges, L. V., & Valentine, J. C. (Eds.). (2009). *The handbook of research synthesis and meta-analysis* (2nd ed.). New York: Sage.

Glass, G. V. (1976). Primary, secondary, and meta-analysis of research. *Educational Researcher*, 5(10), 3–8.

Green, J. L., Camilli, G., & Elmore, P. B. (Eds.). (2012). *Handbook of complementary methods in education research*. Routledge.

Noblit, G. W., & Hare, R. D. (1988). *Meta-ethnography: Synthesizing qualitative studies*. Newbury Park: Sage.

Suri, H. (2014). *Towards methodologically inclusive research synthesis*. UK: Routledge.

Suri, H., & Clarke, D. J. (2009). Advancements in research synthesis methods: From a methodologically inclusive perspective. *Review of Educational Research*, 79(1), 395–430.

ACKNOWLEDGEMENTS

Research syntheses are always collective endeavors. We would like to thank and acknowledge colleagues and graduate research assistants who helped us with various aspects of this project including Dr. Peter Smagorinsky and Mrs. Tairan Qiu, both at the University of Georgia. We recognize the intellectual communities at each of our respective Universities – the University of South Carolina, the University of Missouri–St. Louis, and the University of Georgia – and appreciate the support, space, and time that were necessary to write this book. To the many anonymous reviewers, editors, and readers of our research syntheses, we owe a debt of gratitude for inspiring our collective research imagination. We would also like to thank Karen Adler for her support of this project, as well as Annette Woods and Barbara Comber for their insightful and helpful reviews of this volume. We particularly thank Dr. Harsh Suri for her intellectual contribution to our work and especially for being willing to write the Foreword to this volume.

AUTHORS

Catherine Compton-Lilly is the John C. Hungerpiller Professor at the University of South Carolina. As a professor in the College of Education, Dr. Compton-Lilly's research focuses on family literacy practices, particularly the literacy practices of children from communities that have been underserved by schools. In her initial work, she documented the home and school literacy practices of eight of her former first grade students as they moved from elementary school through high school. In an ongoing study, now in its twelfth year, she is exploring the family literacy practices of children from immigrant families. Dr. Compton-Lilly has edited or authored nine books and has authored multiple articles related to family literacy in major literacy journals including the *Reading Research Quarterly*, *Research in the Teaching of English*, *The Reading Teacher*, *Journal of Early Childhood Literacy*, *Written Communication*, and *Journal of Literacy Research and Language Arts*.

xiv Authors

Dr. Compton-Lilly's scholarly contribution is recognized in the most recent volume of the Garn Press' Great Women Scholars Series, *Time in Education: Intertwined Dimensions and Theoretical Possibilities* (Kabuto & Compton-Lilly, 2020).

Rebecca Rogers is the E. Desmond Lee Endowed Professor in Tutorial Education and a Curators' Distinguished Research Professor in the College of Education at the University of Missouri–St. Louis, USA. Her research specializes in literacy studies, teacher learning, and critical discourse studies. She is the author of seven books including the 2018 book "Reclaiming Powerful Literacies: New Horizons for Critical Discourse Analysis." Her publications have appeared in national and international journals such as *Reading Research Quarterly*, *Anthropology & Education Quarterly*, *Linguistics & Education*, *Journal of Literacy Research*, *Race, Ethnicity, and Education*, and *Urban Education*. Rebecca is the Past-President of the *Literacy Research Association* and a Fulbright Fellow. She is a publicly engaged scholar and former elected school board member, co-founder of *Educators for Social Justice*, and involved with parent organizing for racial justice.

Tisha Lewis Ellison is an associate professor in the Department of Language and Literacy Education at The University of Georgia. Her research explores the intersections of family literacy, multimodality, and digital and STEM literacy practices among Black and Latinx families and adolescents. Dr. Lewis Ellison has been the recipient of the Spencer Postdoctoral Fellowship from the National Academy of Education, the Early Career Achievement and J. Michael Parker awards from the Literacy Research Association, and the Promising Researcher Award from the National Council of Teachers of English. Her numerous grants, awards, and research studies are advancing the field of families' digital literacies and STEM literacies across lifespans, in homes and community settings, and in ways that inform parents, adolescents, and teachers. Her work has appeared in the selected peer-reviewed journals: *Reading Research Quarterly*, *Research in the Teaching of English*, *Journal of Literacy Research*, *Written Communication*, *The Reading Teacher*, *Journal of Adolescent and Adult Literacy*, *Urban Education*, and *Journal of Education*. She received her Ph.D. degree in Reading at the University at Albany, State University of New York.

INTRODUCTION

Reviewing Bodies of Literacy Scholarship:
Practices, Possibilities, and Potentials

Why Write a Book on Research Syntheses?

People carry out research syntheses for various reasons. **Research syntheses** can clarify how a domain or subdomain of scholarship engages with theoretical or social constructs, survey the landscape of a body of scholarship, identify gaps and/or silences in available research, identify theoretical shortcomings, synthesize findings across studies, and/or help scholars, practitioners, and policymakers to understand what supports literacy learning.

Aren't All Research Syntheses the Same?

In this section, we describe various types of research syntheses. We will start with **traditional literature reviews** including **dissertation literature reviews**, literature reviews within articles, and stand-alone literature reviews, including handbook, chapters, and **integrative literature reviews.** Differences among these traditional forms of literature reviews are identified and explored. We then explore other, less traditional, forms of research syntheses, including qualitative meta-ethnography and metasynthesis. These forms of research syntheses are detailed in Chapters 2 through 6.

We use the term research synthesis to reference any form of review that looks across primary studies. Research syntheses analyze and interpret research reports rather than collecting raw data. A synthesis is connective in that it tells a story of what is known across the findings of a study. We agree with Suri (2014) who argues that the purpose of syntheses is to create new knowledge by making connections or *integration* across primary studies. As evidenced by our glossary (Appendix A), there are several sub-types of integrative research syntheses

2 Reviewing Bodies of Literacy Scholarship

including **conceptual literature reviews**, **integrative literature reviews**, **meta-ethnographies**, and **qualitative metasummaries.** Suri (2014) argued that research syntheses could draw on both quantitative and qualitative methodologies, including statistical research syntheses, **systematic reviews**, and qualitative research syntheses. In this book, we focus on quantitative research syntheses.

In our reading of books and articles that address various types of research syntheses, we found a dizzying array of terms. In part, this reflects the growth of syntheses as academic enterprises. We have noted that different scholars use different terms to refer to the same or similar types of research syntheses and sometimes use the same term to refer to larger categories of research synthesis. For example, Shanahan (2001) argues that the following terms can be interchangeable: research synthesis, integrative review, research integration, and literature review. He notes that these terms are all used to refer to "methods of inquiry used to derive generalizations from the collective findings of a body of existing studies" (p. 133).

In contrast, Thorne, Jensen, Kearney, Noblit, and Sandelowski (2004) explicitly distinguish integrative literature reviews from **metasyntheses**, which they describe as including **meta-ethnography**, **grounded formal theory**, and **metastudy.** Unlike integrative reviews, metasyntheses aspire toward the development of new knowledge through rigorous analysis of the findings from existent qualitative research. Complicating the use of these terms, Samnani, Vaska, Ahmed, and Turin (2017) describe metasynthesis as a review of literature reviews, sometimes referred to as *a tertiary review*. They then differentiate between various approaches to research synthesis and identify the strengths and weaknesses of each (p. 638). Their categories of research syntheses include **literature reviews, scoping reviews**, critical reviews, systematic reviews, **meta-analyses**, mapping analyses, and metasyntheses. Further complicating this discussion of terminology is the fact that meta-review categories are constantly evolving in response to the bodies of research studied, the questions asked, and synthesists' purposes. This evolution is both unstoppable and potentially productive as it can lead to new possibilities for making sense of large bodies of scholarship

Terms related to research synthesis are further complicated by the possibility of hybrid forms of review. For example, while we did not originate the term "critical integrative literature review" (Thorne et al., 2004), we used this term to refer to our research synthesis published in 2012 (Compton-Lilly, Rogers, & Lewis, 2012). Our review qualifies as an integrative literature reviews because it views a particular phenomenon – family literacy – through a diversity equity lens. We used the term "critical" because we appraised family literacy scholarship in terms of strengths, weaknesses, and gaps related to equity, representation, and bias.

While we were "comprehensive" in searching across databases for reviews of scholarship, we did not refer to the review as "systematic". In part, this reflected the epistemological frame from which our review was conceived and our resistance to post-positivist claims. However, as discussed in Chapter 4, despite our critical orientation and review of critically oriented scholarship, our process certainly included post-positivistic tendencies (e.g., citation counting). For now, our point is that research synthesists often refer to their reviews using hybrid terminology to capture the purpose and design of the review.

Hart (1998) argued that synthesis involve "making connections between the parts identified in analysis. It is not simply a matter of reassembling the parts back into the original order, but looking for a new order" (p. 110). He continued, writing that syntheses require "a comprehensive knowledge of the subject and the capacity to think in broad terms because a range of viewpoints, methodologies, and stances often require connecting" (p. 110). Thus, research syntheses help scholars to order, name, sequence, integrate, map, story, and conceptualize complex and elusive bodies of knowledge. This is particularly essential when dealing with the unwieldy, inherently complicated, and deeply contextualized situations and experiences that characterize qualitative research. While this book focuses primarily on qualitative research syntheses, it is important to point out that some quantitative syntheses draw on qualitative evidence. Likewise, some qualitative syntheses include quantified qualitative evidence (e.g., citation counting). Thus, the boundaries between qualitative and quantitative are not fixed (Suri, 2014). In addition, all research syntheses have paradigmatic commitments and it is conceivable that both qualitative and quantitative research synthesis could reflect post-positivist, interpretive, critical, or participatory traditions.

Across this volume, we emphasize that the terms used to describe research syntheses are consequential and reference intentions, purposes, and traditions. Thus, it is important for synthesists to understand the landscape of different types of research syntheses. We close this chapter by reflecting on the significance of research syntheses not just for educators, but for scholars across all disciplines, especially scholars pursuing global social justice.

What Possible Reasons Might Scholars Have for Writing Research Syntheses?

In this volume, we explore various purposes for writing research syntheses. In particular, we explore motivations that include establishing credibility for particular claims; identifying gaps, trends, and historical patterns; highlighting areas of controversy or suggesting resolutions; and reflecting on historical or current ways of thinking that provide a mirror on a given body of work. We argue that research syntheses can present arguments about what we know and what we need to learn. Specifically, we argue that a scholarly review can persuade, convince, direct policy, serve busy educators, synthesize large bodies of work, or reveal invisible patterns (Suri, 2014).

4 Reviewing Bodies of Literacy Scholarship

Synthesists as Reflexive Researchers

As with every other form of qualitative research, attention to the biases and assumptions that qualitative research synthesists bring to projects is critical. Just as qualitative researchers must recognize and reveal their alliances, affiliations, and experiences, the same is true of scholars who aspire to review scholarship within a field. Thus, research syntheses always reflect particular experiences, bodies of knowledge, and positionings. They are intrinsically tentative and open to negotiation, reinterpretation, and debate.

Reflexivity is a critical consideration for research synthesists. Savin-Baden and Major (2010) explain:

> Reflexivity in qualitative synthesis therefore means seeking to continually challenge our biases and examining our stances, perspectives, and views as a researcher. This is not meant to be a notion of 'situating oneself' as formulaic as pronouncing a particular positioned identity connected with class, gender or race for example, but rather situating oneself in order to interpret data demands so to engage with critical questions (p. 82).

Threaded throughout this book is our own reflexive analysis of our journeys as research synthesists – from novice doctoral researchers to seasoned academic scholars. We use examples from our own research syntheses as touchstones to make our decisions, logic, process, and procedures transparent. We use these examples to critique our own assumptions, bias, and silences. We make the case that refining our understanding of the available types of research synthesis designs will support conceptual, methodological, and ethical advances in the field of literacy studies.

Attending to researcher reflexivity has not always been considered relevant in conducting research syntheses. Research synthesists began explicitly attending to selection and publication biases starting in the 1980s (e.g., Wade, 1983) and more commonly in the 2000s (e.g., Slavin & Cheung, 2005; Swanson, Trainin, Necoechea, & Hammill, 2003; Torgerson, Porthouse, & Brooks, 2005) that could affect what types of research studies were published. However, it was not until the most recent decade when research synthesists began to acknowledge personal and cultural biases within the context of their published synthesis (e.g., Compton-Lilly et al., 2012; Wetzel et al., 2019; Rogers & Schaenen, 2014). Fisher (2005) – in a review of teacher-child interactions during the teaching of reading – argued that research syntheses are limited by not only who the authors are but also by who they are *not*. He wrote, "it is important to recognize that the present paper is written from the perspective of a researcher in literacy education. I am not a linguist, a psychologist, a sociologist, or a philosopher – all of whom have contributed to our understanding of speech in the classroom and how it may impact the teaching of reading" (pp. 16–17).

Considering the History and Scope of Research Syntheses

Sandelowski and Barroso (2007) argue that since the 1990s there has been a rising interest in evidence-based practices and in methodologies for synthesizing bodies of research. Because, evidence in education is accessed through multiple methodologies and across decades, making sense of bodies of scholarship requires tools that enable researchers to look across studies conducted in different spaces, with differing methodologies, and at varying points in time (Suri, 2014). Historically, quantitative and qualitative researchers have relied on traditional literature reviews to analyze research chronologically or in relation to particular themes or perspectives. These reviews generally highlight a selected set of studies that are linked to support a compelling account or argument related to a particular issue.

In quantitative research, research syntheses have often assumed the form of **meta-analysis** (Randolph, 2009) in which secondary researchers calculate effect sizes for particular interventions, particularly across randomized control group studies. Specifically, quantitative meta-analysis involves researchers using common metrics to analyze effect sizes across carefully selected studies that purport to have measured the same issue or effect. This method is used to measure the effects of particular interventions. Quantitative meta-analyses aspire to produce a level of knowledge and generalizability that extends beyond the claims made by single studies. In short, they focus on emerging bodies of knowledge that draw on cycles of research across time to establish generalizable claims.

Despite claims about the increased generalizability of meta-analysis findings, it is widely recognized that synthesist's perspectives affect how quantitative studies are selected, the arguments used to link the studies, and the synthesist's conclusions (Suri, 2014). In particular, Light and Pillemer (1984) argue that different researchers reviewing the same set of studies can come to very different conclusions.

Quantitative meta-analysts often apply stringent criteria (e.g., the use of control groups, sample size, internal validity, and replicability) that are associated with high-quality studies. In contrast, qualitative studies take many forms and synthesists must remain sensitive to local research contexts as well as the people involved. Thus, applying lists of defined criteria to identify high-quality qualitative research studies is problematic and narrow definitions of high-quality research could easily exclude important and influential studies in a field.

Just as quantitative meta-analysis has been used to move beyond a particular set of findings toward the identification of more generalizable claims, there has been increased interest in synthesis methods that can be used with qualitative research studies. Over the past 30 years, qualitative methods have gained a strong foothold in academic circles based on their ability to explore factors that can be identified, but not sufficiently explored, using quantitative methods. By drawing on observations in learning spaces, interviews with participants, and artifacts produced by teachers and students, qualitative researchers identify patterns across data sources, revealing critical insights for educators. However, questions have been consistently raised about the generalizability of qualitative findings.

6 Reviewing Bodies of Literacy Scholarship

The traditional critique that qualitative findings are never generalizable is called into question with the ongoing cumulation of qualitative studies that have been conducted over time. For example, scholars have studied family literacy for decades and hundreds of papers have been published. While the specific findings of each study are clearly limited in terms of their direct generalizability to other populations, it is clear that there is much we have learned about families and literacy. When researchers consider bodies of research cumulatively, patterns can be discerned. Specifically, based on our own wide reading of studies in family literacy, we argue that generalizable claims can be made about the diversity of literacy practices, the multiple purposes that these literacy practices serve, important intersections between literacy practices and identity construction, and the stable, yet evolving, nature of literacy practices within technologically informed communities and classrooms.

Perhaps the question is not whether qualitative studies are generalizable, but rather, what insights from across studies help us to understand people's experiences and perspectives, and how those ways of being interface with educational practices. As we look across qualitative studies, we recognize patterns across studies, methodologies that appear particularly helpful, and findings that materialize differently in different contexts while pointing to consistencies and commonalities. These generalizations must always be understood in dialogue with local contexts and histories, the perspectives of local participants, and the resources and opportunities that are available in those contexts.

The question taken up by this book is how might we, as literacy education scholars, synthesize and organize what we know about literacy as we grapple with our own abilities to make claims based on large bodies of qualitative work. Specifically, qualitative research synthesists provide tools to help researchers recognize patterns across studies in order to identify and name what we know about literacy purposes, practices, and learning.

This is significant work. Too often qualitative studies are dismissed as anecdotal or thought-provoking examples rather than as important and scholarly contributions. Qualitative research has the potential to help researchers to recognize and attend to the diversity of literacy practices in diverse educational settings, the various purposes of literacy, the significance of participant identities, and the effects of technology. This book takes on this challenge by presenting the reader with a range of methodologies for not only reviewing literature but also for exploring what we know as a field and what types of information might be generalizable as we look across qualitative studies.

Types of Research Syntheses Featured in This Book

While there are many forms of qualitative research syntheses, we focus on the following: dissertation literature reviews, traditional literature reviews, integrative literature reviews, metasyntheses, and meta-ethnographies. Although we present these types of syntheses in separate chapters and as discrete methodologies, there is significant overlap across these traditions. Part of our goal is to demonstrate how different forms of qualitative research syntheses entail various types of claims, sampling processes, forms of representation, types of findings, methodologies, perspectives, and purposes. A fairly complete listing of research synthesis approaches is presented in Appendix A.

Dissertation literature reviews and traditional literature reviews are assumedly familiar to literacy scholars and will be addressed through examples presented in Chapters 2 and 3. In Chapters 4, 5, and 6, we introduce three approaches to research synthesis that may be less familiar to many literacy scholars: integrative literature reviews, meta-ethnographies, and qualitative metasyntheses. Examples of these research syntheses and discussions of the collaborative processes that have led to the writing of these research syntheses are shared. Below we offer a brief introduction to each of these synthesis types.

Dissertation Literature Reviews

While dissertation literature review is a form of the traditional literature review described in the section below, we discuss them separately here, and in Chapter 2, not only because the forms of literature review present a particular set of challenges, but also because we suspect that many of our readers are particularly interested in this form of review. Descriptions of dissertation literature reviews target graduate student audiences. These texts generally highlight the process for reviewing literature in the service of writing a thesis or dissertation. In general, these texts provide guidance for writing a literature review chapter and provide information about content and organization.

There are many texts that focus on writing a dissertation literature review (e.g., Galvan & Galvan, 2017; Hart, 1998; Machi & McEvoy, 2009; Randolph, 2009; Ridley, 2012). For example, Ridley (2012) described her text as a *step-by-step* guide designed for graduate students. Written in the United Kingdom, where universities follow different processes for preparing graduate students and present slightly different expectations about what dissertations entail, the primary focus of this book is to prepare graduate students for their dissertation literature review process. After defining the dissertation literature review genre, describing literature reviews as entailing both process and practice, distinguishing between the types of literature reviews that might be expected at the undergraduate, graduate, and doctoral levels, and presenting various ways in which the literature can be situated within dissertations, Ridley offers advice on conducting literature searches and evaluating sources.

Like many texts in this genre, Ridley's text (2012) focuses on *how to*. A closing chapter briefly addresses the "systematic literature review" (p. 188), where Ridley describes the purposes and methodologies for crafting more extensive and stand-alone literature reviews. She described quantitative meta-analyses and

8 Reviewing Bodies of Literacy Scholarship

stand-alone traditional literature reviews providing definitions for and descriptions of these texts. This chapter provides a brief introduction, but does not explore systematic reviews in sufficient detail that would enable researchers to conduct these types of reviews.

Other publications describe various ways to organize and present a dissertation literature review. For example, Randolph (2009) described the various types of dissertation literature reviews. His typology differentiated between literature reviews that are framed in regard to topic, goals (e.g., integrate/generalize findings, resolve a debate, and bridge areas of study), perspectives, coverage in a given field, or audience. Randolph recommends that writers of literature reviews attend carefully to the decisions they make in order to craft a review that adequately supports the argument presented in their dissertations. Unlike Ridley (2012), Randolph argues that literature reviews involve methodologies that must be clearly described by the author. For example, authors should state research questions and issues, identify how they selected the studies that were included in their review, and describe their processes for analyzing those studies. Randolph differentiates between quantitative and qualitative literature reviews providing overviews of the history and methods for each.

Unfortunately, the dissertation literature review is often where many scholars end their literature review journey. While most scholars continue to write literature reviews for articles and book chapters, these latter texts tend to echo the practices learned during the dissertation process. In this text, we treat the qualitative research syntheses as distinct methodological processes that, like other forms of research, can assume multiple forms, involve explicit methodological procedures, and address various types of research questions.

Traditional Literature Reviews

Traditional literature reviews analyze a body of scholarship to reveal themes, trends, gaps, controversies, and areas of confluence. The goal is to raise awareness of various patterns and/or to argue for or against positions in a field. Traditional literature reviews can comprise portions of larger texts (i.e., articles, books, and dissertations) or can be stand-alone articles such as those represented in handbooks or journals dedicated to the publication of literature reviews (i.e., *Review of Educational Research*). Additionally, traditional literature reviews can share epistemological and methodological features with other kinds of reviews (e.g., critical integrative reviews). Chapter 3 of this book describes two traditional literature reviews written by Rebecca Rogers and her colleagues focused on critical discourse analysis.

Integrative Literature Reviews

An integrative literature review is premised on an interest in investigating a body of research through a particular lens or terms of particular questions or perspectives (Thorne et al., 2004). As with the other forms of research synthesis, researchers use methodologies and carefully delineated analytic steps as they describe driving questions, the sampling of primary studies, and relevant patterns. While approaching a body of literature with a particular question or in terms of a particular issue can provide important information about a topic and/or the field, there are also challenges and limits associated with this approach. In particular, by focusing on specific issues or questions, other significant considerations may be neglected. In addition, all of the studies in any given sample may not have been specifically designed to investigate the issue chosen by the secondary reviewer; thus, the analysis is dependent on the information and perspectives made available, which may or may not reflect the full scope of issues relevant to the secondary reviewer's questions.

An integrative literature review (Thorne et al., 2004) can be described as critical when reviewers "aspire to comment on an entire body of the work, making claims about the political or ideological nature of previous inquiries, exposing theoretical assumptions on which methodological approaches have been built or raising questions with regard to the motive and intent of previous investigators" (p. 1345). The analytic focus is on variations in approach, vision, and interpretation across research reports and reflects the critical lens of the secondary analysis. These reviewers draw conclusions about a body of scholarship in order to shift perspectives, extend thinking, or challenge readers. We discuss our critical integrative review of family literacy studies in Chapter 4 of this book.

Meta-Ethnographies

Meta-ethnography is a particular form of metasynthesis that is designed to analyze language, specifically the metaphors researchers use to describe and present their work. Meta-ethnography reveals ways of thinking about a particular topic or body of work. While developed by educators, meta-ethnographies are most commonly found in the field of nursing and generally take the form of full-length articles.

Originated by Noblit and Hare (1988), meta-ethnography is sometimes described as a form of metasynthesis. However, rather than focusing explicitly on findings from ethnographic studies, meta-ethnography involves analyzing the metaphors used to present and frame findings with the goal of comparing, synthesizing, and creating new understandings.

Meta-ethnography aims to "account for all important similarities and differences in language, concepts, images and other ideas around a target experience" (Sandelowski, Docherty, & Emden, 1997, p. 369). Specifically, meta-ethnographers identify and translate across key metaphors in existent research studies to trace the development, refinement, and expansion of conceptual frameworks that frame and define a body of scholarship. Translating key metaphors across studies provides descriptive evidence and reveals patterns of thought and sense-making within bodies of scholarship (Noblit & Hare, 1988).

10 Reviewing Bodies of Literacy Scholarship

Noblit and Hare (1988) argue that "translations of studies will vary with the translators" (p. 31) in the same way that researchers working with the same data produce different findings; they describe meta-ethnography as involving "interpretations of interpretations of interpretations" (p. 35) that reveal cultural phenomena and understandings operating in and across studies. As described in Chapter 6 of this volume, Noblit and Hare suggest seven overlapping methodological phases for conducting a meta-ethnography. We discuss our meta-ethnography of family literacy studies in Chapter 5 of this book.

Qualitative Metasyntheses

Thorne and her colleagues (2004) clearly distinguish critical integrative literature reviews from metasyntheses citing the commitment that metasynthesis researchers have to "develop[ing] new knowledge based on rigorous analysis of existing qualitative research findings" (p. 1343). Qualitative metasyntheses deal directly with findings from and across qualitative studies that investigate the same or similar issues. The goal is to look across studies to identify what we know about a particular topic and highlight areas for further research. Due to the detailed nature of these analyses, metasyntheses are generally stand-alone articles.

Some scholars have compared qualitative metasynthesis to quantitative meta-analysis; both processes focus on the findings of primary studies that share a particular focus. However, we recognize that qualitative metasynthesis and quantitative meta-analysis are grounded in very different epistemological assumptions. In short, quantitative meta-analysis focuses on measurable effect sizes of particular variables while qualitative metasynthesis methods deal directly with findings from and across qualitative studies. In this book, we use the term metasynthesis to refer to qualitative research synthesis methodologies that focus specifically on the integration and synthesis of research findings.

In their review of various types of metasyntheses, Thorne et al. (2004) describe qualitative metasynthesis as "a family of methodological approaches for developing new research based on rigorous analysis of existing qualitative findings" (p. 1343). Sandelowski and her colleagues (1997) describe metasynthesis as "[t]he theories, grand narratives, generalizations, or interpretive translations produced from the integration or comparison of findings from qualitative studies (Sandelowski et al., 1997, p. 366). Sandelowski and Barroso (2007) warn that the "interpretive integration of qualitative findings that are themselves interpretive syntheses of data, including the phenomenologies, ethnographies, grounded theories, and other coherent descriptions or explanations of phenomena, events, or cases that are the hallmark findings of qualitative research" (p. 151). Thus, Thorne and her colleagues (2004) describe attempts to "create overarching or synoptic claims on the basis of various analytic and synthetic strategies applied to the bodies of extant qualitative research" (Thorne et al., 2004, p. 1342).

Reviewing Bodies of Literacy Scholarship **11**

Conceptualizations of metasyntheses differ in terms of their expressed goals. McCormick, Rodney, and Varcoe (2003) describe qualitative metasyntheses as "another 'reading' of the data, an opportunity to reflect on the data in new ways" (p. 936) while Beck (2009) highlights the opportunity to "delve deeper into the research to reveal some new information that may increase our understanding" (p. 702). Metasyntheses can take a variety of forms including meta-ethnography, which is discussed below and in Chapter 6. Other forms of metasynthesis include the following: grounded formal theory, metastudy, and **qualitative research integration.** All of these research synthesis approaches share an interest in findings and collective knowledge across various research studies (see Appendix A for a more complete listing of research synthesis approaches).

- The goal of *grounded formal theory* is to "create a model explaining variations arising from differences in time and context that the contributing researchers could not have captured in their more circumscribed venues" (Thorne et al., 2004, p. 1355). Thus, grounded formal theory involves looking reflexively across research studies to identify conditions under which findings and emergent generalizations might be warranted.
- *Metastudy* involves a three-pronged process that includes "metatheory, meta-method and meta-data analysis" (Thorne et al., 2004, p. 1355). It involves a "set of detailed guidelines for search and retrieval, for creating an analytic dialogue, and for interpreting the findings deriving from a diverse set of studies into one another and into the possibilities of a coherent new whole" (Thorne et al., 2004, p. 1356).
- *Qualitative research integration* references empirical studies that are directed "toward the combination of research findings in reports of qualitative studies" (Thorne et al., 2004, p. 1357). Unlike metasummaries, which are simply an aggregation of qualitative findings, qualitative research integration references the "interpretive integration of qualitative findings... that offer novel interpretations" (Thorne et al., 2004, p. 1358).

Despite variation in methodologies and expressed goals, scholars generally agree on the significance and power of qualitative metasyntheses. As Sandelowski and her colleagues (1997) maintain:

> Qualitative metasynthesis is not a trivial pursuit, but rather a complex exercise in interpretation: Carefully peeling away the surface layers of studies to find their hearts and souls in a way that does the least damage to them (p. 370).

However, attempts at metasynthesis have been plagued with difficulties. McCormick et al. (2003) note that the techniques for conducting metasyntheses are new and poorly developed; in addition, conducting a metasynthesis is complex and time consuming, which may contribute to the lack of practical

12 Reviewing Bodies of Literacy Scholarship

examples of metasyntheses (McCormick et al., 2003). In Chapter 6 of this volume, we describe our process for conducting a metasynthesis that draws on findings from across studies related to family literacy conducted by BIPOC scholars.

What Role Do Qualitative Research Syntheses Play in Academic Fields?

While we write this book from our perspectives as literacy educational scholars, we recognize that the compilation of qualitative information and scholarship has implications across disciplines. Some of the most important questions faced by our world have been examined and partially addressed through the compilation and synthesis of qualitative data. Questions related to climate change, global health, and social justice are addressed not only by numbers but also through observations, interviews, and compelling cases across contexts and countries.

For example, *The Lancet Countdown* (Watts et al., 2018) – a collaboration among 24 academic institutions and inter-governmental organizations, based in every continent, and representing a vast range of disciplines and data sources – concluded that the "human symptoms of climate change are unequivocal and potentially irreversible – affecting the health of populations around the world, today. Whilst these effects will disproportionately impact the most vulnerable in society, every community will be affected" (p. 10). Reports related to social justice (e.g., Baudot, 2006) and global health inequalities (e.g., Quinn & Kumar, 2014) raise similar concerns about the fate of people living in poverty. While these reports ostensibly privilege numbers and quantitative data, they also reflect historical and current practices, observations of scientists, and the experiences of people around the globe.

Research syntheses are important tools for addressing inequities in all its forms. It is neither the murder of George Floyd that singly inspired a global racial justice movement, nor was Hurricane Katrina the sole harbinger of global warming. It is the cumulation and synthesis of these experiences over time that is activating change and resistance. Thus, we argue for the significance of research syntheses and the need to make patterns visible across contexts, cases, and spaces in order to reveal the inequities that define not only education but all facets of people's lives around the world.

Related Appendix

Appendix A: Common Qualitative Research Synthesis Designs

References

Baudot, J. (2006). *Social Justice in an Open World The Role of the United Nations*. United Nations.

Beck, C. T. (2009). A meta-synthesis of qualitative research. *The American Journal of Maternal/Child Nursing*, 27(4), 214–221.

Compton-Lilly, C., Rogers, R., & Lewis, T. (2012). Analyzing epistemological considerations related to diversity: An integrative critical literature review of family literacy scholarship. *Reading Research Quarterly*, 47(1), 33–60.

Fisher, R. (2005). Teacher-child interaction in the teaching of reading: A review of research perspectives over twenty-five years. *Journal of Research in Reading*, 28(1), 15–27.

Galvan, J. L., & Galvan, M. C. (2017). *Writing literature reviews: A guide for students of the social and behavioral sciences*. Taylor & Francis Group.

Hart, C. (1998). *Doing a literature review: Releasing the social science research imagination*. Sage.

Light, R. J., & Pillemer, D. B. (1984). *Summing up; the science of reviewing research*. Harvard University Press.

Machi, L. A., & McEvoy, B. T. (2009). *The literature review: Six steps to success*. Corwin Press.

McCormick, J., Rodney, P., & Varcoe, C. (2003). Reinterpretations across studies: An approach to meta-analysis. *Qualitative Health Research*, 13(7), 933–944.

Noblit, G. W., & Hare, R. D. (1988). *Meta-ethnography: Synthesizing qualitative studies*. Sage.

Quinn, S. C., & Kumar, S. (2014). Health inequalities and infectious disease epidemics: A challenge for global health security. *Biosecurity and Bioterrorism: Biodefense Strategy, Practice, and Science*, 12(5), 263–273.

Randolph, J. J. (2009). A guide to writing the dissertation literature review. *Practical Assessment, Research, and Evaluation*, 14(13), 1–13.

Ridley, D. (2012). *The literature review: A step-by-step guide for students* (2nd ed.). Sage.

Rogers, R., & Schaenen, I. (2014). Critical discourse analysis in literacy education: A review of the literature. *Reading Research Quarterly*, 49(1), 121–143.

Samnani, S. S., Vaska, M., Ahmed, S., & Turin, T. C. (2017). Review typology: The basic types of reviews for synthesizing evidence for the purpose of knowledge translation. *Journal of the College of Physicians and Surgeons Pakistan*, 27(10), 635–641.

Sandelowski, M., & Barroso, J. (2007). *Handbook for synthesizing qualitative research*. Springer Publishing Company.

Sandelowski, M., Docherty, S., & Emden, C. (1997). Focus on qualitative methods: Qualitative metasynthesis: Issues and techniques. *Research in Nursing and Health*, 20, 365–371.

Savin-Baden, M., & Major, C. H. (Eds.). (2010). *New approaches to qualitative research: Wisdom and uncertainty*. Routledge.

Slavin, R. E., & Cheung, A. (2005). A synthesis of research on language of reading instruction for English language learners. *Review of Educational Research*, 75(2), 247–284.

Shanahan, T. (2001). Research syntheses and making sense of the accumulation of knowledge related to reading. In M. L. Kamil, P. B. Mosenthal, P. D. Pearson, & R. Barr (Eds.), *Methods of literacy research: The methodology chapters from the handbook of reading research* (Vol. 3, pp. 143–160). Routledge.

Suri, H. (2014). *Towards methodologically inclusive research syntheses: Expanding possibilities*. Routledge.

Swanson, H. L., Trainin, G., Necoechea, D. M., & Hammill, D. D. (2003). Rapid naming, phonological awareness, and reading: A meta-analysis of the correlation evidence. *Review of Educational Research*, 73(4), 407–440.

Thorne, S., Jensen, L., Kearney, M. H., Noblit, G., & Sandelowski, M. (2004). Qualitative metasynthesis: Reflections on methodological orientation and ideological agenda. *Qualitative Health Research*, 14(10), 1342–1365.

Torgerson, C., Porthouse, J., & Brooks, G. (2005). A systematic review of controlled trials evaluating interventions in adult literacy and numeracy. *Journal of Research in Reading*, 28(2), 87–107.

Wade, S. E. (1983). A synthesis of the research for improving reading in the social studies. *Review of Educational Research*, 53(4), 461–497.

Watts, N., Amann, M., Ayeb-Karlsson, S., Belesova, K., Bouley, T., Boykoff, M., … Cox, P. M. (2018). The Lancet Countdown on health and climate change: From 25 years of inaction to a global transformation for public health. *The Lancet*, 391(10120), 581–630.

Wetzel, M., Vlach, S., Svrcek, N., Steinitz, E., Omogun, L., Salmerón, C., … Villarreal, D. (2019). Preparing teaches with sociocultural knowledge in literacy: A literature review. *Journal of Literacy Research*, 51(2), 138–157.

1

SURVEYING THE LANDSCAPE OF PUBLISHED QUALITATIVE RESEARCH SYNTHESES IN LITERACY STUDIES

Sandelowski, Docherty, and Emden (1997) have described research synthesis designs as ranging from traditional literature reviews to conceptual and systematic reviews including metasyntheses and meta-ethnographies. Within this body of scholarship, there are **traditional literature reviews**, including those found in dissertations and scholarly handbooks. These traditional reviews are often organized chronologically or thematically and generally do not include detailed methodological descriptions. There are also what Norris and Ortega (2007) described as **systematic research syntheses**, which entail thoughtful, rationalized, and explicated processes for selecting primary studies, analyses that focus on the original data/evidence presented in primary studies rather than the claims of researchers, and data analysis methods that allow research synthesists to look consistently and exhaustively within and across primary studies. We use the term **research synthesis scholarship** to refer to both traditional and systematic reviews.

In this chapter, we survey the landscape and history of research syntheses in literacy studies. As discussed in our introductory chapter, a broad array of terminology is associated with various types of research syntheses. Our goal in this chapter is to sift through these terms and the multiple approaches and theoretical and empirical commitments that they entail. We then propose working definitions for various terms as we enter this conversation (see Appendix A).

As a team of research synthesists, we have individually and collectively written several published research syntheses. With accessibility and distribution of knowledge in mind, we have also published a range of *spin-off* reports to ensure that our research syntheses are widely distributed. These efforts are presented in the text boxes at the beginning of each chapter. As scholars we have also written and published shorter literature reviews within published reports on empirical studies. We have also had our own empirical research cited in research syntheses authored

16 Qualitative Research Syntheses in Literacy Studies

by colleagues and have served as peer reviewers for research syntheses written by colleagues. After working individually and collaboratively on research syntheses – as authors, editors, reviewers, and consumers – we find ourselves focusing on research syntheses as intellectual, theoretical, and methodological activities.

In preparing to write this book, we reviewed hundreds of research syntheses involving literacy to explore the landscape of our field. We asked a series of questions including the following:

> What kinds of research syntheses have been published?
> What methodologies do synthesists seem to rely on?
> What research syntheses have been most widely cited?

During this process, several things have become clear. We noted that the genre of research synthesis has changed dramatically over the past 80 years. While attempts at early research synthesis were generally annotated lists or summaries of research studies related to particular dimensions of literacy – particularly reading, more recent research syntheses take various methodological forms, including meta-analyses, integrative reviews, metasyntheses, and meta-ethnographies. Furthermore, the number of syntheses that address literacy has exploded over the past 20 years. This proliferation in methodology and number begs careful attention to traditions, designs, methods, modes of representation, and the interpretations that characterize these reviews.

Despite our extensive reading in this area, we could not find a book squarely located within literacy studies that focused specifically on various approaches to research syntheses. Certainly, such a book would have been useful as we envisioned and wrote our independent and collaborative research syntheses. Each of us recalls asking "What kind of research syntheses is this?" As we drafted our reviews, we searched bodies of scholarship, defined inclusion criteria selected primary studies, read and reread selected studies, coded and analyzed the studies, and reported the syntheses of our findings. As a result, we began to conceptualize and understand the types of research syntheses that we were writing. Each attempt to write a research synthesis was a quintessential process of *building the car while driving it* as we made critical decisions in the moment and encountered challenges as we worked. Part of our dilemma was that authors of research syntheses were not always clear about the types of research synthesis they were conducting. As we looked across published research syntheses, scholars were inconsistent in the terms they used to describe and characterize their work. In addition, across our reviews of primary studies in literacy education, we noted that many authors did not refer to their research syntheses by type, genre, or methodology and their review designs and methods were often not described. Early literature reviews read like annotated bibliographies and were treated as neutral and objective reviews of research, while more recent research syntheses sometimes described sampling processes, methodological descriptions, and analytical procedures.

Indeed, only after reading and re-reading studies and reflecting on the field did we discern what was interesting and salient about particular types of syntheses – to us and assumedly to fellow researchers. We have found this emergent approach to analyzing research synthesis scholarship clarifying and helpful as we continue our efforts to synthesize qualitative scholarship.

In addition to our concerns about how particular terms are used, we simultaneously caution against rigidly categorizing types of research syntheses. In our own work, we have sometimes found it useful, if not necessary, to draw on multiple designs. With that said, as research synthesists, we think it is helpful for fellow synthesists – including reviewers and editors – to have a general sense of the landscape of research syntheses. Thus, in this book, we explore five different types of research syntheses: dissertation reviews, traditional literature reviews, integrative reviews, metasyntheses, and meta-ethnographies. The first three are among the most common qualitative research synthesis approaches in literacy studies. Metasyntheses and meta-ethnography, on the other hand, hold a great deal of potential for the field but, as of yet, has been underutilized in education and in literacy research. Thus, we took a deep dive into each of these review designs. In doing so, we unpacked the decisions we made, the questions we asked, and the challenges we faced as synthesists.

As we read methodological and theoretical discussions of research syntheses processes – often from outside the field of education – we became increasingly aware of additional types of research synthesis designs and methodologies. Appendix A presents a list of common qualitative research synthesis designs. Norris and Ortega (2006) suggests that these types comprise "a reviewing continuum" (p. 5) with each type of research synthesis having different purposes, methods, and representational practices.

To explore issues related to writing research syntheses, we revisited syntheses that we have written and published. We found ourselves dipping into folders – both manila and electronic – that contained materials and documents related to our process that never made it into our published reports. In Chapters 2, 3, 4, 5, and 6, we explore the structures, purposes, and review designs of five of these approaches. We demystify each research synthesis by making transparent our decision making at key stages in our work. Indeed, there were many implicit and explicit choices made across the lifespan of our research syntheses processes. In addition, we provide a sense of the feedback we received from reviewers and critically reflect on silences, missed opportunities, and strengths in each of our published products. Finally, we share ideas for disseminating findings from research syntheses to reach multiple audiences.

The Contribution of Research Syntheses

We make a case for the scholarly integrity of research syntheses and their contributions as academic enterprises. Sometimes, research syntheses are treated

18 Qualitative Research Syntheses in Literacy Studies

as "means to an end" – that is, a body of scholarship is reviewed in order to build an argument to support a line of empirical research in a book, article, or dissertation. These types of syntheses are often treated as technical undertakings – necessary hurdles void of novel, conceptual, and intellectual contributions. Our volume extends conversations about research synthesis scholarship in ways that push beyond supporting particular projects or positions or as tests of novice scholar competence. We explore research syntheses as important scholarly texts that make critical and unique contributions to academic fields. Research syntheses can assume multiple forms, serve various purposes, speak to multiple audiences, and have wide-ranging effects (Sandelowski, 2014; Sandelowski et al., 1997; Suri, 2013). As Suri (2013) notes, "it is crucial that synthesists share, discuss, debate, and critique different aspects of research synthesis processes to improve the quality of research syntheses" (p. 28).

Research syntheses do important theoretical and philosophical work. Some research syntheses highlight areas of controversy within a given body of work; sometimes syntheses suggest resolutions or compromises, at other times they argue for the salience of particular perspectives. Other research syntheses invite reflection on historical and/or contemporary ways of thinking. Others document change over time focusing on the emergence of scholarly stances and conceptual shifts. These research syntheses act as mirrors on bodies of research to reveal problematic trends, questionable ways of thinking, silences, or reified conceptualizations that may be embedded in scholarship. Still other research syntheses incite action – advocating new methodological directions, new metaphors for thinking, or novel practices.

In 1976, Glass made a particularly strong argument for the significance of research syntheses. While this article pointed most directly to quantitative meta-analyses and the use of statistical measures to identify compelling patterns across primary studies, Glass argued that while educators have accumulated vast stores of research, "We need methods for the orderly summarization of studies so that knowledge can be extracted from the myriad of individual researches" (p. 4) and the "best minds are needed to integrate the staggering number of individual studies" (p. 4). Glass notes that with the proliferation of research related to literacy, researchers in the 1970s identified a need for research methods that would allow them to look across primary research studies to consider the cumulation of knowledge related to various aspects of education. As Norris and Ortega (2006) described, various forms of research syntheses emerged as a "methodological movement in the 1970s in response to dissatisfaction with several major weaknesses inherent in traditional approaches to reviewing" (p. xi). They explained that traditional research syntheses tended to be narrative summaries of fields and/or bodies of research without attention to the designs, methods, or theories that guided the syntheses.

In the 1970s, quantitative researchers began to explore the potential of meta-analysis and the use of effect sizes to make claims across studies. Thus, the history of research syntheses entails a long quest to understand phenomena by looking across various research studies and learning contexts. Research syntheses, as an academic enterprise, are continually growing and developing as evidenced by ongoing conceptual dialogues in journals dedicated to scholarly review, including *Educational Researcher* (e.g., Glass, 1976; Kennedy, 2007), *British Educational Research Journal* (e.g., Foster & Hammersley, 1998), and *Review of Educational Research* (e.g., Apple, 1999; Grant & Graue, 1999; Lather, 1999).

Medical journals have had particular focus on the affordances of qualitative research synthesis (i.e., Sandelowski et al., 1997). These syntheses raise important issues related to the cumulation of evidence, cross-case comparisons, and the accumulation of patient reports. We enter this dialogue as qualitative literacy researchers and experienced research synthesists with the intention of expanding possibilities for educational researchers to engage with qualitative research syntheses in order to identify patterns related to findings, trends, and silences within bodies of scholarship and to identify directions for future research.

While some qualitative studies have been highly cited (see Compton-Lilly, Rogers, & Lewis, 2012; Compton-Lilly, Rogers, & Lewis Ellison, 2020), these qualitative studies are often described as anecdotal and not generalizable. However, as Stake (1978) explained, qualitative studies mimic the understandings that people gain "through direct and vicarious experience" (p. 5) and emulate the advantages of learning through "natural experience acquired in ordinary personal involvement" (p. 5). Over time, qualitative researchers working in a vast range of fields have contributed to the accumulation of information related to particular or similar phenomena across research contexts. Collectively these studies contribute to important understandings about phenomena, including literacy. Dyson and Genishi (2005) argued that qualitative research wove ideas together creating "quilts" (p. 115) of understanding. They pointed out for the significance of naturalistic generalization as readers generalize "in private, personal ways, modifying, extending, or adding to their generalized understandings of how the world works" (p. 115).

A Brief History of Research Syntheses in Literacy Studies

Traditional research syntheses related to literacy date back to the late 1800s (Venezky, 1984). In 1897, Quantz wrote a monograph in which he reviewed the findings from a handful of studies completed in a laboratory at the University of Wisconsin Madison related to the reading process, including eye movements, reading speed, and lip movement during reading. In another monograph published in 1906, Dearborn reviewed emerging findings related to eye movements and perceptual span while reading. Two years later, Huey (1908) published a book, which at that time, was the most comprehensive review of reading scholarship ever published. Like Quantz (1897) and Dearborn (1906), this review addressed the perception of words and reading rate, while also reporting on primary studies that

20 Qualitative Research Syntheses in Literacy Studies

examined subvocal speech, the nature of meaning making, and reading instruction. These monographs and books were followed by an ever-increasing number of summaries and syntheses that have been published in research journals.

To gain a sense of the range and nature of published research syntheses in literacy, we conducted an extensive search of literacy journals and journals that publish research syntheses related to literacy. To search literacy journals, we searched the online holdings of each literacy journal archive; we searched both titles and abstracts with combinations of the terms "review," "meta-analysis," "meta-ethnography/metaethnography," and "meta-synthesis/metasynthesis." We searched all major literacy journals including the *Reading Research Quarterly, Journal of Literacy Research, Research in the Teaching of English*, and *Written Communication*. For generalist journals, we used search engines (JSTOR, ProQuest, Academic Search, and Education Full Text) to search titles and abstracts with the terms "review," "meta-analysis," "meta-ethnography/metaethnography," and "meta-synthesis/metasynthesis" in conjunction with each of the following terms – "literacy," "reading," and "writing." Generalist journals included the *Harvard Educational Review, Review of Educational Research, Review of Research in Education*, and *Teachers College Record*.

As we identified research syntheses, with the help of graduate students, we read and analyzed each article using an Analytical Review Template (ART) (see Appendix B) to record characteristics of each article. We then reread articles, added missing information, and removed articles that were not research syntheses related to literacy. We ended up with a sample of 144 qualitative research syntheses related to literacy (Table 1.1). The earliest reviews that we found were published in 1937 (e.g., Breed, 1937; Gray, 1937).

In the course of our analysis, we stumbled across an early set of reviews, which we have tracked on a separate list – the *Summary of Investigations Relating to Reading*. We analyzed these reviews separately for three reasons. First, the *Summary of Investigations* were conducted by one person for 35 consecutive years – William S. Gray. Second, the summaries do not address particular bodies of literacy scholarship, but aspire to summarize all research related to reading, and later language arts, each year. Finally, unlike the other reviews, these summaries were solicited by the journals and are not peer-reviewed publications.

Summaries of Investigations Relating to Reading

Over an impressive 35 years (1925–1960), Gray wrote the *Summary of Investigations Relating to Reading*. The first summary monograph was published in 1925 and references 436 "reading investigations made in England and America prior to July, 1924." Gray noted that he also included "certain studies carried on in Germany and in France" (Good, 1925, p. 628). The following year, the summaries began to be published as journal articles, first in the *Elementary School Journal* and later in the *Journal of Educational Research, The Reading Teacher*, and the *Reading Research Quarterly*, and finally again as a monograph published by the International Reading Association.

Qualitative Research Syntheses in Literacy Studies **21**

TABLE 1.1 Topics Addressed by 144 Qualitative and Quantitative Research Syntheses

Topics	144 Qualitative and Quantitative Research Syntheses (1930–2015)
1930s	
Reading, Reading Research and Instruction, and Reading Psychology 1937–1967	(Gray, 1937) (Porter, Shafer, & Monroe, 1946) (Durrell & Murphy, 1949) (Sheldon, 1955) (Gilbert & Holmes, 1955) (McCullough, 1958) (Clymer & Robinson, 1961) (Williams, 1965) (Summers, 1967) (Kerfoot, 1967)
Spelling 1937–2002	(Breed, 1937) (Torgerson & Elbourne, 2002)
1940s	
Reading Difficulties and Reading Intervention 1943–2016	(Kopel & De Boer, 1943) (Torgerson, Porthouse, & Brooks, 2005) (Torgerson, 2007) (Edmonds et al., 2009) (Wanzek et al., 2013) (Reed, Cummings, Schaper, & Biancarosa, 2014) (Wexler, Pyle, Flower, Williams, & Cole, 2014) (Scammacca et al., 2016)
1950s	
Writing and Teaching Writing 1952–2018	(Gunn & Barlow, 1952) (Schmieder, 1958) (West, 1967) (Marksheffel, 1964) (Mosenthal, 1983) (Humes, 1983) (Applebee, 1984) (Hidi & Anderson, 1986) (DiPardo & Freedman, 1988) (Durst & Newell, 1989) (Smagorinsky & Smith, 1992) (Igland & Ongstad, 2002) (Bangert-Drowns, Hurley, & Wilkinson, 2004) (Newell, Beach, Smith, & VanDerHeide, 2011) (Williams & Mayer, 2015) (Kent & Wanzek, 2016) (Graham et al., 2018)
Oral and Written Language 1955–1996	(DeBoer, 1955) (Sperling, 1996)

(Continued)

22 Qualitative Research Syntheses in Literacy Studies

TABLE 1.1 Continued

1960s	
Instructional Materials, Methods, and Programs 1965–2009	(Barnes, 1965) (Clifford, 1984) (Stahl & Miller, 1989) (Slavin, Lake, Chambers, Cheung, & Davis, 2009)

1970s	
Multisensory, Multimodality 1975	(Silverston & Deichmann, 1975)
Language Variation, African American Language 1975–1976	(Somervill, 1975) (Harber & Bryen, 1976)
Assessment 1977–1990	(Kulhavy, 1977) (Huot, 1990)
Orthography, Phonology, Phonics, and Morphology 1977–2018	(Richardson, DiBenedetto, & Bradley, 1977) (Swanborn & De Glopper, 1999) (Mesmer, 2001) (Ehri, Nunes, Stahl, & Willows, 2001) (Macmillan, 2002) (Swanson, Trainin, Necoechea, & Hammill, 2003) (Carlisle, 2010) (Bowers, Kirby, & Deacon, 2010)s (Weiser & Mathes, 2011) (Al Ghanem & Kearns, 2015) (Hadley & Dickinson, 2020)

1980s	
Reading and Content Areas 1983–2011	(Wade, 1983) (Cavagnetto, 2010) (Sinatra & Broughton, 2011)
Vocabulary and Academic Language 1983–2017	(Mezynski, 1983) (Marulis & Neuman, 2010) (Nagy & Townsend, 2012) (Ford-Connors & Paratore, 2015) (Wright & Cervetti, 2017)
Politics, Ethics, Civics, and Ideology 1984–1997	(Erickson, 1984) (Brantlinger, 1997)
Play and Literacy 1985–2001	(Pellegrini, 1985) (Roskos & Christie, 2001)
Special Needs, Special Education 1986–2013	(Lipson & Wixson, 1986) (Schirmer & McGough, 2005) (Swanson & Hsieh, 2009) (Griffiths & Stuart, 2013)

Multilingualism, Bilingualism 1989–2018	(Hornberger, 1989) (Fitzgerald, 1995) (Slavin & Cheung, 2005) (Janzen, 2008) (Reyes, 2012) (Cheung & Slavin, 2012) (Prevoo, Malda, Mesman, & van IJzendoorn, 2016) (Bacon, 2017) (Fitton, McIlraith, & Wood, 2018)

1990s

Comprehension 1991–2018	(Dole, Duffy, Roehler, & Pearson, 1991) (Kucan & Beck, 1997) (Gersten, Fuchs, Williams, & Baker, 2001) (García & Cain, 2014) (Spencer & Wagner, 2018)
Digital Literacies and Technological Practices (including Television) 1991–2019	(Cochran-Smith, 1991) (Bangert-Drowns, 1993) (Fabos & Young, 1999) (Blok, Oostdam, Otter, & Overmaat, 2002) (Lankshear & Knobel, 2003) (Kuiper, Volman, & Terwel, 2005) (Moses, 2008) (Burnett, 2010) (Mills, 2010) (Miller, 2013) (Pandya & Ávila, 2017) (Singer & Alexander, 2017) (Kucirkova, 2019)

Particular Publications
1992–1999
	(Baldwin et al., 1992) – NRC publications:
	    1952–1991
	(Guzzetti, Anders, & Neuman, 1999) – 30 years of
	    JRB/JLR

Theoretical 1995–2009	(Greene & Ackerman, 1995) (Smagorinsky, 2001) (McVee, Dunsmore, & Gavelek, 2005) (Weis, Jenkins, & Stich, 2009)
Family Literacy, Parent Literacy, Home Literacy Practices 1995–2020	(Bus, Van Ijzendoorn, & Pellegrini, 1995) (Sénéchal & Young, 2008) (Mol, Bus, & De Jong, 2009) (Reese, Sparks, & Leyva, 2010) (Van Steensel, McElvany, Kurvers, & Herppich, 2011) (Compton-Lilly et al., 2012). (Compton-Lilly et al., 2020)

(Continued)

24 Qualitative Research Syntheses in Literacy Studies

TABLE 1.1 Continued

2000s	
Fluency and Speed 2001–2010	(Fuchs, Fuchs, Hosp, & Jenkins, 2001) (Kirby, Georgiou, Martinussen, & Parrila, 2010) (Kuhn, Schwanenflugel, & Meisinger, 2010)
Out-of-School Literacies 2001–2009	(Hull & Schultz, 2001) (Petchauer, 2009)
Teacher Preparation 2001–2019	(Roskos, Vukelich, & Risko, 2001) (Mosely Wetzel et al., 2019) (Fowler-Amato, LeeKeenan, Warrington, Nash, & Brady, 2019) (Hikida et al., 2019) (Bomer, Land, Rubin, & Van Dike, 2019) (Flores, Vlach, & Lammert, 2019) (Hoffman et al., 2019) (Lysaker & Handsfield, 2019) (Bomer & Maloch, 2019)
Teacher/Child Interactions 2005	(Fisher, 2005)
Discourse Analysis 2005–2014	(Rogers, Malancharuvil-Berkes, Mosley, Hui, & Joseph, 2005) (Rex et al., 2010) (Rogers & Schaenen, 2014)
Adolescent Literacy 2006–2009	(Franzak, 2006) (Faggella-Luby, Ware, & Capozzoli, 2009)
International Reading Instruction 2007	(Commeyras & Inyega, 2007)
Children's Literature 2009	(Brooks & McNair, 2009)
2010s	
Neuroscience and Reading 2011	(Hruby & Goswami, 2011)
Transnationalism 2012	(Lam & Warriner, 2012)
Motivation, Voice, Engagement 2012–2018	(Schiefele, Schaffner, Möller, & Wigfield, 2012) (Sperling & Appleman, 2011) (Unrau et al., 2018)
Low SES students 2013	(Kim & Quinn, 2013)
Literacy Practices 2014	(Juzwik, 2014)
Reading Development 2014	(Pfost, Hattie, Dörfler, & Artelt, 2014)
Literacy Coaching 2020	(Robertson, Padesky, Ford-Connors, & Paratore, 2020)

In each early summary, Gray provided citations and one sentence descriptions of studies that had been conducted during the prior year. Findings from these studies were not reported. For example, the 1927 report summarized 56 studies; Gray concluded that summary with a one paragraph gloss:

> There are two interesting preliminary facts which merit attention. First, there has been marked improvement during the past year in the quality of the studies published. In general, each study relates to a single specific problem; the data presented are more reliable; and the interpretations are keener and better defended. Second, a relatively large number of investigations of reading in the so-called "content" subjects have been reported. This fact indicates that reading as it relates to the various school subjects and activities is now challenging some of the attention that it has long deserved (p. 464).

By 1954, Gray's annual reviews were becoming more similar to traditional literature reviews familiar to contemporary readers. These later summaries also included summaries existing reviews of literacy related to scholarship. Gray opened his 1954 summary with the following statement (1954):

> Ten of the references are devoted exclusively to summaries of published research relating to specific areas or problems. They have been included because of their value in guiding practice and in planning further research. Due to their character, they should be read in detail by those interested in the topics discussed. Accordingly, they are referred to briefly in the statements that follow with no attempt to summarize their contents (p. 401).

Gray then listed ten articles that reviewed various dimensions of reading including readiness, differentiated instruction in reading, relationships between personality and language arts, eye-movement studies, and reading disability. Next, Gray guided the reader through a review of other primary studies published between 1950 and 1951 which he summarized under the following headings: The Sociology of Reading, The Physiology and Psychology of Reading, and the Teaching of Reading. Starting in 1953, the *Summary of Investigations Relating to Reading* were published in *The Reading Teacher* and the *Reading Research Quarterly* (Shanahan, 2002). Following Gray's death in 1960 – the same year he published his final summary – Helen M. Robinson and later Sam Weintraub served as the first author for the *Summaries*.

Between 1961 and 1963, *Summary of Investigations Relating to Reading* was published in both the *Journal of Educational Research* and *The Reading Teacher* by different scholars. In some years, *Summary of Investigations* specific to English language arts in elementary education (Petty & Burns, 1964; *Elementary English*) and English language arts in secondary education (Strom, 1964; *The English Journal*) were also published. These summaries addressed broad areas of interest including spelling, reading problems, English composition, materials, methods, and programs.

By the mid-1990s, the last few *Summaries* were published by International Reading Association (now the International Literacy Association) as monographs. For example, the 1996 summary (Weintraub, 1996) – the last one that we were able to locate – summarizes approximately 500 reports of reading research published between summer 1994 and spring 1995. The summary had sections dedicated to teacher's preparation and practice, the sociology of reading, the physiology and psychology of reading, the teaching of reading, and the reading of atypical learners. The studies are grouped into subcategories. Citations and abstracts of approximately 200 words are presented for each study. An author index and a list of journals that were "monitored" are presented at the end of the monograph. The opening section of the monograph continued to be dedicated to summaries of reading research and was by far the shortest section of the book – with only three entries, including the Annual *Summary of Investigations Relating to Reading* from the prior year (Weintraub, 1996).

Peer-Reviewed Research Syntheses Related to Literacy

In order to capture the range of topics addressed by literacy scholars, we include both qualitative and quantitative research syntheses in Table 1.1. In this table, we identify bodies of research that have been reviewed in journal articles to reveal evolving research interests and to serve contemporary scholars who are interested in exploring the historical development of these bodies of research. This analysis does not include books, book chapters, or handbook chapters.

Over time, research syntheses related to literacy have become increasingly specific in terms of focus. While early reviews often addressed broad areas – including *reading* or *reading research* – more recent reviews focus on particular areas of interest (e.g., motivation, teacher preparation, and adolescent literacy). The most reviewed area of literacy research is writing and the teaching of writing (17 reviews). Research syntheses related to writing first appeared in 1952 and have been consistently published since then. Another highly reviewed area involves digital and technological literacies. Thirteen reviews have been published since 1991. Research syntheses with the longest presence are reviews related to reading difficulties and reading interventions with eight reviews spanning 73 years (1943–2016). However, seven out of eight of these reviews were published after 2004. Finally, some areas of literacy scholarship have had only one research synthesis (e.g., multisensory/multimodality, children's literature, neuroscience, and reading) or have only been published during a limited span of time; for example, two research syntheses related to language variation/African American language were published in 1976 and 1978, but not since. More recent reviews have focused on more specialized topics including digital literacy, reading programs for Spanish speakers, scientific literacy, and morphological instruction.

Qualitative Research Syntheses in Literacy Studies 27

In a historical review of the content of the *Review of Educational Research* — a journal dedicated to review-oriented scholarship, Grant and Graue (1999) note that early journal editors identified lists of topics to be addressed every 3 years. Thus, the content published in these volumes reflects the preferences of the editors. They note that early reviews generally "took the form of annotated bibliographies organized by category" and "little was done in terms of synthesis" (p. 389). The journal was explicitly designed to include practitioner and scholarly audiences.

Over time, editors of journals became increasingly concerned about the quality of the studies published and worked to implement "rigorous standards for the nature of appropriate research evidence" (Grant & Graue, 1999, p. 388). By the early 1970s, editors pursued a policy of publishing unsolicited reviews of research on topics identified by contributors. During this time, the *Review of Educational Research* increasingly published reviews that relied on statistical procedures. As a result, teacher access and interest was limited by unfamiliar analytical methods, terms, and topics that were only marginally applicable to classroom teaching.

At present, the most definitive source of research syntheses in literacy research may be literacy handbooks, including the *Handbooks of Reading Research* (Shanahan, 2002). Handbooks are not discussed in this chapter. A research synthesis presentation is also featured annually at the *Literacy Research Association* conference and is published annually in *Literacy Research: Theory, Method, and Practice* (formerly the NRC/LRA yearbook).

Special issues of journal can also be important forums for presenting research syntheses. For example, the 2019 issue of the *Journal of Literacy Research* featured a collection of research syntheses related to literacy teacher education culled from the *CITE-ITEL* database. The CITE-ITEL database — an ongoing public knowledge project — continues to operate as a repository for storing and accessing research related to literacy teacher education. By making research related to literacy teacher education available, this site provides a comprehensive resource for research synthesists who want to access primary studies to understand how literacy educators are prepared and supported. This data base includes more than 650 research articles published since 2000. The special issue included six research syntheses that addressed a range of issues related to literacy teacher preparation. Reflecting emerging trends in the types of research syntheses being published, these syntheses qualify as either integrative reviews or metasyntheses, rather than traditional literature reviews. In their tertiary review of this special issue, Lysaker and Handsfield (2019) make the case that integrative research syntheses can be sites of disruption and dialogue by revealing synthetic findings that require scholars to reconsider assumptions and beliefs. Syntheses can also be rewritten for practitioners. For example, we reworked our critical integrative review as a column for *Language Arts* (Compton-Lilly et al., 2019). Other research syntheses, such as the *National Reading Panel Report* (2000) and its

28 Qualitative Research Syntheses in Literacy Studies

accompanying summary presented a road map for literacy education that – 20 years later – continues to affect what happens in United States classrooms.

As Shanahan (2002) reported, over time research syntheses have moved away from presenting simple summaries of primary research toward reviews that feature "clear selection standards in the identification of relevant research, explicit criteria for judgments, operational definitions, and replicability of methods" (p. 137). In short, Shanahan (2002) argued that reviews "should rise above authoritative opinion" (p. 137) to reveal trends and patterns to support literacy scholars and educators. In sum, the genre of literature reviews in literacy studies has changed dramatically over the last 80 years.

Types of Literature Reviews Related to Literacy

In addition to tracking the issues addressed by research syntheses, we also explored the level of methodological detail presented in published reports. Within our entire sample, we excluded 35 reviews that synthesized quantitative studies; most of these were quantitative meta-analyses that reported effect sizes. These quantitative studies are not included in Table 1.2. We also did not include the four tertiary reviews that involved analysis across research syntheses. Table 1.2 lists the types of qualitative research syntheses published since 1937, which are discussed below. Again, this analysis focuses on journal articles and does not include books, book chapters, or handbook chapters.

Based on our analysis, it was rare for research synthesists to describe the methods used to conduct their studies prior to 2000. We located only five research syntheses published in journals prior to 2000 that provided detailed descriptions of methodologies they used to review primary scholarship. Thus, Breed (1937) presented a compelling case. One of the very earliest research syntheses included in our data set, Breed, provided notable detail about his methods. He noted that his review took "cognizance not only of quantitative reports, but also of critical discussions" (p. 519) conducted between 1934 and 1937. He explained that he reviewed 79 studies and described his collaborative analytic method which entailed the preparation of a tentative bibliography "prepared by the writer and submitted to the other members of the committee for corrections and additions. On the basis of a revised bibliography the first draft of the chapter was prepared by the writer, submitted to the other members of the committee for suggestions, then modified to take account of these suggestions" (p. 519). He noted that in his analysis "words heretofore reported in studies of the writing vocabulary of children have been selected on the basis of frequency of use in themes, frequency of misspelling in themes, frequency of use in letters written outside of school, and frequency of occurrence in free or controlled association" (p. 519).

Qualitative Research Syntheses in Literacy Studies **29**

TABLE 1.2 Analysis of 105 Qualitative Research Syntheses Related to Literacy

	Definitions	Methodological Descriptions	
77 Traditional Literature Reviews 1937–2017	These reviewers reported on particular bodies of work via chronological/ historical, thematic, and narrative reviews.	47 reviews did not include a methodological description 30 reviews included a methodological description	Five methodological descriptions before 2000 25 methodological descriptions after 2000
28 Integrative Reviews 2001–2019	These reviewers brought a stated lens or perspective to the research and/or attended to particular questions.	15 reviews did not include a methodological description 13 reviews included a methodological description	Zero methodological descriptions before 2000 13 methodological descriptions after 2000
5 Qualitative Metasyntheses 1991–2020	Meta-syntheses examine the findings of high-quality qualitative research studies to identify patterns and trends (Thorne et al., 2004).	One synthesis did not include a methodological description Four syntheses included a methodological description	Zero methodological descriptions before 2000 Four methodological descriptions after 2013
1 Meta-Ethnography	Reviews of ethnographic research (Noblit & Hare, 1988; Urrieta & Noblit, 2018) that involve metaphoric analyses.	This meta-ethnography included a methodological description (2020)	

30 Qualitative Research Syntheses in Literacy Studies

This level of specificity is rare in early research syntheses and does not appear again until 1983 when Wade published a synthesis related to "improving reading in the social studies" (p. 461). Her analysis identified a brief selection process, years included in the study, the number of articles reviewed, and a brief description of the coding process used.

Traditional Literature Reviews

In our review of published research syntheses, traditional literature reviews were the most common. Eisenhart (1998) describes these as reviews that "establish the dimensions of a field so that the width and breadth of the field are defined" (p. 394). Traditional literature reviews, like other kinds of research syntheses, can be thought of as "independent research studies are held to the same evaluative standards used with other forms of research" (Shanahan, 2002, p. 134). Indeed, Table 1.2 illustrates that of the 105 qualitative research syntheses we reviewed, we classified 77 as traditional literature reviews. Forty-seven of these traditional literature reviews did not include a clear description of how primary studies were sampled, selected, or analyzed. Of the 30 traditional literature reviews that included a methodological description, only five were published before 2000. More recent literature reviews – those published in or after 2000 – tended to include more methodological detail.

Examples of traditional literature reviews with detailed methodologies include Al Ghanem, and Kearns (2015), Roskos, Vukelich, and Risko (2001), Schiefele, Schaffner, Möller, and Wigfield (2012). For example, Burnett (2010) described her review as including "only empirical studies, rather than project descriptions, analyses of programs or guidelines for practice [that] included a clear statement of methodology" (p. 252). She clarified that while all articles were derived from peer-reviewed articles and chapters from edited collections that "there was no further screening in relation to rigor, originality or significance" (p. 252). She named the data bases and search terms she used to conduct her search, the years sampled, and the number of articles included. Her review highlighted the need for more exploratory research that considered how digital practices were used within educational settings and how digital practices related to other dimensions of literacy learning. Her goal was to better understand how new technologies contributed to children's literacy learning. Burnett clearly described the limitations of her analysis.

While traditional literature reviews related to literacy continue to be published, since 2000, increasing numbers of reviews have assumed the forms of integrative literature reviews and metasyntheses. These forms of research syntheses consistently include detailed methodological descriptions. In Chapter 3 of this volume, Becky describes two linked traditional literature reviews she conducted with colleagues (Rogers, et al., 2005; Rogers & Schaenen, 2014).

Integrative Literature Reviews

Integrative literature reviews investigate a body of research through a particular lens or in terms of a particular question or perspective (Thorne et al., 2004). While several integrative literature reviews have been published in literacy studies, they are far less common than traditional literature reviews. In contrast to the 77 traditional literature reviews we identified, we located only 28 integrative literature reviews. Integrative literature reviews do not aspire to comment on a comprehensive body of scholarship, instead they ask particular questions or impose particular perspectives on a set of primary studies. Identifying integrative literature reviews into our sample was challenging because most authors do not use the term "integrative literature review" to identify their work. As research synthesists, we carefully read each research synthesis to ascertain whether authors focused on a particular issue or question, or imposed a particular lens or perspective on a body of scholarship.

The integrative literature reviews that we analyzed were published after 1985 and most provided clear details related to search procedures, selection, and analytic techniques. For example, Newell, Beach, Smith, and VanDerHeide (2011) published an integrative review of primary studies related to the teaching and learning of argumentative writing. While the authors did not describe their reviews as an integrative review, they clearly state a particular purpose, "we use this critical review to make the case for more research on teaching and learning argumentative reading and writing that integrates a range of research perspectives for how and why to conduct studies of this important aspect of academic learning" (p. 274).

The authors described a detailed sampling process that included "empirical studies of teaching and learning argumentative reading and writing in grades K–12 in English language arts classrooms and in college-level writing contexts published between 1985 and 2011" (p. 275) and clear criteria for selecting primary studies. Search procedures included both "manual shelf and online searches" (p. 276). Targeted journals and search terms were identified. Their analysis reflected their goal of synthesizing a range of research perspectives; in particular they adopted a "dialogic approach to explore alternative frameworks of a cognitive perspective and a social perspective on argumentation to consider useful contributions of both frameworks as well as tensions between the two" (p. 276). Their findings identified gaps in the field and explored the degree to which argumentative reading and writing instruction reflected either the adoption of cognitive tasks or social practice positions and discourses. In Chapter 4, we discuss our critical integrative literature review related to family literacy (Compton-Lilly et al., 2012).

Meta-Ethnographies

We identified only one meta-ethnography in literacy studies (Compton-Lilly et al., 2020). For the sake of transparency, we note that this meta-ethnography of family literacy scholarship was conducted by the authors of this volume.

32 Qualitative Research Syntheses in Literacy Studies

Our meta-ethnography used procedures described by Noblit and Hare (1988) to design and conduct an analysis of primary research in the field of family literacy. The published version included a detailed description of our search procedures, selection, and analytic techniques. Suri (2013) would characterize our search procedure as an example of snowball sampling that attended to the most cited qualitative studies in the field of family literacy. While our research and writing processes are detailed in Chapter 5, we present a brief description below.

Specifically, we analyzed the metaphors that highly cited scholars have used to present and describe family literacy. Meta-ethnography, as described by Noblit and Hare (1988), treats metaphors as linguistic tools that allow metasynthesists to compare and synthesize understandings across ethnographic studies of family literacy. Specifically, we identified key metaphors to trace the development, refinement, and expansion of epistemological stances that have informed and continue to frame family literacy scholarship. Our meta-ethnography highlighted generally invisible changes in understandings and emerging lines of argument related to family literacy. This analysis led to the identification of a problematic silence related to racism and systemic oppression, which we treat as a significant meta-ethnographic finding. In Chapter 5, we discuss our meta-ethnographic process (Compton-Lilly et al., 2020).

Qualitative Metasyntheses

We draw on Sandelowski and Barroso's (2007) definition of metasyntheses as research syntheses that look across the findings of primary studies. For the analysis presented in Table 1.2, we reread the research syntheses included in our sample (see Table 1.2) to identify reviews that explicitly attended to findings across primary studies in order to make claims about knowledge in relation to a particular body of scholarship. In literacy studies, we identified five research syntheses that we classified as qualitative metasyntheses.

For example, Bacon (2017) attended to how primary studies conceptualized and operationalized critical literacy in English language teaching classrooms. His review outlined the current state of the field and provided illustrations of promising pedagogical approaches. Bacon explicitly described his research synthesis as drawing on the "methodology of qualitative metasynthesis, an inductive approach to synthesizing research through summarizing findings from empirical studies, while also viewing the reviewed literature as a structure, or cultural artifact, by which to offer interpretations about the field" (p. 428). He explained his sampling process, including his intentional focus on "countries in which English is widely spoken as well as countries where English is learned as a 'foreign' or secondary language" (p. 428). Bacon's criteria for primary study inclusion were not based on country of origin, language(s) spoken by participants, learner age groups, or English-ability levels. Bacon identified both the databases he used and the particular journals he searched. In all, 68 studies were analyzed by attending

Qualitative Research Syntheses in Literacy Studies **33**

to "larger units of cultural knowledge" (p. 429) identified by Bacon and informed by "theoretical frameworks underlying critical literacies in ELT" (p. 429). Bacon then constructed a "preliminary taxonomy" (p. 429). Bacon found that findings coalesced "around five key topics: teacher beliefs, learner beliefs, course design, specific practices, and language-emphatic designs" (p. 424). Based on this metasynthesis, Bacon argued that "critical literacies, enacted through a variety of pedagogies and techniques, can motivate and inspire critical engagement among teachers and learners alike across a vast array of age groups, cultures, and pedagogical contexts" (p. 446). In Chapter 6, we discuss our experiences with an ongoing metasynthesis project.

General Process for Conducting Research Syntheses

Suri (2013) assumed the monumental task of identifying critical aspects of high-quality research syntheses. Specifically, she identifies three guiding principles: "informed subjectivity and reflexivity, purposely informed selective inclusivity, and audience-appropriate transparency" (p. i). Suri (2013) argued that similar design phases could be applied to syntheses of both qualitative and quantitative primary studies. She argued that qualitative, quantitative, and mixed methods research syntheses could include both qualitative and quantitative primary research. Suri was particularly interested in review methodologies that looked across and moved beyond the epistemological, theoretical, and methodological differences operating in primary studies. In short, Suri described a *methodologically inclusive research synthesis method* that was "intended as a coherent conceptualization of research synthesis methods, expressed through the identification of critical decisions and thorough discussion of varied options associated with individual decisions in the process of rigorous research synthesis" (p. xix). She identified review phases that transcend types of research synthesis and the types of primary studies involved:

- Identifying an appropriate epistemological orientation,
- Identifying an appropriate purpose,
- Searching for relevant literature,
- Evaluating, interpreting, and distilling evidence from selected articles, and
- Communicating with audiences.

While we draw on Suri's design phases, in the sections below, we describe how we have adapted these phases to focus on the synthesis of qualitative literacy educational scholarship.

Identifying an Epistemological Orientation

As Suri (2013) noted, epistemologies and paradigms facilitate our understandings of phenomena by providing frameworks to guide and direct research syntheses. However, epistemologies also restrict our gaze and limit what we might consider

34 Qualitative Research Syntheses in Literacy Studies

relevant to our work. Suri noted that the epistemological orientations that drive research synthesis projects must be compatible with the intended purpose of a project. Epistemologies guide sampling and searching processes for primary studies, how primary studies are represented, how primary studies are placed in conversation with each other, and how synthesis findings are presented.

In our own work with family literacy, we intentionally adopted an epistemology that honored a vast range of families from many different backgrounds, respected the knowledge they brought, and recognized the strengths and best intentions of parents. These epistemological premises were critical to our work. In order to craft research syntheses that honor both our academic colleagues and the participants of their primary studies, we sought to ensure that what we do, what we write, and how we bring ideas together contributed to understanding families in ways that raise important insights yet also lead to productive changes for families and family literacy educators. Epistemologically, we aspired toward a stance that honored the logic and intentions that drove the primary researcher, while simultaneously highlighting the voices of study participants.

Identifying a Purpose

Epistemology is tightly linked to purpose. For example, in our empirical work, we insist on epistemologies that contribute to a more socially just world. For us, this entails conducting research syntheses that ultimately serve children and families. Thus, our critical integrative literature review examined how family literacy researchers addressed diversity, while our meta-ethnography revealed a relative lack of attention to race and racism in the work of highly cited scholars. These findings are particularly crucial given the fact that family literacy researchers generally serve Families of Color from historically underserved communities.

Review designs are also intricately connected to the purposes of research syntheses. Suri (2013) identified interpretive, critical, and participatory purposes for qualitative research syntheses.

- Interpretive research synthesists recognize the world as socially constructed and acknowledge the tacit knowledge, views, and experiences that researchers and study participants bring to research studies. Their goal is to contribute to understanding and communication across communities by attending to the experiences and interests of multiple stakeholders.
- Critical metasynthesists subscribe to explicitly emancipatory goals by challenging grand narratives and dominant discourses while attending to the voices of people who have not been well-represented.
- Participatory research synthesists recognize that individuals and community members construct understandings of the world; within a participatory tradition, practitioners are invited to analyze and re-envision their own practices

and positions. The intentional purpose for a research synthesis is to improve practice – including teaching – through careful reflection and attention to the lived experiences of people.

These purposes operate in both primary studies and in research syntheses. As with all qualitative research, the purposes for qualitative research syntheses may morph and change as synthesists become immersed in primary study analysis and recognize what is salient to study participants, primary researchers, and themselves as research synthesists.

Searching for Relevant Literature

Suri (2013) noted that how research synthesists search and sample primary studies is critical. The search process for research syntheses involves asking the following questions:

- *Which terms will be used?*
- *How much time will be covered in the search?*
- *Which search channels and databases will be used?*
- *What are the affordances and constraints of the database vendor and databases I am searching?*
- *How will studies be sampled for review?*
- *What will be the inclusion/exclusion criteria?*
- *How will I overcome search biases (e.g., language bias, availability bias, and familiarity bias)?*
- *How will I end or close the search?*

Often, although not always, these questions are addressed in the methodology sections of published research syntheses.

Search Terms

Choosing search terms for locating primary studies that fit the interests of research synthesists is critical. Search terms that are too broad or imprecise will require research synthesists to review and vet large bodies of potential studies. In contrast search terms that are too narrow may fail to locate relevant studies. The process of identifying search terms is complicated by the use of multiple search engines and the viability of a particular terms across multiple platforms and databases (i.e., ProQuest EBSCO, Google Scholar, Amazon, and university library catalogue). In order to identify viable search terms research synthesists must test the usefulness of particular terms, combinations terms, and formatting that affects how terms operate within databases. For example, quotation marks the use of "and" versus "or," and particular forms of punctuation affect how search terms operate in databases. For example, the use of an asterisk (★) will search multiple forms of a word allowing the searcher to locate any word that has a particular root (e.g., child★ will search childhood, children, and childish). The use of a question mark (?) in the middle of a word will bring up various spellings of a word; thus "organi?e" will elicit both American and British spellings – "organise" and "organize." This is particularly significant if research synthesists intend to search international publications.

The Timeframe Sampled

Research synthesists also make decisions about the timeframe that will be sampled. Some research syntheses (Baldwin et al., 1992; Guzzetti et al., 1999; Juzwik, 2014; Roskos & Christie, 2001; Whitehead & Wilkinson, 2008; Schiefele et al., 2012) include multiple decades of literature to address where has the field been and/or address current and future needs. For example, a study by Roskos and Christie (2001) exemplified one purpose of a longitudinal review. Their study was designed to examine the role of reflection in the professional education of reading teachers and inform future research in reading teacher preparation. They focus on "likenesses and differences that might help to clarify the reflection construct for research work and inform instruction in reflection during the preparatory years" (p. 597). Thus, they review scholarship to not only gain a sense of what is known but also to propose implications for future research.

Scammacca et al. (2016) "undertook the task of synthesizing 100 years of published research on reading interventions for students in Grades 4 to 12" (p. 757). Their goal was to "systematically review the published literature in a way that highlights the lessons of the past to inform present and future research and practice" (p. 757). In other cases, scholars use research syntheses to explore the contribution of a particular publication or the state of knowledge on a particular topic. For example, Mills (2010) looked across various publications to examine long-term trends in New Literacy Studies. Some research syntheses straddle multiple purposes. Comber's stated purposes (2014) included both reviewing "several decades of literacy research in schools in high-poverty environments" and exploring "what matters in young people's education" (p. 115). Gersten et al.'s (2001) stated purposes included conducting "a comprehensive review of intervention research conducted over the past 20 years" to inform "comprehension instruction for students with learning disabilities" (p. 279). In short, these authors synthesized multiple decades of scholarship to identify best practices.

Search Channels and Databases

What continues to be omitted in many discussions of research syntheses is the logic related to why and how particular search decisions are made. In this section, we introduce readers to differences between database vendors and databases.

Qualitative Research Syntheses in Literacy Studies **37**

We also review popular databases and the strengths and weaknesses of these databases (see Appendix C).

Across research syntheses listed in Table 1.2, 63 different databases were consulted. Databases are the online platforms provided by database vendors that bundle publications so that they can be simultaneously searched. Database vendors such as ProQuest and EBSCO are companies that compile and host various databases; they sell access to these databases to universities, libraries, and other organizations. Database vendors use different interfaces and provide various bundled packages of publications. Database vendors may offer special features including the provision of non-American and/or non-English databases.

Appendix C presents an annotated list of databases that are commonly used by university scholars for literacy education research. Many of these databases index scholarship and provide downloadable full text/PDF copies of research articles. Full text databases include ERIC, JSTOR, and Lexis Nexis Academic. These databases also allow scholars to search the digital content of journals.

Some databases are index-only, which means that they provide citations to articles, which then need to be located through other means (i.e., university library and online network). Web of Science and PsycInfo are examples of index databases. Academic Search Complete is a mixed database, which means it offers a combination of citations and downloadable publications. Some databases are open-access (i.e., ERIC), but most require an institutional subscription (i.e., university or library).

All databases exclude scholarship for a variety of reasons including traditions, myopic cultural norms, licensing issues, and available funds. The United States, being the largest economy, has a significant effect on what is available through databases. Reviewers should always be aware that there are powerful economic, political, and cultural forces that affect data bases and recognize that knowledge and power operate at the core of these systems.

For example, South Africa is an important space for scholars who are interested in critically oriented literacy studies. Unlike the United States and most other countries, South Africa hosts multiple national databases that are owned by different companies; only some of these are listed in major search engines, such as Scopus. The University of Cape Town lists these databases on their university homepage, but many of these databases are not integrated into ProQuest or EBSCO because South African scholars value being able to retain their rights to these databases. In contrast, in the United States, Summon is a shared *library federated search engine*. Summon operates at the top layer of the funneling system that serves various search engines, including Google Scholar. Because of this, scholars who search using Summon or Google Scholar often turn up more journal articles in addition to references to book chapters and dissertations.

Complexities related to search engines and access to scholarship, are illustrated by Dixon (in review) in her bibliometric analysis of South African language and literacy scholarship. Specifically, she identifies the advantages of using the

38 Qualitative Research Syntheses in Literacy Studies

international database Scopus because it provides more access to social sciences, arts, and humanities research than most major databases. However, she reminds readers that not all South African journals are included in that database; which limits the ability of scholars to access and search the full range of South African scholarship related to language and literacy.

Overcoming Search Bias

Search bias is an important consideration for scholars who conduct research syntheses. In short, search engines and databases often present biases related to what is included or excluded, the representation of international scholars, and the publication of research in languages other than English (Suri, 2013). Suri (2013) warned that "reports published in international English language journals... may not be representative of all the studies conducted on the topic" (p. 93). Thus, research synthesists must consider how to expand searches to better access the full set of scholarship related to issues of interest. Table 1.3 provides advice on internationalizing searches. Other ideas – including bibliographic branching and backward searching – are discussed in Chapters 2 through 6. In each chapter, we reflect on the inevitable partiality of research syntheses due to time, access, and database limits, as well as biases introduced by experiences and assumptions that affect our reading and interpretation of primary studies.

We suggest that research synthesists actively attempt to decolonize their research syntheses by posing the following questions:

- To what extent is research from around the world intentionally sought in order to avoid search biases related to language, accessibility, and geographic locale?
- To what extent do synthesists attend to the voices and experiences of participants in empirical studies?

TABLE 1.3 Ways to Internationalize a Search Despite the Limitations of Database Vendors

---

- Search online, open access databases, such as Redalyc, SciELO, and African Journals Online. Many of these databases provide an option to sign up to receive emails when articles are published in selected journals.
- Consult with colleagues who work in a range of geographical locales; ask about database norms, journal indexing, and alternate databases. This is particularly important if the topic under review (e.g., critical literacy) has a long international history (e.g., South Africa and Latin America).
- Explicitly search by key word and country
- Note that several databases (i.e., PsycINFO) provide the option to search in Spanish language journals.
- Search out specific databases that are known to have an international scope (e.g., SCOPUS).

Qualitative Research Syntheses in Literacy Studies **39**

These issues are particularly important for researchers who engage in critical traditions of literacy research. As was the case with the CDA in education dataset examined by Rogers and her peers (Rogers, et al., 2005; Rogers & Schaenen, 2014; see Chapter 3) and in the family literacy research syntheses examined by the authors (Compton-Lilly et al., 2012; Compton-Lilly et al., 2020; see Chapters 4 and 5, respectively), critically oriented scholarship is often conducted with historically minoritized communities. Depending on the questions research synthesists ask, they may attend differently to the voices and experiences of the people who participated in the primary research studies.

Evaluating, Interpreting, and Distilling Evidence from Primary Studies

Research synthesists engage in varied and detailed methods for evaluating, interpreting, and distilling evidence across primary studies and other forms of published scholarship. In some cases, analytic methods are determined by particular syntheses methodologies. In other cases, research synthesists design their own analytical processes, applying them reiteratively to the selected corpus of studies. Thus, the method used is contingent on the type of review conducted, the questions asked, and the methodology adapted.

If a synthesis project is designed to evaluate research studies, review synthesists might identify evaluative criteria to guide that analysis. Criteria might be based on analyses of exemplar studies, characteristics of highly cited studies, and/or methodological design elements recommended by expert researchers.

If the research synthesists focus on the findings presented in primary studies, they require different analytical tools. These tools must help the researcher to identify claims and patterns within primary studies as well as categories of findings across the studies. This might entail comparing and analyzing findings and attending to findings reiterated across studies, time, and epistemology to understand the targeted phenomenon. Finally, as is the case for meta-ethnography, research synthesists might attend to the metaphors that primary researchers use to reference the phenomenon of interest.

Thus, research syntheses do not end with analyses of individual primary studies. Synthesists look across the corpus of identified studies and the patterns they have discerned to compare and contrast how primary scholars have collectively made sense of the phenomenon of interest. As part of this cross-case analytic process, research synthesists might reveal disagreements, confluences of findings, and emerging lines of argument across studies and over time. Looking across studies may reveal voices and perspectives that have been ignored and or place attention on critical issues that have defined people's lives and experiences.

40 Qualitative Research Syntheses in Literacy Studies

Communicating with Audiences

Audience is an important consideration for research synthesists. In our own work, we have sometimes revisited our research syntheses to craft what we have learned for a new audience. This requires careful rethinking of how information is framed and presented. For example, we recently re-wrote our critical integrative literature review (Compton-Lilly et al., 2012), which was published in a highly ranked scholarly journal, for a teacher audience (Compton-Lilly et al., 2019). As part of this process, we omitted much of our methodological detail, adopted a more conversational voice, and identified implications for teachers and educators working with families. Public knowledge projects which aim to make research syntheses accessible to multiple audiences are becoming more common. CITE-ITEL – a repository for storing and accessing research related to teacher education – is an example of one such public knowledge project.

The Use of Research Syntheses

The ways we conducted our research syntheses were informed by our use of research syntheses in our roles as university faculty, teacher educators, and community members.

Research syntheses are generally recognized by journal editors as among the most cited genres of scholarly articles. In our review of 144 of literature reviews in literacy studies, the average number of Google citations was just over 206 per review; three reviews had over a thousand citations – Bus et al. (1995, 2491 citations), Dole et al. (1991; 1289 citations), and Gersten et al. (2001; 1066 citations). Some journal editors – for example, Bloome and Wilkinson during their terms as editors for the *Reading Research Quarterly* – worked to include a research synthesis in each issue (2010–2015). Well-written and highly cited research syntheses positively affect the impact factor for journals, which are in constant competition with other journals.

Ultimately, syntheses play an important role in making sense of the landscape of scholarly research. It is important to keep in mind that research syntheses are written from a theoretical perspective and have a methodological design, although the degree to which procedures are described and followed varies. Indeed, the inner workings of research syntheses are not always transparent and, thus, syntheses can reproduce silences and inequities as they are circulated and distributed, contributing to assumedly definitive accounts of *what is known* instead of questioning, extending, and challenging what we think we know. We have been fortunate as research synthesists – although we did not always feel fortunate at the time – to have submitted manuscripts to editors and journals with thoughtful reviewers who challenged us to strengthen and tighten various aspects of our research syntheses. Our experiences in negotiating journal review processes are addressed in the chapters that follow.

Related Appendices

Common Qualitative Research Synthesis Designs

Appendix B: Final Analytic Review Template (ART)

Appendix C: Databases Used by University Scholars for Educational Research

References

Al Ghanem, R., & Kearns, D. M. (2015). Orthographic, phonological, and morphological skills and children's word reading in Arabic: A literature review. *Reading Research Quarterly*, 50(1), 83–109.

Apple, M. W. (1999). What counts as legitimate knowledge? The social production and use of reviews. *Review of Educational Research*, 69(4), 343–346.

Applebee, A. N. (1984). Writing and reasoning. *Review of Educational Research*, 54(4), 577–596.

Bacon, C. K. (2017). Multilanguage, multipurpose: A literature review, synthesis, and framework for critical literacies in English language teaching. *Journal of Literacy Research*, 49(3), 424–453.

Bangert-Drowns, R. L. (1993). The word processor as an instructional tool: A meta-analysis of word processing in writing instruction. *Review of Educational Research*, 63(1), 69–93.

Bangert-Drowns, R. L., Hurley, M. M., & Wilkinson, B. (2004). The effects of school-based writing-to-learn interventions on academic achievement: A meta-analysis. *Review of Educational Research*, 74(1), 29–58.

Baldwin, R. S., Readence, J. E., Schumm, J. S., Konopak, J. P., Konopak, B. C., & Klingner, J. K. (1992). Forty years of NRC publications: 1952–1991. *Journal of Reading Behavior*, 24(4), 505–532.

Barnes, R. F. (1965). Materials, methods, and programs for literacy education. *Review of Educational Research*, 35(3), 218–223.

Blok, H., Oostdam, R., Otter, M. E., & Overmaat, M. (2002). Computer-assisted instruction in support of beginning reading instruction: A review. *Review of Educational Research*, 72(1), 101–130.

Bomer, R., Land, C. L., Rubin, J. C., & Van Dike, L. M. (2019). Constructs of teaching writing in research about literacy teacher education. *Journal of Literacy Research*, 51(2), 196–213.

Bomer, R., & Maloch, B. (2019). Lessons for leaders on the preparation of literacy educators. *Journal of Literacy Research*, 51(2), 259–264.

Bowers, P. N., Kirby, J. R., & Deacon, S. H. (2010). The effects of morphological instruction on literacy skills: A systematic review of the literature. *Review of Educational Research*, 80(2), 144–179.

Brantlinger, E. (1997). Using ideology: Cases of nonrecognition of the politics of research and practice in special education. *Review of Educational Research*, 67(4), 425–459.

Breed, F. (1937). Spelling. *Review of Educational Research*, 7(5), 519–525.

Brooks, W., & McNair, J. C. (2009). "But this story of mine is not unique": A review of research on African American children's literature. *Review of Educational Research*, 79(1), 125–162.

Burnett, C. (2010). Technology and literacy in early childhood educational settings: A review of research. *Journal of Early Childhood Literacy*, 10(3), 247–270.

42 Qualitative Research Syntheses in Literacy Studies

Bus, A. G., Van Ijzendoorn, M. H., & Pellegrini, A. D. (1995). Joint book reading makes for success in learning to read: A meta-analysis on intergenerational transmission of literacy. *Review of Educational Research*, 65(1), 1–21.

Carlisle, J. F. (2010). Effects of instruction in morphological awareness on literacy achievement: An integrative review. *Reading Research Quarterly*, 45(4), 464–487.

Cavagnetto, A. R. (2010). Argument to foster scientific literacy: A review of argument interventions in K–12 science contexts. *Review of Educational Research*, 80(3), 336–371.

Cheung, A. C., & Slavin, R. E. (2012). Effective reading programs for Spanish-dominant English language learners (ELLs) in the elementary grades: A synthesis of research. *Review of Educational Research*, 82(4), 351–395.

Clifford, G. J. (1984). Buch und lesen: Historical perspectives on literacy and schooling. *Review of Educational Research*, 54(4), 472–500.

Clymer, T., & Robinson, H. M. (1961). Reading. *Review of Educational Research*, 31(2), 130–144.

Cochran-Smith, M. (1991). Word processing and writing in elementary classrooms: A critical review of related literature. *Review of Educational Research*, 61(1), 107–155.

Comber, B. (2014). Literacy, poverty and schooling: What matters in young people's education? *Literacy*, 48(3), 115–123.

Commeyras, M., & Inyega, H. N. (2007). An integrative review of teaching reading in Kenyan primary schools. *Reading Research Quarterly*, 42(2), 258–281.

Compton-Lilly, C., Lewis Ellison, T., & Rogers, R. (2019). The promise of family literacy: Possibilities and practices for educators. *Language Arts*, 97(1), 25–35.

Compton-Lilly, C., Rogers, R., & Lewis Ellison, T. (2020). A meta-ethnography of family literacy scholarship: Ways with metaphors. *Reading Research Quarterly*, 55(2), 271–289.

Compton-Lilly, C., Rogers, R., & Lewis, T. (2012) Analyzing epistemological considerations related to diversity: An integrative critical literature review of family literacy scholarship. *Reading Research Quarterly*, 47(1), 33–60.

Dearborn, W. F. (1906). The psychology of reading: An experimental study of the reading pauses and movements of the eye. *Monograph* 14(1), Columbia University.

DeBoer, J. J. (1955). Oral and written language. *Review of Educational Research*, 25(2), 107–120.

DiPardo, A., & Freedman, S. W. (1988). Peer response groups in the writing classroom: Theoretic foundations and new directions. *Review of Educational Research*, 58(2), 119–149.

Dole, J. A., Duffy, G. G., Roehler, L. R., & Pearson, P. D. (1991). Moving from the old to the new: Research on reading comprehension instruction. *Review of Educational Research*, 61(2), 239–264.

Durrell, D. D., & Murphy, H. A. (1949). Research in reading, 1946–1948. *Review of Educational Research*, 19(2), 95–106.

Durst, R. K., & Newell, G. E. (1989). The uses of function: James Britton's category system and research on writing. *Review of Educational Research*, 59(4), 375–394.

Dyson, A. H., & Genishi, C. (2005). *On the case* (Vol. 76). Teachers College Press.

Edmonds, M. S., Vaughn, S., Wexler, J., Reutebuch, C., Cable, A., Tackett, K. K., & Schnakenberg, J. W. (2009). A synthesis of reading interventions and effects on reading comprehension outcomes for older struggling readers. *Review of Educational Research*, 79(1), 262–300.

Ehri, L. C., Nunes, S. R., Stahl, S. A., & Willows, D. M. (2001). Systematic phonics instruction helps students learn to read: Evidence from the National Reading Panel's meta-analysis. *Review of Educational Research*, 71(3), 393–447.

Eisenhart, M. (1998). On the subject of interpretive reviews. *Review of Educational Research*, 68(4), 391–399.

Erickson, F. (1984). School literacy, reasoning, and civility: An anthropologist's perspective. *Review of Educational Research*, 54(4), 525–546.

Fabos, B., & Young, M. D. (1999). Telecommunication in the classroom: Rhetoric versus reality. *Review of Educational Research*, 69(3), 217–259.

Faggella-Luby, M. N., Ware, S. M., & Capozzoli, A. (2009). Adolescent literacy—Reviewing adolescent literacy reports: Key components and critical questions. *Journal of Literacy Research*, 41(4), 453–475.

Fisher, R. (2005). Teacher-child interaction in the teaching of reading: A review of research perspectives over twenty-five years. *Journal of Research in Reading*, 28(1), 15–27.

Fitton, L., McIlraith, A. L., & Wood, C. L. (2018). Shared book reading interventions with English learners: A meta-analysis. *Review of Educational Research*, 88(5), 712–751.

Fitzgerald, J. (1995). English-as-a-second-language learners' cognitive reading processes: A review of research in the United States. *Review of Educational Research*, 65(2), 145–190.

Flores, T. T., Vlach, S. K., & Lammert, C. (2019). The role of children's literature in cultivating preservice teachers as transformative intellectuals: A literature review. *Journal of Literacy Research*, 51(2), 214–232.

Ford-Connors, E., & Paratore, J. R. (2015). Vocabulary instruction in fifth grade and beyond: Sources of word learning and productive contexts for development. *Review of Educational Research*, 85(1), 50–91.

Fowler-Amato, M., LeeKeenan, K., Warrington, A., Nash, B.L., & Brady, R.B. (2019). Working toward a socially just future in the ELA methods class. *Journal of Literacy Research*, 51(2), 158–176.

Foster, P., & Hammersley, M. (1998). A review of reviews: Structure and function in reviews of educational research. *British Educational Research Journal*, 24(5), 609–628.

Franzak, J. K. (2006). Zoom: A review of the literature on marginalized adolescent readers, literacy theory, and policy implications. *Review of Educational Research*, 76(2), 209–248.

Fuchs, L. S., Fuchs, D., Hosp, M. K., & Jenkins, J. R. (2001). Oral reading fluency as an indicator of reading competence: A theoretical, empirical, and historical analysis. *Scientific Studies of Reading*, 5(3), 239–256.

García, J. R., & Cain, K. (2014). Decoding and reading comprehension: A meta-analysis to identify which reader and assessment characteristics influence the strength of the relationship in English. *Review of Educational Research*, 84(1), 74–111.

Gersten, R., Fuchs, L. S., Williams, J. P., & Baker, S. (2001). Teaching reading comprehension strategies to students with learning disabilities: A review of research. *Review of Educational Research*, 71(2), 279–320.

Gilbert, L. C., & Holmes, J. A. (1955). Chapter I: Reading: Psychology. *Review of Educational Research*, 25(2), 77–91.

Glass, G.V. (1976). Primary, secondary, and meta-analysis of research. *Educational Researcher*, 5(10), 3–8.

Good, C.V. (1925). A notable summary and interpretation of reading investigations. *The School Review*, 33(8), 627–629.

Graham, S., Liu, X., Bartlett, B., Ng, C., Harris, K. R., Aitken, A., Barkel, A., Kavanaugh, C., & Talukdar, J. (2018). Reading for writing: A meta-analysis of the impact of reading interventions on writing. *Review of Educational Research*, 88(2), 243–284.

Grant, C. A., & Graue, E. (1999). (Re)viewing a review: A case history of the review of educational research. *Review of Educational Research*, 69(4), 384–396.

44 Qualitative Research Syntheses in Literacy Studies

Gray, W. S. (1954). Summary of Reading Investigations July 1, 1952 to June 30, 1953. *The Journal of Educational Research*, 47(6), 401–439.

Gray, W. S. (1937). Chapter 7: Reading. *Review of Educational Research*, 7(5), 493–507.

Gray, W. S. (1927). Summary of Reading Investigations (July 1, 1925, to June 30, 1926), part I. *The Elementary School Journal*, 27(6), 456–466.

Gray, W. S. (1925). *Summary of Investigations Relating to Reading. Supplementary Educational Monographs, No. 28.* Department of Education, University of Chicago Press.

Greene, S., & Ackerman, J. M. (1995). Expanding the constructivist metaphor: A rhetorical perspective on literacy research and practice. *Review of Educational Research*, 65(4), 383–420.

Griffiths, Y., & Stuart, M. (2013). Reviewing evidence-based practice for pupils with dyslexia and literacy difficulties. *Journal of Research in Reading*, 36(1), 96–116.

Gunn, M. A., & Barlow, E. R. (1952). Chapter IV: English Composition. *Review of Educational Research*, 22(2), 96–101.

Guzzetti, B., Anders, P. L., & Neuman, S. (1999). Thirty years of JRB/JLR: A retrospective of reading/literacy research. *Journal of Literacy Research*, 31(1), 67–92.

Hadley, E. B., & Dickinson, D.K. (2020). Measuring young children's word knowledge: A conceptual review. *Journal of Early Childhood Literacy*, 20(2), 223–251.

Harber, J. R., & Bryen, D. N. (1976). Black English and the task of reading. *Review of Educational Research*, 46(3), 387–405.

Hidi, S., & Anderson, V. (1986). Producing written summaries: Task demands, cognitive operations, and implications for instruction. *Review of Educational Research*, 56(4), 473–493.

Hikida, M., Chamberlain, K., Tily, S., Daly-Lesch, A., Warner, J. R., & Schallert, D. L. (2019). Reviewing how preservice teachers are prepared to teach reading processes: What the literature suggests and overlooks. *Journal of Literacy Research*, 51(2), 177–195.

Hoffman, J. V., Svrcek, N., Lammert, C., Daly-Lesch, A., Steinitz, E., Greeter, E., & DeJulio, S. (2019). A research review of literacy tutoring and mentoring in initial teacher preparation: Toward practices that can transform teaching. *Journal of Literacy Research*, 51(2), 233–251.

Hornberger, N. H. (1989). Continua of biliteracy. *Review of Educational Research*, 59(3), 271–296.

Hruby, G. G., & Goswami, U. (2011). Neuroscience and reading: A review for reading education researchers. *Reading Research Quarterly*, 46(2), 156–172.

Huey, E. B. (1908). *The Psychology and Pedagogy of Reading.* The Macmillan Company.

Hull, G., & Schultz, K. (2001). Literacy and learning out of school: A review of theory and research. *Review of Educational Research*, 71(4), 575–611.

Huot, B. (1990). The literature of direct writing assessment: Major concerns and prevailing trends. *Review of Educational Research*, 60(2), 237–263.

Humes, A. (1983). Research on the composing process. *Review of Educational Research*, 53(2), 201–216.

Igland, M. A., & Ongstad, S. (2002). Introducing Norwegian research on writing. *Written Communication*, 19(3), 339–344.

Janzen, J. (2008). Teaching English language learners in the content areas. *Review of Educational Research*, 78(4), 1010–1038.

Juzwik, M. M. (2014). American evangelical Biblicism as literate practice: A critical review. *Reading Research Quarterly*, 49(3), 335–349.

Kennedy, M. (2007). Defining a literature. *Educational Researcher*, 36 (3), 139–147.

Qualitative Research Syntheses in Literacy Studies **45**

Kent, S. C., & Wanzek, J. (2016). The relationship between component skills and writing quality and production across developmental levels: A meta-analysis of the last 25 years. *Review of Educational Research*, 86(2), 570–601.

Kerfoot, J. F. (1967). Reading in the elementary school. *Review of Educational Research*, 37(2), 120–133.

Kim, J. S., & Quinn, D. M. (2013). The effects of summer reading on low-income children's literacy achievement from kindergarten to grade 8: A meta-analysis of classroom and home interventions. *Review of Educational Research*, 83(3), 386–431.

Kirby, J. R., Georgiou, G. K., Martinussen, R., & Parrila, R. (2010). Naming speed and reading: From prediction to instruction. *Reading Research Quarterly*, 45(3), 341–362.

Kopel, D., & De Boer, J. J. (1943). Chapter I: Reading Problems of Pressing Importance. *Review of Educational Research*, 13(2), 69–87.

Kucan, L., & Beck, I. L. (1997). Thinking aloud and reading comprehension research: Inquiry, instruction, and social interaction. *Review of Educational Research*, 67(3), 271–299.

Kucirkova, N. (2019). Socio-material directions for developing empirical research on children's e-reading: A systematic review and thematic synthesis of the literature across disciplines. *Journal of Early Childhood Literacy* (online pre-publication).

Kuhn, M. R., Schwanenflugel, P. J., & Meisinger, E. B. (2010). Aligning theory and assessment of reading fluency: Automaticity, prosody, and definitions of fluency. *Reading Research Quarterly*, 45(2), 230–251.

Kuiper, E., Volman, M., & Terwel, J. (2005). The Web as an information resource in K–12 education: Strategies for supporting students in searching and processing information. *Review of Educational Research*, 75(3), 285–328.

Kulhavy, R. W. (1977). Feedback in written instruction. *Review of Educational Research*, 47(2), 211–232.

Lam, W. S. E., & Warriner, D. S. (2012). Transnationalism and literacy: Investigating the mobility of people, languages, texts, and practices in contexts of migration. *Reading Research Quarterly*, 47(2), 191–215.

Lankshear, C., & Knobel, M. (2003). New technologies in early childhood literacy research: A review of research. *Journal of Early Childhood Literacy*, 3(1), 59–82.

Lather, P. (1999). To be of use: The work of reviewing. *Review of Educational Research*, 69(1), 2–7.

Lipson, M. Y., & Wixson, K. K. (1986). Reading disability research: An interactionist perspective. *Review of Educational Research*, 56(1), 111–136.

Lysaker, J. T., & Handsfield, L. J. (2019). Integrative research syntheses as sites of disruption in literacy teacher education. *Journal of Literacy Research*, 51(2), 252–258.

Macmillan, B. M. (2002). Rhyme and reading: A critical review of the research methodology. *Journal of Research in Reading*, 25(1), 4–42.

Marksheffel, N. D. (1964). Composition, handwriting, and spelling. *Review of Educational Research*, 34(2), 177–186.

Marulis, L. M., & Neuman, S. B. (2010). The effects of vocabulary intervention on young children's word learning: A meta-analysis. *Review of Educational Research*, 80(3), 300–335.

McCullough, C. M. (1958). Reading. *Review of Educational Research*, 28(2), 96–106.

McVee, M. B., Dunsmore, K., & Gavelek, J. R. (2005). Schema theory revisited. *Review of Educational Research*, 75(4), 531–566.

Mesmer, H. A. (2001). Examining the theoretical claims about decodable text: Does text decodability lead to greater application of letter/sound knowledge in first-grade readers? In J.V. Hoffman, D.L. Schallert, C.M. Fairbanks, J. Worthy, B. Maloch (Eds), *Yearbook of the National Reading Conference, Volume 50* (pp. 444–459). National Reading Conference.

Mezynski, K. (1983). Issues concerning the acquisition of knowledge: Effects of vocabulary training on reading comprehension. *Review of Educational Research*, 53(2), 253–279.

Miller, S. M. (2013). A research metasynthesis on digital video composing in classrooms: An evidence-based framework toward a pedagogy for embodied learning. *Journal of Literacy Research*, 45(4), 386–430.

Mills, K. A. (2010). A review of the "digital turn" in the new literacy studies. *Review of Educational Research*, 80(2), 246–271.

Mol, S. E., Bus, A. G., & De Jong, M. T. (2009). Interactive book reading in early education: A tool to stimulate print knowledge as well as oral language. *Review of Educational Research*, 79(2), 979–1007.

Mosely Wetzel, M., Vlach, S. K., Svrcek, N., Steinitz, E., Omogun, L., Taylor, L. A., & Villarreal, D. (2019). Preparing teaches with sociocultural knowledge in literacy: A literature review. *Journal of Literacy Research*, 51(2), 138–157.

Mosenthal, P. (1983). Defining classroom writing competence: A paradigmatic perspective. *Review of Educational Research*, 53(2), 217–251.

Moses, A. M. (2008). Impacts of television viewing on young children's literacy development in the USA: A review of the literature. *Journal of Early Childhood Literacy*, 8(1), 67–102.

Nagy, W., & Townsend, D. (2012). Words as tools: Learning academic vocabulary as language acquisition. *Reading Research Quarterly*, 47(1), 91–108.

National Reading Panel. (2000). *National Reading Panel: Teaching Children to read: An evidence-based assessment of the scientific research literature on reading and its implications for reading instruction: Reports of the subgroups.* Washington, DC: U.S. Department of Health and Human Services, Public Health Service, National Institutes of Health, National Institute of Child Health and Human Development.

Newell, G. E., Beach, R., Smith, J., & VanDerHeide, J. (2011). Teaching and learning argumentative reading and writing: A review of research. *Reading Research Quarterly*, 46(3), 273–304.

Noblit, G. W., & Hare, R. D. (1988). *Meta-ethnography: Synthesizing Qualitative Studies.* Sage.

Norris, J. M., & Ortega, L. (Eds.). (2006). *Synthesizing Research on Language Learning and Teaching* (Vol. 13). John Benjamins Publishing.

Norris, J. M., & Ortega, L. (2007). The future of research synthesis in applied linguistics: Beyond art or science. *TESOL Quarterly*, 41(4), 805–815.

Pandya, J. Z., & Ávila, J. (2017). Inequitable variations: A review of research in technology, literacy studies and special education. *Literacy*, 51(3), 123–130.

Pellegrini, A. D. (1985). The relations between symbolic play and literate behavior: A review and critique of the empirical literature. *Review of Educational Research*, 55(1), 107–121.

Petchauer, E. (2009). Framing and reviewing hip-hop educational research. *Review of Educational Research*, 79(2), 946–978.

Petty, W. T., & Burns, P. C. (1964). A summary of investigations relating to the English language arts in elementary education: 1963. *Elementary English*, 41(2), 119–137.

Pfost, M., Hattie, J., Dörfler, T., & Artelt, C. (2014). Individual differences in reading development: A review of 25 years of empirical research on Matthew effects in reading. *Review of Educational Research*, 84(2), 203–244.

Porter, R. B., Shafer, H., & Monroe, E. (1946). Chapter I: Research in Reading During the War Years. *Review of Educational Research*, 16(2), 102–115.

Prevoo, M. J., Malda, M., Mesman, J., & van IJzendoorn, M. H. (2016). Within-and cross-language relations between oral language proficiency and school outcomes in bilingual children with an immigrant background: A meta-analytical study. *Review of Educational Research*, 86(1), 237–276.

Quantz, J. O. (1897). Problems in the psychology of reading. *The Psychological Review: Monograph Supplements*, 2(1), i–51.

Reed, D. K., Cummings, K. D., Schaper, A., & Biancarosa, G. (2014). Assessment fidelity in reading intervention research: A synthesis of the literature. *Review of Educational Research*, 84(2), 275–321.

Reese, E., Sparks, A., & Leyva, D. (2010). A review of parent interventions for preschool children's language and emergent literacy. *Journal of Early Childhood Literacy*, 10(1), 97–117.

Rex, L. A., Bunn, M., Davila, B. A., Dickinson, H. A., Ford, A. C., Gerben, C., Orzulak, M. J. M., & Thomson, H. (2010). A review of discourse analysis in literacy research: Equitable access. *Reading Research Quarterly*, 45(1), 94–115.

Reyes, I. (2012). Biliteracy among children and youths. *Reading Research Quarterly*, 47(3), 307–327.

Richardson, E., DiBenedetto, B., & Bradley, C. M. (1977). The relationship of sound blending to reading achievement. *Review of Educational Research*, 47(2), 319–334.

Robertson, D. A., Padesky, L. B., Ford-Connors, E., & Paratore, J. R. (2020). What does it mean to say coaching is relational? *Journal of Literacy Research*, 52(1), 55–78.

Rogers, R., & Schaenen, I. (2005). Critical discourse analysis in literacy education: A review of the literature. *Reading Research Quarterly*, 49(1), 121–143.

Rogers, R., Malancharuvil-Berkes, E., Mosley, M., Hui, D., & Joseph, G. O. G. (2005). Critical discourse analysis in education: A review of the literature. *Review of Educational Research*, 75(3), 365–416.

Roskos, K., & Christie, J. (2001). Examining the play–literacy interface: A critical review and future directions. *Journal of Early Childhood Literacy*, 1(1), 59–89.

Roskos, K., Vukelich, C., & Risko, V. (2001). Reflection and learning to teach reading: A critical review of literacy and general teacher education studies. *Journal of Literacy Research*, 33(4), 595–635.

Sandelowski, M. (2014). Unmixing mixed-methods research. *Research in Nursing and Health*, 37(1), 3–8.

Sandelowski, M., & Barroso, J. (2007). *Handbook for Synthesizing Qualitative Research*. Springer Publishing Company.

Sandelowski, M., Docherty, S., & Emden, C. (1997). Qualitative metasynthesis: Issues and techniques. *Research in Nursing & Health*, 20(4), 365–371.

Scammacca, N. K., Roberts, G. J., Cho, E., Williams, K. J., Roberts, G., Vaughn, S. R., & Carroll, M. (2016). A century of progress: Reading interventions for students in grades 4–12, 1914–2014. *Review of Educational Research*, 86(3), 756–800.

Schiefele, U., Schaffner, E., Möller, J., & Wigfield, A. (2012). Dimensions of reading motivation and their relation to reading behavior and competence. *Reading Research Quarterly*, 47(4), 427–463.

Schirmer, B. R., & McGough, S. M. (2005). Teaching reading to children who are deaf: Do the conclusions of the National Reading Panel apply? *Review of Educational Research*, 75(1), 83–117.

48 Qualitative Research Syntheses in Literacy Studies

Schmieder, F. J. (1958). English composition: Writing—Spelling. *Review of Educational Research*, 28(2), 117–126.

Sénéchal, M., & Young, L. (2008). The effect of family literacy interventions on children's acquisition of reading from kindergarten to grade 3: A meta-analytic review. *Review of Educational Research*, 78(4), 880–907.

Shanahan, T. (2002). Research synthesis: Making sense of the accumulation of knowledge in reading. In M. Kamil, P. B. Mosenthal, P. D. Pearson, & R. Barr (Eds.) *Methods of Literacy Research* (pp. 133–150). Lawrence Erlbaum.

Sheldon, W. D. (1955). Reading: Instruction. *Review of Educational Research*, 25(2), 92–106.

Silverston, R. A., & Deichmann, J. W. (1975). Sense modality research and the acquisition of reading skills. *Review of Educational Research*, 45(1), 149–172.

Sinatra, G. M., & Broughton, S. H. (2011). Bridging reading comprehension and conceptual change in science education: The promise of refutation text. *Reading Research Quarterly*, 46(4), 374–393.

Singer, L. M., & Alexander, P. A. (2017). Reading on paper and digitally: What the past decades of empirical research reveal. *Review of Educational Research*, 87(6), 1007–1041.

Slavin, R. E., & Cheung, A. (2005). A synthesis of research on language of reading instruction for English language learners. *Review of Educational Research*, 75(2), 247–284.

Slavin, R. E., Lake, C., Chambers, B., Cheung, A., & Davis, S. (2009). Effective reading programs for the elementary grades: A best-evidence synthesis. *Review of Educational Research*, 79(4), 1391–1466.

Smagorinsky, P. (2001). If meaning is constructed, what is it made from? Toward a cultural theory of reading. *Review of Educational Research*, 71(1), 133–169.

Smagorinsky, P., & Smith, M. W. (1992). The nature of knowledge in composition and literary understanding: The question of specificity. *Review of Educational Research*, 62(3), 279–305.

Somervill, M. A. (1975). Dialect and reading: A review of alternative solutions. *Review of Educational Research*, 45(2), 247–262.

Spencer, M., & Wagner, R. K. (2018). The comprehension problems of children with poor reading comprehension despite adequate decoding: A meta-analysis. *Review of Educational Research*, 88(3), 366–400.

Sperling, M. (1996). Revisiting the writing-speaking connection: Challenges for research on writing and writing instruction. *Review of Educational Research*, 66(1), 53–86.

Sperling, M., & Appleman, D. (2011). Voice in the context of literacy studies. *Reading Research Quarterly*, 46(1), 70–84.

Stahl, S. A., & Miller, P. D. (1989). Whole language and language experience approaches for beginning reading: A quantitative research synthesis. *Review of Educational Research*, 59(1), 87–116.

Stake, R. E. (1978). The case study method in social inquiry. *Educational Researcher*, 7(2), 5–8.

Strom, I. M. (1964). Summary of investigations relating to the English language arts in secondary education: 1962–1963. *The English Journal*, 53(2), 110–135.

Summers, E. G. (1967). Reading in the secondary school. *Review of Educational Research*, 37(2), 134–151.

Suri, H. (2013). *Towards Methodologically Inclusive Research Syntheses: Expanding Possibilities*. Routledge.

Swanborn, M. S., & De Glopper, K. (1999). Incidental word learning while reading: A meta-analysis. *Review of Educational Research*, 69(3), 261–285.

Swanson, H. L., & Hsieh, C. J. (2009). Reading disabilities in adults: A selective meta-analysis of the literature. *Review of Educational Research*, 79(4), 1362–1390.

Swanson, H. L., Trainin, G., Necoechea, D. M., & Hammill, D. D. (2003). Rapid naming, phonological awareness, and reading: A meta-analysis of the correlation evidence. *Review of Educational Research*, 73(4), 407–440.

Thorne, S., Jensen, L., Kearney, M. H., Noblit, G., & Sandelowski, M. (2004). Qualitative metasynthesis: Reflections on methodological orientation and ideological agenda. *Qualitative Health Research*, 14(10), 1342–1365.

Torgerson, C. J. (2007). The quality of systematic reviews of effectiveness in literacy learning in English: A 'tertiary' review. *Journal of Research in Reading*, 30(3), 287–315.

Torgerson, C. J., & Elbourne, D. (2002). A systematic review and meta-analysis of the effectiveness of information and communication technology (ICT) on the teaching of spelling. *Journal of Research in Reading*, 25(2), 129–143.

Torgerson, C., Porthouse, J., & Brooks, G. (2005). A systematic review of controlled trials evaluating interventions in adult literacy and numeracy. *Journal of Research in Reading*, 28(2), 87–107.

Unrau, N. J., Rueda, R., Son, E., Polanin, J. R., Lundeen, R. J., & Muraszewski, A. K. (2018). Can reading self-efficacy be modified? A meta-analysis of the impact of interventions on reading self-efficacy. *Review of Educational Research*, 88(2), 167–204.

Urrieta, Jr, L., & Noblit, G. W. (Eds.). (2018). *Cultural Constructions of Identity: Meta-Ethnography and Theory*. Oxford University Press.

Van Steensel, R., McElvany, N., Kurvers, J., & Herppich, S. (2011). How effective are family literacy programs? Results of a meta-analysis. *Review of Educational Research*, 81(1), 69–96.

Venezky, R. L. (1984). The history of reading research. In P. D. Pearson (Ed.) *Handbook of Reading Research* (pp. 3–38). Lawrence Erlbaum.

Wade, S. E. (1983). A synthesis of the research for improving reading in the social studies. *Review of Educational Research*, 53(4), 461–497.

Wanzek, J., Vaughn, S., Scammacca, N. K., Metz, K., Murray, C. S., Roberts, G., & Danielson, L. (2013). Extensive reading interventions for students with reading difficulties after grade 3. *Review of Educational Research*, 83(2), 163–195.

Weintraub, S. (1996). *Annual Summary of Investigations Relating to Reading, July 1, 1994 to June 30, 1995*. International Reading Association.

Weis, L., Jenkins, H., & Stich, A. (2009). Diminishing the divisions among us: Reading and writing across difference in theory and method in the sociology of education. *Review of Educational Research*, 79(2), 912–945.

Weiser, B., & Mathes, P. (2011). Using encoding instruction to improve the reading and spelling performances of elementary students at risk for literacy difficulties: A best-evidence synthesis. *Review of Educational Research*, 81(2), 170–200.

West, W. W. (1967). Written Composition. *Review of Educational Research*, 37(2), 159–167.

Wexler, J., Pyle, N., Flower, A., Williams, J. L., & Cole, H. (2014). A synthesis of academic interventions for incarcerated adolescents. *Review of Educational Research*, 84(1), 3–46.

Whitehead, K., & Wilkinson, L. (2008). Teachers, policies and practices: A historical review of literacy teaching in Australia. *Journal of Early Childhood Literacy*, 8(1), 7–24.

Williams, J. P. (1965). Reading Research and Instruction. *Review of Educational Research*, 35(2), 147–153.

Williams, C., & Mayer, C. (2015). Writing in young deaf children. *Review of Educational Research*, 85(4), 630–666.

Wright, T. S., & Cervetti, G. N. (2017). A systematic review of the research on vocabulary instruction that impacts text comprehension. *Reading Research Quarterly*, 52(2), 203–226.

2

REFLECTING ON AND REDEFINING APPROACHES TO WRITING DISSERTATION LITERATURE REVIEWS

Introduction

> The literature review has been described as a "report of primary or original scholarship" (Cooper, 1988b, p. 107) and "an interpretation and synthesis of published work" (Merriam, 1988, p. 6). It is also helpful in establishing "a backdrop for the problem or issue that has led to the need for the study."
>
> (Creswell, 2014, p. 30)

Writing a dissertation can be daunting, especially the challenges of compiling, composing, conceptualizing, and synthesizing the literature into a workable review. In this book, we define a literature review as an analysis of a body of scholarship within a particular field of study. This analysis includes theoretical and methodological procedures for exploring relevant themes, patterns, trends, gaps, and inconsistencies in scholarly literature. A review is not only a requirement when writing a dissertation; it is the foundation for current research, which helps scholars understand important ideas from various studies and compile them in a cohesive order. Most dissertation committee members want to know if the scholar knows and understands their field. Additionally, as Hart (1998) explains, "the literature will help you to provide evidence and substance for justifying your choice [of project]" (p. 16). Scholars outside the literacy field have also argued that describing the methodology for a literature review "creates a firm foundation for advancing knowledge and facilitating theory development," and "by integrating findings and perspectives from many empirical findings," "a literature review can address research questions with a power that no single study has" (Snyder, 2019, p. 333).

52 Reflecting on and Redefining Approaches

As Boote and Beile (2005) state, it is impossible to conduct relevant research without first understanding the literature in the field. Thus, researchers must identify and understand what has been previously written and then build on that literature, and in so doing contribute to the field of study. It is relevant to note that more premier journals, including the *Review of Educational Research*, have legitimated "state-of-the-art literature reviews" as scholarly work that is recognized as real research (LeCompte et al., 2003, p. 124).

My (Tisha's) dissertation focused on addressing and understanding the dyadic relationship between an African American mother and son as they engaged in daily digital literacy practices (see Table 2.1). I sought to answer the following three questions:

- In what ways does a family enact "digital literacies" at home?
- How might digital literacies shape a family's relational practices, how do these practices reshape, and how do the family members relate to each other?
- In what ways did this particular mother and her children interchangeably apprentice one another when engaging in digital literacies?

As I reviewed existing literature, my role was to find pertinent research that would support my topic and relate to those questions. I sought to build upon what and how past and present scholars spoke about the everyday (digital) literacy practices that occurred across various contexts for different purposes among adolescents and families.

While writing my literature review, I relied on the craft of qualitative methodologists such as Creswell (1994), Glesne (1999), Merriam (2001), Patton (2002), Shanahan (2002), and Wolcott (2001). These methodological "elders" were recommended by professors, assigned in doctoral courses, and identified by colleagues and peers as the go-to resources for qualitative research design and theory in relation to literature reviews. While these scholars helped me get through my literature review processes and concretize my ideas, it was much later, during and after my dissertation writing processes, that I was introduced to a more diverse group of scholars (e.g., Bhattacharya, 2009; Patel, 2015; Smith, 1999/2012; Tuck & Yang, 2012). Such scholars spoke against the colonizing discourses of Anglo-Americans who believed that Western perspectives and ideas were legitimate and that colonialism and oppression could exist in states that claimed to value social justice, equality, and freedom (Tuck, 2015). I found these

TABLE 2.1 Related Scholarship

Lewis, T. (2009). *Family literacy and digital literacies: A redefined approach to examining social practices of an African American family* [unpublished doctoral dissertation]. State University of New York, Albany.

decolonizing methodologists through conferences, workshops, and webinars, and they deprogrammed my thinking about colonizing discourses. In my doctoral program, there were very few scholars of color whose work was displayed in courses or recommended by my professors. Now, to be clear, I do not believe that these above scholars' work would have been unwelcomed as part of my research repertoire; however, I was taught by mostly white male professors in my doctoral program who taught their own information and viewpoints about research methodology, projected their own methodological references as suggestions, and continued to use those colonizing ideologies in course discussions. The following section describes some of the main misconceptions I experienced as a doctoral writer as I tried to understand the task, demonstrate the required criticality, and negotiate the large amount of information involved when writing a **dissertation literature review**.

Misconceptions About Literature Reviews

> One of the biggest challenges seems to be the notion that the literature review needs to be an exhaustive summary of everything that has ever been written on the topic under investigation.
>
> (Guerin, n.d.)

There are many misconceptions and misunderstandings about the messiness of writing a literature review for a dissertation. Some qualitative researchers believe that reviewing the literature should not occur until after the data collection has begun, fearing that pre-existing theories and research designs would inform or influence the writer (Glesne, 1999). While this is possible, reading literature throughout the research processes – including before data collection phases – provides a more stable grounding, which, in turn, extends individuals' knowledge in the field.

While there were no specific doctoral courses on writing literature reviews during my doctoral program, each course provided a broad orientation of literacy research and research methodology that prepared me for writing my literature review. I found that reading throughout my research process was more helpful to me since I was gaining more knowledge and understanding about family literacy and technology (digital literacies) that was useful very early during my class assignments, my comprehensive examinations, and, eventually, my dissertation.

The quandaries below are the impetus for this chapter, which was written and designed with novice and established doctoral students in mind. It is designed to help scholars avoid some of the most common mistakes and assumptions made when searching, selecting, and writing a dissertation literature review. While no review is perfect, this chapter aims to offer considerations that can support readers during this writing process.

54 Reflecting on and Redefining Approaches

My process of writing a literature review was challenging for a number of reasons, as stated below:

- I did not know how much literature I should review.
- I did not know the length of the dissertation review.
- I thought I could predict the number of articles that I would focus on in my review.
- I feared that I would miss pertinent literature that was important to the field.
- I did not know how far back I should search the topic.
- I did not know when/how I would reach **saturation** (see Table 2.2).

- I was confused about the organization/formatting of the reviews (e.g., **synthesizing** vs. **summarizing**) (see Tables 2.3–2.4).
- I participated in **"data dumping"** when citing scholarship (see Table 2.5).
- I did not readily establish a critical argument related to the literature I found.
- I did not find a significant body of research in my specific field of study, so I had to expand my parameters and consider interdisciplinary literacy studies.
- I relied on secondary sources rather than primary sources when reviewing the literature.
- I did not state clear findings of the studies as related to my study.

TABLE 2.2 Saturation

Saturation
The process of exhausting what you have researched, where nothing else is added to your topic.

TABLE 2.3 Synthesizing

Synthesizing
Linking together a cohesive set of ideas, relationships, and patterns.

TABLE 2.4 Summarizing

Summarizing
Identifying the key points within a text.

TABLE 2.5 Data Dumping

Data dumping
Compiling a large number of sources in your review without explanation, flow, or clarity of thought.

Reflecting on and Redefining Approaches **55**

These misconceptions occurred because I had preconceived understandings of what a literature review should look like before first understanding my process and knowledge about the field. Certain researchers, such as Creswell (1994), have maintained that writing literature reviews should meet the following three criteria:

- present results of similar studies,
- relate the present study to the ongoing dialogue in the literature, and
- provide a framework for comparing the results of a study with other studies.
  - He also suggested the following:
- identify terms to be used in the literature search;
- locate literature;
- read and assess the relevance of the literature;
- organize the literature selected; and
- begin writing the review (Creswell, 2002).

However, these steps are broad, and they neither reveal complexities nor recognize differences between writing a dissertation literature review or writing a literature review for a traditional academic paper (Boote & Beile, 2005; Bruce, 1994). I paraphrase Hart (1998), who provided a more robust set of criteria for writing dissertation literature reviews. In them, a scholar should be:

- distinguishing what has been done from what needs to be done,
- discovering important variables relevant to the topic,
- synthesizing and gaining a new perspective,
- identifying relationships between ideas and practices,
- establishing the context of the topic or problem,
- rationalizing the significance of the problem,
- enhancing and acquiring relevant vocabulary,
- understanding the structure of the subject,
- relating ideas and theories to applications,
- identifying the main methodologies and research techniques that have been used, and
- placing research within a historical context to demonstrate familiarity with state-of-the-art developments.

While stating step-by-step processes in writing a literature review was not the focus of this chapter, nor was it a key component to my knowledge of writing a review for my dissertation, it is important to understand how reviews written by doctoral students can apply to Cooper's (1988b) Taxonomy of Literature Reviews (Randolph, 2009).

Cooper (1988b) describes six characteristics of literature reviews: *focus, goal, perspective, coverage, organization,* and *audience.* "Focus" is when one identifies

56 Reflecting on and Redefining Approaches

that there are gaps in the research that a scholar desires to fill with the study. There are many "goals" for a literature review, but after critically reviewing and analyzing the research, one can identify the key issues and ideas, and create a bigger picture of the research in an effort to compose an argument. Cooper (1988a) argues that "perspective" is important when writing a literature review because it forces us to be neutral when we present the findings as accurate facts. "Coverage" focuses on choosing select pieces of research that are manageable for the reviewer. In other words, students may choose to purposively sample empirical studies in peer-reviewed journals instead of conference papers. While this is true, and since my topic was new to the field of family digital literacy practices among African American families and adolescents, I have found online articles and conceptual work beneficial to my understanding of the topic, and thus contributed to the field.

When thinking about the many formats to organize a review, Cooper (1988b) states that "organization" represents how reviews should be organized through the following formats: (1) historical, in which the review is chronological and examines research over periods of time with the hopes of identifying directions for future research; (2) conceptual, as organized by the theories in the literature; or (3) methodological, which is similar to an empirical article in that it does not always have to relate to the content of what was said in the review, but to the method of analysis (i.e., introduction, methods, results, and discussion). Lastly, Cooper describes "audience" as the individuals slated to read the review. For a dissertation literature review, the audience will be dissertation committee members, not a general non-academic population.

New Research Topic: Thinking About the Literature Review

> So it's not that there is no literature for the pretend researcher on their topic, it's rather that they have to think more broadly about what they might need and use. They have to map the possible areas that are linked to their question and then sort out, by skimming and noting, what's most relevant and related. They must then bring these selected literatures together in a way that supports the research they are going to do.
>
> (Thomson, 2015)

As I completed my data collection and began my literature review in 2007, literacy research was continuing to develop and adopt various changes in terminology to refer to my work, including: "family/parental involvement," "family literacy," "technology," "technology(ies)," "multiliteracy(ies)," "multimodal(ity/ies)," "information literacy" (Bawden, 2008), "computer literacy," "media literacy," "network literacy," "e-literacy," and "digital literacy(ies)" (Gilster, 1997). The literature on African American family's digital literacy practices was scant in the literacy field; thus, I had to expand the scope of my interest and topic (e.g., to digital literacies,

Reflecting on and Redefining Approaches **57**

adolescents' digital literacies/tools, practices, new literacies, and meaning-making). I mistakenly believed I had to read everything on my topic, but soon found that it was not realistic to expect that my review would include an exhaustive list of everything that had been written, or even of everything I had read or written. Consequently, I had to ask myself: *which literature would advance my knowledge of my topic? The (digital) literacy field? Or African American families?*

Although I read multiple examples of dissertation and **traditional literature reviews**, it took time for me to identify and review the literature that made sense to me and was relevant for my intended topic. Having a plan for the articles I searched and read were important, but attempting to predict an outcome of how many articles I would read and peruse was an impossible feat. A common misstep is believing that every article needs to be in your review. The benefit of reviewing the literature is to explore how *what* is said is advancing the conversation on your topic, and to let the research force you to answer questions and take you by surprise when reading and writing. In my current courses, I like to "bring in" the scholars we are reading, pretend they are in the discussion with us, and explore how their perspectives and arguments are contributing to the field.

One earlier report I read that became an important review of some of the prevailing issues in the family literacy field was Vivian Gadsden's (1994) *Understanding Family Literacy: Conceptual Issues Facing the Field*. I was impressed with Gadsden's style of writing and how she synthesized the body of scholarship around family literacy. As a Black woman, she humanized Black intergenerational families' voices, literacy practices, and their value of literacy access. She did not ignore the fact that "race, class, and culture" were important concepts in family literacy (Gadsden, 1996, p. 31). Via a report of empirical work, her conceptual work greatly contributed to the field because it discussed relevant work regarding intergenerational literacy, parent–child literacy, emergent literacy, and family support. In addition, it was easier to trust her perspectives over some white researchers', who researched family literacy practices within the Black community from a deficit model. This conceptual work was one of the many models I attempted to use when writing both my literature review and my future work.

Early in my doctoral program, I took a Families course in the sociology department. This course focused on research literature concerning families, parent–child relations, extended families, and family policy. The literature assigned for this course came from allied fields such as sociology, communication and gender studies, and anthropology; however, for my dissertation search, I relied on allied journals with a literacy focus, such as *Anthropology and Education Quarterly* and *Adult Education Quarterly*. I chose these journals because they were recognized in my field of study, and the sociology journals from my course, at times, did not coincide with my research topic. I did find helpful literature from business and medical-related journals (e.g., *Journal of American Academy of Child and Adolescent Psychiatry, Journal of Attention Disorders, Journal of Academy of Business and Economics*, and *Psychiatric News*) that increased my knowledge of these concepts,

58 Reflecting on and Redefining Approaches

as the participants of my study were from a particular social class and the focal son from my study was diagnosed with attention deficit hyperactivity disorder.

Research in my field concerning African American families and digital literacies neither overtly recognized nor humanized the narratives and literacy practices of Black families in decolonizing ways. As a result, I sought out literature that explored how families communicated and interacted with each other (i.e., Edwards, 2009; Gadsden, 1994; McAdoo, 2006; Taylor & Dorsey-Gaines, 1988). In addition, I sought literature that documented how adolescent boys and girls generally engaged with and were shaped by digital literacy practices in their daily lives (Chandler-Olcott & Mahar, 2003; Jacobs, 2006; Lewis & Fabos, 2005) and in both national and international spaces (Cairney & Ruge, 1998; Marsh, 2006). Occasionally, I found studies that addressed African American and Latinx families, but focused on the digital divide, parental guidance, how parents communicated with their children in the home concerning technology (Ba et al., 2002), how discursive and unique literacy patterns among families formed barriers between home and school (Compton-Lilly, 2003), and how African American families dealt with issues of identity, inequity, and power relationships through their interactions with literacy across homes and communities (Rogers, 2003).

An important objective of my research was to acknowledge and rectify the omission of Black families' representation in literacy education research. Thus, studying a family's digital literacy practices in the home was significant to me, both as an African American woman and a researcher. Situating my research within a framework of sociocultural traditions of New Literacy Studies (NLS) and multimodality, I was interested in understanding and reviewing current theories that addressed literacy practices and literacy events, family literacy and digital literacies, apprenticeship, and meaning-making and identity construction. I believed these key components were vital for examining family literacy and digital literacy practices in the twenty-first century. I also described, through my review of relevant research studies, how these contemporary issues related to and were constituted in the lives of adolescents and families and their everyday social practices. I also sought to examine what family literacy looked like in the digital literacy age. After I passed my comprehensive exams, I compiled a draft of a concept map to highlight some of the above variables I was interested in for my pending research (see Figure 2.1).

Figure 2.1 shows my beginning thoughts on ways to organize my dissertation literature review. At that time, I had not yet changed my topic to family literacy and digital literacies. When I sent the map to one of my committee members, she stated the following:

- The categories/boxes seem to be "uneven"; that is, some are areas of focus and others are dealing with theory or method. Perhaps you could decide which you want to focus on and then develop subcategories?

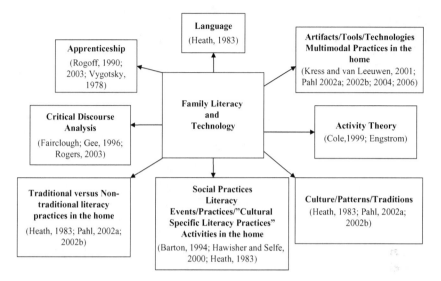

FIGURE 2.1 Concept Map

- It seems like the studies that specifically address family literacy and technology should be included in this concept map. Which studies have you reviewed that specifically address family literacy and technology?
- You might consider the notion of "design," as the New London Group uses it in their book *Multiliteracies*. I think you will find this theoretical concept useful in terms of linking the family literacy piece with the technology piece.

I found my committee's comments very helpful. While this map was a way to understand my thoughts and the topics for my review, it provided me with a better understanding to categorize the key headings for my literature review and overall dissertation. I suggest this same method for doctoral students, even if it is a simple draft of a concept map. The next section describes some of the key points I used when I searched for relevant literature for my dissertation topic. In addition, I share the approaches I used to search the literature (e.g., database searches using keywords) and describe how my search helped me identify the knowledge gaps related to African American families' digital literacy practices.

Searching the Literature

> The process of searching for qualitative research reports can be messy and those ah-hah moments that irrevocably change the course of a literature search are difficult to immediately record or to retrospectively retrace.
>
> (Finfgeld-Connett & Johnson, 2012, p. 8)

60 Reflecting on and Redefining Approaches

Searching the literature was a recursive process throughout my doctoral program; however, during the years of 2005–2009, I searched for relevant literature specifically during my comprehensive exams. For instance, I used educational search engines such as ERIC, JSTOR, ProQuest, Google, and Google Scholar, and I reviewed bibliographies from selected research articles to extend my research knowledge and reach saturation. In addition, I used a combination of terms to describe my areas of interest (i.e., *African American family and digital literacy(ies)*, *Black family and digital literacies/tools*, *family's digital literacy practices*, *families and technology*, *families and digital tools*, *adolescents and digital literacy*, *adolescents and digital literacy practices*, *family involvement*, *parental involvement*, and *digital texts/tools*). I initially kept track of my searches using EndNote, and later created a literature review matrix using MS Word (see Table 2.6).

Over time, I came to prefer the old-school approach of manually composing a literature matrix over EndNote because I was able to freely label my categories and searches in ways that were appropriate for my study. While EndNote has been the industry standard for research and reference management software, there are many free products that students can use to store and manage research papers and generate bibliographies for scholarly articles (e.g., www.mendeley.com and www.qiqqa.com).

During this search process, I organized studies by authors in ascending alphabetical order for easy location. I would read or skim each article that I either found or that was sent to me from my committee members and peers. I repeatedly scanned and sifted through the articles that were relevant to my research topic and categorized them within the matrix. Then I printed and placed the ones that I did not immediately use in a large binder and compiled them in a crate for later use. On occasions, I returned to those articles to revisit and review them. I organized the most relevant articles I read and stored them in a Dropbox and email folder labeled, "Dissertation Articles." Since Dropbox has a storage limit, I wanted to find storage without a fee, so my email folder was a likely solution.

I started reading articles from top-tier, renowned literacy journals that were recognized in my field, including *Reading Research Quarterly*, *Journal of Literacy Research*, *Research in the Teaching of English*, *Journal of Adolescent and Adult Literacy*, *Adult Education Quarterly*, and *Language Arts*. In addition, I located conceptual research, reports, and online articles. For instance, I found such literature through the National Center for Family Literacy (NCFL), a nonprofit organization providing educational and economic support solutions for families. The literature from NCFL included reports about family literacy and parental school engagement. I read these reports and conceptual data differently than published articles because some were not entirely based on empirical research. However, these materials provided a baseline of knowledge about how community leaders, policy makers, and family-centered coalitions viewed family literacy. These resources were free and readily available. I also read online articles from Google Scholar. I spent a great deal of time carefully searching, reading, and rereading

TABLE 2.6 Literature Review Matrix

Categories/ Keywords In article searching	References (APA)	Abstract	Theoretical Framework/ Perspectives	Methodology	Findings	Search Engine
I. African American Fathers	Gadsden, V., Wortham, S., & Turner, H. (2003). Situated identities of young, African American fathers in low-income urban settings. *Family Court Review*, *41*(3), 381–399.	Young, low-income, African American fathers have been at the center of research, practice, and policy on families over the past decade. This article uses a "voicing" analytic technique to examine identities among young, low-income, African American fathers living in an urban setting; the intersections of these identities; and the fathers' perceptions of the influences of familial, peer, and legal systems as barriers and resources in their development as fathers and the sustainability of their fathering roles. The primary questions	African American, fathers; minority fathers; young, low-income; urban fathers	Young, low-income, African American fathers have been at the center of research, practice, and policy on families over the past decade. This article uses a "voicing" analytic technique to examine identities among young, low-income, African American	Results from a survey, focus groups, and interviews suggest that the fathers seek to reinvent themselves and reconstruct their identities by separating from street life, redefine	Google

62 Reflecting on and Redefining Approaches

the bibliography sections of relevant articles and formulated new lists of literature to locate. As a result, I considered why the author(s) cited particular studies, the main focus of each search, as well as each search's apparent gaps. I began to notice how other researchers wrote about similar bodies of literature and how some scholars presented summarized lists of scholarship, while others discussed or highlighted particular texts. I mention this because choosing to read other colleagues and peers' dissertation literature reviews was, for me, an intentional learning process about the literature review genre. In this search, I noticed vast differences between how these colleagues synthesized and analyzed literature to make sense of their data. I often sought out colleagues and professors to recommend literature reviews. In addition, two other colleagues and I would often meet to discuss literature over lunch or dinner; we also read and offered feedback of each other's reviews. Additionally, I was the vice president of the Graduate Student Literacy Forum, by which doctoral students from our department provided research support to the graduate school's entire student body. This forum hosted literacy symposiums, professional development sessions, weekly dissertation discussion groups, brown bag lunches, and monthly methodological work sessions where students shared articles, read, and constructed feedback on works-in-progress, research proposals, and literature reviews of each other's work. This creative research outlet was a very helpful part of engendering conversations around the literature in scholarly and critical ways, and in finding literature for my research topic.

Finfgeld-Connett and Johnson (2012) stated that reaching the end of a literature search is a judgment call because it is literally impossible to know what literature has not been reviewed. For instance, since there were few studies that directly examined African American families' digital literacy practices from NLS and multimodality stances, I sought out studies that were closely linked to adolescents' meaning making and identity formation concerning digital literacy practices, and these studies generated further inquiries about digital literacy in family literacy studies, such as studies on adolescent girls' digital literacy practices in online spaces (Cammack, 2002; Chandler-Olcott & Mahar, 2003; Norton-Meier, 2004). In addition, some literature I found explored young children's engagement in digital literacy practices in the home, and how adults' use of multiple modes of literacy practices around texts illustrated multimodality in home contexts from international perspectives (Marsh & Thompson, 2001). Lewis and Fabos' (2005) work was key to my research, as it examined how seven adolescents engaged in instant messaging (IMing), and how their social identities were shaped by this digital literacy. This work was very similar to the practices that my participants, Larnee and Gerard (mother and son), engaged in when they texted and IMed each other at home (Lewis, 2013). This process of searching relevant literature about adolescents' digital literacy practices allowed me to find some studies (albeit from other cultural populations) until saturation was reached.

Making Arguments with the Literature

> To give an argument means to offer a set of reasons or evidence in support of a conclusion.
>
> (Weston, 2000, p. xii)

The art of making an argument is critical when writing a literature review. The literature review process drives the argument's possibilities (Boote & Beile, 2005). For instance, an argument needs to present a main idea about a position and offer evidence to support that idea. Evidence should reflect claims made about a particular topic and be persuasive for the intended audience (Boote & Beile, 2005; Weston, 2000). Identifying gaps in the field, developing an unrelated argument, and noting inconsistencies and errors of other scholars is a skill that must be learned over time. While there is no single set of rules about how to make written arguments, there are structures to follow that can help scholars establish strong voices in order to analyze and convey different perspectives in objective ways and avoid subjective intensifiers like "really" and "very," which tend to exaggerate content.

Constructing an argument entails attending to what an author has done and used, and why. Composing a simple argument requires three components: claim, evidence, and warrant (Boote & Beile, 2005; Hart, 1998; Machi & McEvoy, 2012) (see Figure 2.2).

Toulmin's (1969) Argument Model adds to these components to include *data, warrant, backing, qualifier,* and *rebuttal.* Toulmin's model is one example of how arguments might be made and analyzed. To provide reasons for each claim (data), legitimizing the claim as relevant (warrant), and supporting the warrant (backing)

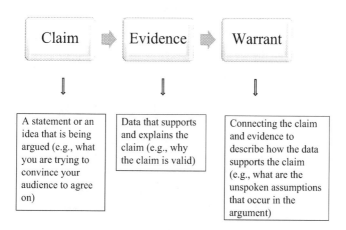

FIGURE 2.2 Three Components of a Simple Argument

64 Reflecting on and Redefining Approaches

indicates the claim with limiting words such as "usually," "most," "some" (qualifiers), and includes counter-arguments that address alternative viewpoints (rebuttals).

The early stages of writing my dissertation literature review (e.g., making arguments and establishing a voice) were challenging. What I thought were clear, consistent, and coherent arguments that were not always comprehensible to my readers. It took me a long time to organize my thoughts and articulate my argument in compelling and systematic ways that supported my claims. I tended to present underexplained constructs that I was actually still defining and trying to understand.

I also had to capture my academic voice. Fuller (2006) argued that it takes time for students in doctoral programs to "master a body of knowledge" and be loyal "to its corresponding practices and central dogmas," which can assume the form of academic bullshitting (p. 245; Smagorinsky et al., 2010). According to Smagorinsky et al. (2010), academic bullshitting is "when students are put in the position of having to sound more learned than they are, [so] they often bullshit their way through their assignments to create the appearance of knowledge according to scholarly specifications, even in its considerable absence" (p. 369). Students from the study demonstrated that they were able to finagle the composition of interpretive essays and papers. According to the authors,

> Bullshit thus involves a degree of risk, of going beyond what one begins the writing process with and stretching one's knowledge so that its articulation meets disciplinary expectations—of performance before competence, as Cazden (1981) asserted in applying Vygotsky (1978) principles to issues of teaching and learning. From this perspective, bullshit is indeed good stuff, perhaps even teachable. Although we have yet to see in any state or district curriculum documents an explicit requirement for students to become better at bullshitting, we do find that the generative potential of bullshitting as we have operationalized it for this study may benefit student writers as they learn to write within disciplinary expectations (p. 402).

It is concluded that students do participate in academic bullshitting while writing literature reviews for dissertations, but as they continue to write and "develop an identity within a community of discourse," they gain "genre knowledge" (p. 402).

In addition to finding my voice when writing, I did a lot of "telling" rather than "showing." Although some writers argue that telling is appropriate, it can be ambiguous and less effective in social science arguments. Below, I present early examples of how I presented my thoughts and arguments related to family literacy scholarship, intergenerational literacy, and digital literacy research.

> First, it is important to report how constructs, *family literacy* and *intergenerational literacy* have been used interchangeably in research. Intergenerational

literacy is highlighted in Gadsden's (2000) report as being "associated often with deficit models and with the idea of 'fixing' problems within families in order to create opportunity for future generations (?)." However, this report suggests that intergenerational literacy not only passes knowledge within the family but opens the door of beliefs, power and literacy. It creates vision and purpose from future generations. She asserts that intergenerational literacy is represented in various forms in the process of learning and teaching, parental involvement with their children and other family members, as well as the values and practices that support those engagements. Gadsden (2000) states that "these processes [of] acts of reading and writing, and beliefs about and valuing of literacy may be used as predictors or consequences of generational practices.

In the above paragraph, I explain my understanding of Vivian Gadsden's 2000 report on intergenerational literacy, but I rely too much on summarizing certain parts without synthesizing key components of her argument. For example, I could have shown more supporting evidence to explain how I arrived at my conclusion, instead of simply repeating conclusions.

Later on in my writing process, this comment from one of my dissertation committee members about one of my drafts included in-depth questions and comments for me to consider. These comments often highlighted what was missing or needed.

Clearly make an argument for why a study on family literacy and technology is important. That is, why now—at this particular social, political, economic, racial juncture—is a study that examines e-family literacy practices important?

A clear review of the literature on family literacy is in order. You describe some studies that have been conducted but **you need to make an argument with your literature review**—that is one you have reviewed [in] the literature—[then] think about the sub-sets that exist in the database. **What differences exist? How do each of the studies define family literacy? Technology? What theoretical frameworks are used in each of the studies? Who are the participants? What are the findings? What methodologies are used?** You might read through all of the studies and determine which aspects of the study you use.

Situated in the New Literacies Studies, the authors point out that very few studies have traced the culturally specific ways in which people use the Internet. I am wondering **how these arguments would play out in terms of technology and family literacies. In what ways do families use technologies in culturally specific ways? In what ways does the presence of technology change cultural patterns?** (March 27, 2007)

66 Reflecting on and Redefining Approaches

I bolded my committee member's comments in order to better understand what was being asked of me. These insights and questions helped me clarify my argument and better organize my literature review. These comments also helped me focus on existing scholarship to recognize how that work informed my intended research. As I reviewed both the comments from my committee members and my drafts, I realized that my main ideas needed to be teased out more and categorized in relation to the research in more compelling ways. Below, I present a snippet of my rationale for why a case study of an African American family was worthy of research.

> In this dissertation, I argue that the void in the research concerning digital literacy practices among African American families is problematic. It is problematic because it suggests that the practices, knowledge, and experiences of African American families are not valued in today's research. It also suggests that because of the digital divide, urban families do not have access to or know how to use the Internet (Banks, 2006). In light of a digitally mediated world in which families constantly use and reuse digital literacies to help them make sense of themselves, their world, and their experiences, these literacy practices among African American families will not only trigger further examinations for literacy research but will open new claims for how research needs to further examine digital literacy practices.
>
> (Lewis, 2009, p. 3)

This section presented an acceptable argument for my dissertation. What I convey in this paragraph is the paucity of research conducted with African American families and how their digital experiences were excluded from family literacy scholarship. I argued for the need for this work to help advance the digital literacy field within these families.

Summarizing Versus Synthesizing Literature

> A literature review is not a summary of various studies, but rather an integration of reviewed sources around particular trends and themes.
>
> (Glesne, 1999, p. 21)

> [Synthesizing literature sums] up the knowledge generated in an area in order to draw conclusions directly relevant to practice or chart directions for future research.
>
> (Sandelowski & Barroso, 2007, p. 23)

Unlike my prior career in journalism, my dissertation involved crafting rich narratives that were not judged by length or story content in order to tell in-depth stories of individual lives. I appreciated and welcomed this style of writing. However, adjusting to academic writing was challenging as I came to understand

Reflecting on and Redefining Approaches **67**

differences between summarizing and synthesizing literature to review for my dissertation. These two aspects of writing a review can be confused by today's doctoral students because summarizing and synthesizing are closely related and both are used as feasible strategies in reading and research (Eaton, 2010). In my novice mind, I found myself providing too much detail when synthesizing studies. I realized that when I found studies that were closely linked to my work or ones I enjoyed, I tended to summarize the entire study, thinking that this was required, as is evident in my above paragraph about Gadsden (2000). Wolcott (1990) calls this the "lump (dump)" (p. 17).

Summarizing studies presents an overview of the main points of a study presented in one's own words. Synthesizing across studies requires reviewing the main points of each study and describing how studies relate to one another to generate new knowledge. Throughout each chapter in this book, we have primarily focused on reviewing & synthesizing empirical studies. However, a synthesis of conceptual work could also be conducted (see Chapter 1). Here is my attempt to synthesize literature on "family literacies and digital literacy practices" in my dissertation:

> For over the past two decades, the field of family literacy has offered significant insight into family literacy practices in the home (Cairney & Ruge, 1998; Heath, 1983; Taylor, 1983; Taylor & Dorsey-Gaines, 1988). These studies examine the emergence of children's understanding of the nature and functions of literacy practices. Family literacy researchers have identified discursive patterns and unique literacy patterns among families and barriers between home and school, especially for children from lower various socioeconomic backgrounds (Compton-Lilly, 2003; Lareau, 1989; McCarthey, 1997; Purcell-Gates, 1995; Shockley-Bisplinghoff, 1995). While these studies have raised awareness of how families understand literacy, family literacy is changing and research must focus on the new ways that families interact with one another and engage in complex literacy practices through digital technologies.
>
> A number of researchers have explored digital literacies or media-related literacy practices (Bruce, 2002; Cairney & Ruge, 1998; Cammack, 2002; Chandler-Olcott & Mahar, 2003; Jacobs, 2006; Lewis & Fabos, 2005; Mahar, 2002; Marsh, 2006; Marsh & Thompson, 2001; Stein & Slonimsky, 2006). These studies examine issues such as pop culture, instant messaging, and the digital literacies and multimodalities that individuals practice on a daily basis in online communities (Hagood, 2000; Marsh, 2006). However, there is still a limited amount of research that focuses on family literacy and digital literacy practices, in particular how they contribute to the increasing technological demands of the home and world and influence how families talk, think, value, and identify themselves when engaging in technologies.
>
> (Lewis, 2009, pp. 16–17)

68 Reflecting on and Redefining Approaches

This section was part of my attempt to answer my first two research questions that drove my dissertation: (1) In what ways does a family enact "digital literacies" at home? and (2) How might digital literacies shape a family's relational practices, and how do these relational practices reshape how the family members relate to each other? While I searched for literature related to these topics, I also focused on literature that had been written over time. While reading these articles and books, I noted that "reading to review" Hart (1998, p. 53) or "reading as a reviewer" (Chapters 3 and 5) required me to categorize various studies that explored how individuals used digital tools as everyday practices to make sense of their worlds.

Below, I address writing a literature review as a recursive process, which is key to the writing process as one rewrites, revises, and rethinks the organization of a review.

Recursive Processes in Writing a Literature Review

> Conducting a literature review is usually recursive, meaning that somewhere along the way, you'll find yourself repeating steps out-of-order.
>
> (University of West Florida Library Studies, 2019)

Writing in general is a recursive process in which identified patterns are continually revised. Over time, these patterns are integrated and ideas become more refined (Zamel, 1982). Elbow (1998) reminds us that "trying to write it right the first time" is a "dangerous method" (p. 39). For instance, I wrote various versions of my literature review as I reworked my drafts until my committee and I were satisfied with "the best version" (Bloomberg & Volpe, 2008). However, my best version did not evolve through linear stages, or across a few weeks. I went back and forth with my committee members, even during the data collection and analysis processes. Across time, we identified nuances in the literature that required me to revise or delete portions of the review. This gentle process meant that reviewing and writing the literature review would not necessarily be completed before the data collection and analysis sections were written. Like me, most novice scholars go through multiple revisions of their dissertation review drafts.

For example, during my doctoral program, my comprehensive examination entailed writing the literature review section for my dissertation. The criterion for the exam was to demonstrate creditable work in examining how literacy researchers have studied the issues related to family literacy and digital literacies, and present a clear argument about how those issues contribute to the field. More specifically, the *Ph.D. Dissertation Handbook* stated,

> The literature review in the proposal should include an introduction to the problem or issue in the field that your study addresses, your research questions, your theoretical framework, and a coherent review of relevant

Reflecting on and Redefining Approaches **69**

literature that provides a rationale for the research questions and methodology. You need to be explicit about the timeliness and relevance of your proposed research... The literature review must be focused and selective, and the focus will be on the rationale for the study, the research questions, the research design, and the data collection and analysis procedures (University at Albany, SUNY, 2014).

When completing the final revision of my dissertation, I located a significant study I had missed in my search that was very relevant to my research (Ba et al., 2002). This study addressed the paucity of studies that examined African American families' literacies and digital literacies. Ba et al. (2002) examined nine low-income and ten middle-income African American and Latinx families with children in grades 7 and 8. The families in this study were similar to my participants, the Alis. Like those families, the Ali family's everyday digital literacy practices influenced their family life. For example, the family purchased an internet connection, the children spent leisure time on the computer, parents used the computer, parents used digital tools to communicate with their children, and family members engaged in troubleshooting when problems arose. Digital literacy practices were influenced by social, technological, and school environments. My study also showed various nuances, and proved that families like the Alis *did* have access to the technologies accessed by families explored in Ba et al.'s (2002) study. This example reveals how the process of writing a literature review is ongoing, and initial searches are inherently partial. Because of this, it is often necessary to update keywords and phrases and keep detailed records in order to manage an up-to-date scholarly search.

My first iteration of my review started with searching literature on the following topics/structures: (a) family literacy; (b) families' cultural, socioeconomic, and discursive literacy practices; (c) families and technologies/new literacies/digital literacies, and (d) family literacy as apprenticeships. My final dissertation headings in my literature review were as follows: (a) Theories of Multimodalities, (b) Origins of Digital Literacies, (c) Literacy Practices/Literacy Events, (d) Family Literacies and Digital Literacy Practices, (e) Apprenticeships in Family Literacies, and (f) Meaning Making and Identities. These themes/topics provided me with specific vantage points to focus on as I examined the most important constructs and analyzed my data.

Conclusion

There are many challenges involved in writing a dissertation literature review. In this chapter, I make explicit the significance of addressing the purpose, goal, structure, and voice of the literature review that doctoral students must write in order to propose the idea that their research is often quite different from the literature that frames their studies' findings. This highlights the recursive nature

70 Reflecting on and Redefining Approaches

of immersing oneself in scholarship as data are collected, analyzed, interpreted, and put into conversation with field/s of study. It is important to address how the literature review is an ongoing process, but through this process, and with guidance, you will enhance and advance your understanding of your own work.

From my retrospective analysis of writing my dissertation literature review and the subsequent syntheses I have conducted over time, I often offer the following recommendations to doctoral students below. This is not an exhaustive list, but does contain key points that I found helpful during and after writing my literature review and dissertation.

Reflecting on and Redefining: Questions/Recommendations to Consider When Writing the Literature Review for Your Dissertation

- What gaps exist in the literature in your field?
- When perusing the literature, in what ways does the researcher provide enough information to reach saturation?
- What questions were/were not asked?
- Comb the reference lists of relevant articles for more exhaustive lists of scholarship in your field of study. One way of knowing if you have reached saturation is when you see the same studies mentioned over again in the review and in the bibliography sections; however, only you can decide to conclude the search for additional literature.
- Consider completing a literature matrix of key scholarship in your field to chart how each study relates to the larger body of literature. Think about the following questions (this is not an exhaustive list, but reading through all of the studies might determine which aspects of the study you use in the chart):
  - What differences exist?
  - How do each of the studies define your topic?
  - What theoretical frameworks are used in each of the studies?
  - Who are the participants?
  - What are the findings?
  - What methodologies are used?
- When searching literature for research topics that are new to the field and finding that there is a lack of articles on your topic, consider journals outside your specific field of study (e.g., sociology, anthropology, and business) when applicable.
- When reading, it is not realistic to read and include every article or report on your research topic, but it is very important to peruse key components of the article for clarity and to demonstrate a clear understanding of the field and how that study has shaped the development of the field.

References

Ba, H., Tally, W., & Tsikalas, K. (2002). Investigating children's emerging digital literacies. *Journal of Technology, Learning and Assessment, 1*, 4.

Banks, A. J. (2006). *Race, rhetoric, and technology: Searching for higher ground.* Lawrence Erlbaum.

Bawden, D. (2008). Origins and concepts of digital literacy. In C. Lankshear & M. Knobel (Eds.), *Digital literacies: Concepts, policies and paradoxes* (pp. 15–32). Peter Lang.

Bhattacharya, K. (2009). Othering research, researching the Other: De/colonizing approaches to qualitative inquiry. In J. Smart (Ed.), *Higher education: Handbook of theory and research* (Vol. XXIV, pp. 105–150). Springer.

Bloomberg, L. D., & Volpe, M. F. (2008). *Completing your qualitative dissertation: A roadmap from beginning to end.* Sage.

Boote, D., & Beile, P. (2005). Scholars before researchers: On the centrality of the dissertation literature review in dissertation preparation. *Educational Researcher, 34*(6), 3–15.

Bruce, B. C. (2002). Diversity and critical social engagement: How changing technologies enable new modes of literacy in changing circumstances. In D. E. Alvermann (Ed.), *Adolescents and literacies in a digital world* (pp. 1–18). Peter Lang Publishing.

Bruce, C. (1994). Research students' early experiences of the dissertation literature review. *Studies in Higher Education, 19*, 217–229.

Cairney, T. H., & Ruge, J. (1998). *Community literacy practices and schooling: Towards effective support for students.* DEET.

Cammack, D. W. (2002). Literacy, technology, and a room of her own: Analyzing adolescent girls' online conversations from historical and technological literacy perspectives. In D. L. Schallert, C. M. Fairbanks, J. Worthy, B. Maloch, & J. V. Hoffman (Eds.), *51st yearbook of the National Reading Conference* (pp. 129–141). National Reading Conference.

Cazden, C. (1981). Performance before Competence: Assistance to child discourse in the zone of proximal development. *Quarterly Newsletter of the Laboratory of Comparative Human Cognition, 3*(1), 5–8.

Chandler-Olcott, K., & Mahar, D. (2003). "Tech-savviness" meets multiliteracies: Exploring adolescent girls' technology-mediated literacy practices. *Reading Research Quarterly, 38*(3), 356–385.

Compton-Lilly, C. (2003). *Reading families: The literate lives of urban children.* Teachers College Press.

Cooper, H. M. (1988a). The structure of knowledge synthesis. *Knowledge in Society, 1*, 104–126.

Cooper, H. M. (1988b). Organizing knowledge synthesis: A taxonomy of literature reviews. *Knowledge in Society, 1*, 104–126.

Creswell, J. W. (1994). *Research design qualitative and quantitative approaches.* Sage.

Creswell, J. W. (2002). *Educational research: Planning, conducting, and evaluating quantitative and qualitative research.* Merrill Prentice Hall.

Creswell, J. W. (2014). *Research design: Qualitative, quantitative, and mixed methods approaches* (4th ed.). Sage Publications.

Eaton, S. E. (2010). *Reading strategy: Differences between summarizing and synthesizing information.* Retrieved from: http://www.scribd.com/doc/38175256/Differences-Between-Summarizing-and-Synthesizing-Information

Edwards, P. A. (2009). *Tapping the potential of parents: A strategic guide to boosting student achievement through family involvement.* Scholastic.

72 Reflecting on and Redefining Approaches

Elbow, P. (1998). *Writing with power: Techniques for mastering the writing process* (2nd ed.). Oxford University Press.

Finfgeld-Connett, D., & Johnson, E. D. (2012). Literature search strategies for conducting knowledge-building and theory-generating qualitative systematic reviews. *Journal of Advanced Nursing*, 69(1), 194–204.

Fuller, S. (2006). Just bullshit. In G. L. Hardcastle & G. A. Reisch (Eds.), *Bullshit and philosophy: Guaranteed to get perfect results every time* (pp. 241–257). Open Court.

Gadsden, V. L. (1994). *Understanding family literacy: Conceptual issues facing the field* (National Center on Adult Literacy Technical Report TR 94-02). Retrieved from http://www.eric.ed.gov/PDFS/ED374339.pdf

Gadsden, V. L. (1996). How do we account for racial, ethnic, religious, and other cultural differences when designing and conducting family literacy programs? In R. LeGrand (Ed.), *Family literacy: Directions in research and implications for practice*. Office of Educational Research and Improvement, U.S. Department of Education.

Gadsden, V. (2000). Intergenerational literacy within families. In M. L. Kamil, P. B. Mosenthal, P. D. Pearson, & R. Barr (Eds.), *Handbook of Reading Research* (Vol. 3, pp. 871–887). Lawrence Erlbaum Associates.

Gilster, P. (1997). *Digital literacy*. John Wiley & Sons.

Glesne, C. (1999). *Becoming qualitative researchers: An introduction* (2nd ed.). Addison-Wesley.

Guerin, C. (n.d.). *Some misconceptions about literature reviews*. Retrieved from https://doctoral-writing.wordpress.com/2019/07/08/some-misconceptions-about-literature-reviews/

Hagood, M. C. (2000). New times, new millennium, new literacies. *Reading Research and Instruction*, 39(4), 311–328.

Hart, C. (1998). *Doing a literature review: Releasing the social science research imagination*. Sage Publications.

Heath, S. B. (1983). *Ways with words: Language, life, and work in communities and classrooms*. Cambridge University Press.

Jacobs, G. E. (2006). Fast times and digital literacy: Participation roles and portfolio construction within instant messaging. *Journal of Literacy Research*, 38(2), 171–196.

Lareau, A. (1989). *Home advantage: Social class and parental intervention in elementary education*. Falmer.

LeCompte, M. D., Klingner, J. K., Campbell, S. A., & Menk, D. W. (2003). Editors' introduction. *Review of Educational Research*, 73, 123–124.

Lewis, C., & Fabos, B. (2005). Instant messaging, literacies, and social identities. *Reading Research Quarterly*, 40(4), 470–501.

Lewis, T. (2009). *Family literacy and digital literacies: A redefined approach to examining social practices of an African American family* [Unpublished doctoral dissertation]. State University of New York, Albany.

Lewis, T. Y. (2013). "We txt 2 sty cnnectd:" An African American mother and son communicate: Digital literacies, meaning-making, and activity theory systems. *Journal of Education*, 193(2), 1–13.

Machi, L. A., & McEvoy, B. T. (2012). *The literature review: Six steps to success* (2nd ed.). Corwin Press.

Mahar, D. (2002). An uncharted journey: Three adolescent technology experts navigate the school system. In D. L. Schallert, C. M. Fairbanks, J. Worthy, B. Maloch, & J. V. Hoffman (Eds.), *51st yearbook of the National Reading Conference* (pp. 287–297). National Reading Conference.

Marsh, J. (2006). Global, local/public, private: Young children's engagement in digital literacy practices in the home. In J. Rowsell & K. Pahl (Eds.), *Travel notes from the new literacy studies: Case studies in practice* (pp. 19–38). Multilingual Matters.

Marsh, J., & Thompson, P. (2001). Parental involvement in literacy development: Using media texts. *Journal of Research in Reading*, 24(3), 266–278.

McAdoo, H. (2006). *Black families.* Sage Publications.

McCarthey, S. (1997). Connecting home and school literacy practices in classrooms with diverse populations. *Journal of Literacy Research*, 29(2), 145–182.

Merriam, S. B. (1988). *Case study research in education: A qualitative approach.* Jossey-Bass Publishers.

Merriam, S. B. (2001). *Qualitative research and case study applications in education.* Jossey Bass Publishers.

Norton-Meier, L. (2004). A technology user's bill of rights: Lessons learned in chat rooms. *Journal of Adolescent and Adult Literacy*, 47(7), 606–608.

Patel, L. (2015). *Decolonizing educational research: From ownership to answerability.* Routledge.

Patton, M. Q. (2002). *Qualitative research and evaluation methods.* Sage Publications.

Purcell-Gates, V. (1995). *Other people's words: The cycle of low literacy.* Harvard University Press.

Randolph, J. (2009). A guide to writing the dissertation literature review. *Practical Assessment, Research, and Evaluation*, 14(13), 1–13.

Rogers, R. (2003). *A critical discourse analysis of family literacy practices: Power in and out of print.* Routledge.

Sandelowski, M., & Barroso, J. (2007). *Handbook for synthesizing qualitative research.* Springer.

Shanahan, T. (2002). Research synthesis: Making sense of the accumulation of knowledge in reading. In M. L. Kamil, P. B. Mosenthal, P. D. Pearson, & R. Barr (Eds.), *Methods of literacy research* (pp. 133–150). Erlbaum.

Shockley-Bisplinghoff, B. (1995). *Engaging families: Connecting home and school literacy communities.* Heinemann.

Smagorinsky, P., Daigle, E. A., O'Donnell-Allen, C., & Bynum, S. (2010). Bullshit in academic writing: A protocol analysis of a senior's process of interpreting Much Ado about Nothing. *Research in the Teaching of English*, 44(4), 368–405.

Smith, L. T. (1999/2012). *Decolonizing methodologies: Research and indigenous peoples.* Zed Books.

Snyder, H. (2019). Literature review as a research methodology: An overview and guidelines. *Journal of Business Research*, 104, 333–339.

Stein, P., & Slonimsky, L. (2006). An eye on the text and an eye on the future: Multimodal literacy in three Johannesburg families. In K. Pahl & J. Rowsell (Eds.), *Travel notes from the New Literacy Studies: Instances of practice* (pp. 118–146). Clevedon, UK: Multilingual Matters Ltd.

Taylor, D. (1983). *Family literacy: Young children learning to read and write.* Heinemann.

Taylor, D., & Dorsey-Gaines, C. (1988). *Growing up literate: Learning from inner-city families.* Heinemann.

Thomson, P. (2015). *I can't find anything written on my topic… Really?* Retrieved from https://patthomson.net/2015/04/06/i-cant-find-anything-written-on-my-topic/

Toulmin, S. (1969). *The uses of argument.* Cambridge University Press.

Tuck, E. (2015). Foreword. In L. Patel (Ed.), *Decolonizing educational research: From ownership to answerability* (pp. xii–xv). Routledge.

74 Reflecting on and Redefining Approaches

Tuck, E., & Yang, K.W. (2012). Decolonization is not a metaphor. *Decolonization: Indigeneity, Education and Society*, 1, 1–40.

University at Albany, SUNY. (2014). *Ph.D. dissertation handbook*. Retrieved from https://www.albany.edu/philosophy/philosophy-graduate-handbook

University of West Florida Library Studies. (2019). *Literature review: Conducting and writing*. Retrieved from https://libguides.uwf.edu/c.php?g=215199&p=1420520

Vygotsky, L. S. (1978). *Mind in society: The development of higher psychological processes*. Harvard University Press.

Webster, J., & Watson, R.T. (2002). Analyzing the past to prepare for the future: Writing a literature review. *Management Information Systems Quarterly*, 26(3), xiii–xxiii.

Weston, A. (2000). *A rulebook for arguments* (3rd ed.). Hackett Publishing Company, Inc.

Wolcott, H. F. (1990). *Writing up qualitative research* (Sage Qualitative Research Methods Series, Vol. 20). Sage.

Zamel, V. (1982). Writing: The process of discovering meaning. *TESOL Quarterly*, 16(2), 195–209.

3
TRADITIONAL LITERATURE REVIEWS AND FOLLOW UP REVIEWS

Introduction

In this chapter, I (Rebecca) draw on the experience of reviewing research in critical discourse analysis in education research across two points in time. This resulted in two literature reviews published in *Review of Educational Research* (2005 and 2016). As with the other chapters in this book, I retrospectively construct my process of conceptualizing and carrying out these related literature reviews. Along the way, I will draw on feedback from reviewers to shine light on how the review process shapes the scholarship of reviews. I also reflexively situate myself in the review to demonstrate how not only the field of scholarship changed across time but also my stance as a scholar had changed vis-à-vis the field. Table 3.1 illustrates scholarship that is connected to the literature reviews discussed in this chapter. To foreshadow one of the findings from the reviews that is salient in our book on synthesizing literature in literacy studies, we learned that amongst subfields in education, literacy scholars were leading the way with CDA research.

Both papers emerged from my work as a literacy scholar and CDA practitioner, teaching graduate students about CDA. The original 2005 review of CDA in education started as a project in a doctoral seminar in discourse analysis that I taught in 2001. The group included myself, Elizabeth Malancharuvil-Berkes, Melissa Mosley, Diane Hui, and Glynis O'Garro Joseph. I presented versions of the manuscript in various seminars and conferences including the following: CDA Conference in Bloomington, Indiana (June, 2004); Critical Approaches to Discourse Analysis Across the Disciplines/*CADAAD* (May, 2004); CDA Workshop at the University of Albany (2004); and CDA Study Group at the National Reading Conference.

The 2016 review team was assembled from Advanced Doctoral Seminar in CDA. A number of people had taken an advanced CDA course with me (Chris Schott,

76 Traditional Literature Reviews and Follow Up Reviews

TABLE 3.1 Traditional Literature Review and Related Scholarship

Literature Review
Rogers, R., Berkes, E., Mosley, M., Hui, & D., O-Garro, G. (2005). A critical review of critical discourse analysis. *Review of Educational Research*, 75(3), 365–416.

Follow Up Literature Review
Rogers, R., Schaenen, I., Schott, C., O'Brien, K., Trigos-Carrillo, L., Starkey, K., & Chasteen, C. (2016). Critical discourse analysis in educational research: A review of the literature, 2004–2012. *Review of Educational Research*, 86(4), 1192–1226.

A Network of Related Scholarship
Rogers, R., & Schaenen, I. (2014). Critical discourse analysis in language and literacy research. *Reading Research Quarterly*, 49(1), 121–143.

Rogers, R. (2017). Critical discourse analysis and discourses of education. In J. Flowerdew & J. Richardson (Eds.) *Handbook of Critical Discourse Analysis* (pp. 465–479). NY: Routledge.

Companion Website for *An Introduction to CDA in Education* (2011)
The website is a new feature of the second edition of the book and is intended to extend inquiry, exploration, and dialogue beyond the chapters in the book. This website was funded by the Innovative Technology Grant through the University of Missouri-St. Louis. I compiled the resources (with the research assistance of Inda Schaenen) for this website. Staff at Routledge designed the site: http://cw.routledge.com/textbooks/9780415874298/

Rogers, R. (2013). Critical discourse analysis: Criteria to consider in reviewing scholarship. In A. Trainor & E. Graue (Eds.) *Publishing qualitative research in the social and behavioral sciences: A guide for reviewers and researchers* (pp. 69–81). NY: Routledge.

Kathryn O'Brien, Kim Starkey, Cynthia Carter Chasteen, Inda Schaenen, and Lina Trigos-Carrillo). As part of the course, we worked together on reviewing recent scholarship in CDA and explored theoretical, methodological, and representational issues.

In the following sections, I use the major procedures of conducting a literature review as a way to organize my description and critique both of the original review and the follow up study. From "Identifying the Purpose and Research Questions," to "Designing a Review," "Searching and Sampling," "Coding and Analyzing the Studies," and "Representing the Synthesis," I describe, historicize, reflect, and critique my process of conducting a **traditional literature review**.

Before proceeding, I will attempt to define what is meant by a traditional literature review. As we already discussed in Chapter 1, the term "literature review" is a broad umbrella term which captures a range of approaches. **Research synthesis** is often used interchangeably with the word "review." I certainly will use them interchangeably in this chapter. Literature reviews collect and organize the findings from a corpus of primary studies to make claims or tell a story about what is known in an area. Eisenhart (1998) describes a traditional literature review as "establish[ing] the dimensions of a field so that the width and breadth of the field are defined" (p. 394). More so than summarizing the studies, literature reviews synthesize what is known so that the review generates new knowledge. Important to point out that literature reviews and research syntheses are always written from a perspective and tradition. Both the original literature review and the follow up review that I focus on in this chapter were written from a critical tradition yet, as I point out, had roots in post-positivism.

Identifying the Purpose and Research Questions

In the early 2000s, when we began the original review, CDA was just beginning to be used by educational researchers. Indeed, CDA of all types comes from fields outside of education and much of it is tied to linguistics in one way or another. As a junior academic myself carrying out CDA work in education, I wanted to take stock of what had been accomplished in this emerging sub-field so I could point to some reasonable next steps for myself and the field. In 2001, I was asked to teach a doctoral seminar in CDA and stepped into that precarious place of novice and expert. As part of that seminar, we began reviewing scholarship in CDA. At this point in my academic career, I had not read much on how to conduct literature reviews; nor did I know that a range of research syntheses approaches existed. My **dissertation literature review**, much like the one described by Tisha Lewis Ellison in Chapter 2, was conducted and represented to make a case for my ethnographic study and covered different domains of knowledge. CDA was the theoretical and methodological framework in my dissertation study and, as such, focused on becoming knowledgeable about the frames and tools by reading primary theoretical work and empirical studies. I did not, however, do a literature review of studies in educational research that used CDA. Several years later, I continued to use CDA and wanted to have a sense of the landscape of theories and methods so I could build on this work.

In the 2005 review, the published research questions asked, "What happens when Critical Discourse Analysis crosses the boundaries into education research? In what ways do education researchers use CDA? How can the use of CDA in educational contexts inform us about method and theory?" (pp. 366–367)

Looking back on these questions, I can unravel some of the assumptions that were built into them. They reflect a review of a relatively new approach in education research. The first question focuses on the movement of CDA into the field of education. This focus was stated in the paper as, "As such work crosses into the boundary of education, interesting and substantive concerns arise about how it is applied to educational issues, how it affects other research and approached in education, and how it might be reviewed in the non-education research traditions from which it came" (p. 366). The second research question is descriptive. The third question assumes there is a reciprocity to CDA scholarship in education that

78 Traditional Literature Reviews and Follow Up Reviews

can inform the broader field and that educational researchers can contribute to the practice of CDA.

By this time, I had already participated in what I now see as pivotal experiences in my development as a scholar – presenting at the first international *Critical Approaches to Discourse Analysis Across the Disciplines* (CADAAD) conference, convening a seminar at my university with leaders in CDA (which resulted in my 2004 edited book "Introduction to Critical Discourse Analysis in Education"), conducting and publishing empirical work in CDA/education, participating in seminars with multi-disciplinary scholars who held different perspectives about the theoretical commitments and roots of CDA. From these experiences, I met CDA scholars from around the world. I also knew the field was ripe with debate and tension. Indeed, reading key collections of papers was important in framing the paper and entering our synthesis into dialogue with a broader global discussion occurring in the field of social sciences (e.g., 2001 special issue of *Critique of Anthropology* and 1999 debate in *Discourse & Society*). Another purpose of the paper was to put CDA in educational research into dialogue with key debates and tensions, making ourselves answerable to critiques that had formed. We wrote,

> CDA has not gone without critique, and the critiques are part of the overall context in which we intend this review to be read (p. 372). The three most common critiques are: that (a) ideologies are read on to the data, (b) there is an imbalance between social theory and linguistic method, and (c) CDA is often separate from social contexts. "How does CDA conducted in educational contexts hold up to these critiques? To answer this question, we reviewed the proliferating database of education research using CDA (p. 372)

These questions and purpose stand in contrast to reviewing an established body of scholarship which is what we undertook with the follow up review. We posed the framing research questions for the follow up review as "What is the nature of CDA in education research from 2004–2012? What are the characteristics of studies that include CDA? What findings emerge from CDA scholarship in education? How does CDA in education research contribute to the field of critical discourse studies?" (p. 1192). Tables 3.2 and 3.3 are questions that synthesists might ask themselves as they begin their review.

The driving force for the follow up review was my curiosity about how the field had changed over time. I remember wondering, specifically, what cumulative insights had been made that could advance educational equity. I intuitively

TABLE 3.2 A Central Question

What is the history of this field? Is it emergent? Established? What is my position as a scholar in relationship to this field? What critiques have emerged about scholarship in this area?

TABLE 3.3 Considering Assumptions

What are my assumptions, biases, and hopes as I design the study?

knew – from my role as a reviewer for journals and conference, conference participant, and reader of this work – that CDA had taken off. CDA in educational research was readily visible in many journals. This was exciting and, at the same time, led me to wonder how all of this " deconstructing" and "critique" had changed the conditions of education. Part of this was a cynicism that I was bringing to my own scholarship. Indeed, at this point in my career, I had been promoted to Professor and I was taking stock of my contributions I had made to the field and my local communities and how I might deepen this impact moving forward. Thus, the impetus for what became a very long literature review journey was, in some ways, quite personal and rooted in a desire to forge a future path as an educational researcher that was meaningful and could contribute to educational equity.

Designing a Review and Assembling a Reviewing Team

Synthesizing qualitative research in literacy studies often includes emergent review designs. That was certainly the case with the original 2005 literature review. I took notes about the steps we took and then read widely in *Review of Educational Research* to get a sense of the genre of literature reviews published in this journal. This helped to concretize and put into writing some of the decisions we had made. I was learning that there was a language to describe the review design we were creating through our searching, sampling, reading and reviewing, synthesizing and comparing, and asking additional questions. This process was iterative. Because we were reviewing a critical tradition of scholarship and doing so in a manner that looked critically at individual studies as well as the cumulative synthesis of findings, I rooted the review design in a critical tradition.

The design of the follow up review was less emergent because I wanted to compare the results of the two reviews and, ultimately, accomplish a longitudinal review of the scholarship. In this way, reviews can be updated over time. However, because of the massive changes and developments that had taken place in the field, we did innovate on the design and include a review of key constructs in the field (e.g., social action, context, reflexivity, and deconstructive–reconstructive stance to inquiry). These constructs had remained important over time and we wanted to make a case for how educational researchers had made advancements in these areas.

For both reviews, I found it helpful to be accompanied by a research team that had a variety of backgrounds and positionalities vis-à-vis the scholarship. From leading the research team, I could tell there were differences in the depth

80 Traditional Literature Reviews and Follow Up Reviews

of coding based on each research team member's level of expertise in the field. For the review of literacy scholarship, for example, several reviewers were literacy, ESOL, and English Education scholars and generated focused points related to literacy studies in their coding. Other reviewers had backgrounds in other sub-fields of education and made different connections. Indeed, having conducted and published many studies using CDA, I could look more deeply at the nuances of this approach and fine tune categories meant for specialists in this area.

Searching and Sampling

For both the original literature review and the follow up review, our search terms were "critical discourse analysis" and "education." We conducted a search of five electronic databases: ERIC (EBSCO), ArticleFirst (OCLC), PsycINFO (American Psychological Association), Modern Language Association (MLA) International Bibliography, and Web of Science (Thomson Reuters). We wanted the search terms and channels to be as similar as possible in the original and follow up review and include international journals. However, we learned that the field of publishing had changed during this time. Thus, our decisions sought to achieve balance between "replicability" and openness to new techniques, databases, and ways of analyzing and organizing data.

For both literature reviews, we searched each database individually so we would have a clear record of results. We searched for peer-reviewed articles and excluded dissertations and book chapters. We then read through the results and eliminated overlaps. For the original review, we searched from 1980 to 2003 to include 20 years of scholarship. For the follow up review, we picked up where the first review left off and searched from 2004 to 2012. Thus, between the two reviews over 30 years of research was reviewed (1980–2012).

One of the reviewers asked us "Is this a review of critical discourse analysis in education or an artifact of the use of particular databases?" This constructive critique led us to explore the geo-politics of database vendors which turned out to be a very useful step not only for the literature review we were working on but also in terms of piquing a future interest in equitable flows of knowledge (Trigos-Carrillo & Rogers, 2017).

To learn more about the geo-politics of databases and vendors, we consulted a reference librarian. We learned that searching different databases sometimes identified different pieces of scholarship. For example, Table 3.4 shows a "Search Memo" that was generated that shows our reflection on the changing nature of one of the databases we searched and our understanding of how it indexes key words from the primary research.

Indeed, this critique thankfully heightened our sensitivity to issues of knowledge and power within the search process. We engaged in other techniques to broaden the international reach of our search. These are shared in Table 3.5. With all of these techniques, it is inevitable that scholarship will get excluded because

Traditional Literature Reviews and Follow Up Reviews **81**

TABLE 3.4 Search Memo

There were international journals included in the Web of Science search including: *South African Linguistics and Applied Language Studies* and *Asia Pacific Journal of Education*. It looks like WOS is more inclusive because it picks up on the secondary key word descriptors.

I noticed in quite a few articles that the authors may not mention CDA in their abstracts but CDA is listed in the key word descriptor. When in doubt, I included it and then when we get the ART done, we can decide if we want to exclude it.

TABLE 3.5 Techniques for Creating an Inclusive Search

- We identified global journals that were included in the databases we searched (e.g., *South African Linguistics*, *Asia Pacific Education*, and *Australian Educational Researcher*). Part of our search process involved asking leading peers to review the comprehensiveness of our corpus. This helped us to turn up additional pieces of scholarship that, for one reason or another, had not been indexed in the databases we searched. We learned that sometimes new journals are not yet indexed in databases or the indexing system pulls up words from the abstract but not the key word descriptors.
- We hand searched a number of journals such as *Linguistics and Education, Discourse & Society, Discurso & Sociedad*, and *Language in Society*. This involved accessing the table of contents and reading the abstracts.
- We read our search results carefully asking, 'What authors are not represented in this search?' 'What journals are excluded that we know publishes this scholarship?' For example, sometimes we could identify people who had published research in CDA and education yet their work was not showing up in our searches.
- In these cases, we would conduct an "author search" in our databases to see if we could locate scholarship that met the inclusion criteria. We would then see how the article had been indexed and if this knowledge would help us to fine tune our search. For example, there are a number of scholars from around the world whose work in Critical Discourse Analysis has been foundational to the field and perhaps they published conceptual pieces not empirical articles.
- We also engaged in what we called "bibliographic branching" which is reading the references of a piece of scholarship included in the review to get additional sources that may not have shown up in the original searches.

of the geopolitics of knowledge, citation segregation, availability bias, language bias, or familiarity bias (Suri, 2014).

Another decision point when searching for scholarship is determining what genre of scholarship to include/exclude from the search. As noted above, we decided to search for peer-reviewed articles. However, one of the reviewers critiqued this decision arguing that some of the best, cutting-edge research and theory on CDA has been published in books, book chapters, or handbooks. This was a solid point and our review team agreed to add books to our review although

82 Traditional Literature Reviews and Follow Up Reviews

our sampling of these books was less systematic than our review of the databases. We also sought out historical overviews such as Blommaert and Bulcaen (2000), Gee and Green (1998), and Luke (1995, 2002).

Finally, it should be noted that sometimes a reviewer will request the sampling and search procedure be revised. One of the reviewers of the follow up study, for example, requested that we search for articles across 2012. The review had been submitted in the middle of the year. If we wanted to claim that the search included the years 2004–2012, we needed to do another search to include additional articles from 2012. This meant searching again, coding, analyzing, re-tabulating, and re-interpreting our findings. In retrospect, we could have ended the search with the year 2011 but we wanted to provide as up-to-date synthesis of the field as possible.

Sampling of Primary Studies

Researchers need to decide which search results will be included or excluded from the sample. In our reviews, for example, we included research that specifically called itself "critical discourse analysis." We excluded research that involved critically oriented discourse scholarship but did not specifically refer to itself as CDA or critical discourse analysis. There was a great deal of scholarship that referenced critical thinking, critical perspectives, and discourse analysis but did not engage with the theory or methods of CDA.

Locating the Research and Ending the Search

Many of the databases we used were full-text databases. However, we did have a fair number of references that needed to be located. We found our library to have many of the articles. We located all of the articles as PDFs, filed them by the author's last name and publication year, and stored them on our computer and in a cloud-based folder for ease of access by the research team. There were a few instances where we needed to contact the author of a search record to access the article.

It is important for research synthesists to check and double-check their search process to be as inclusive as possible. This means asking critical questions about search biases. This is an important step in reducing knowledge segregation which continues to privilege scholarship of the global north over other parts of the world (e.g., Santos, 2014). In both reviews we closed our search when we felt we had satisfied the reviewers and obtained a good representation of the field.

Reading as a Reviewer: Describing, Coding, and Analyzing the Studies

Hart (1998) introduces the idea of "reading to review" (p. 53) which is a very different mode than reading to learn about an area of scholarship. Synthesists 'read to review' which means approaching primary studies with a set of questions.

After locating all of the articles, we began the process of reading as a reviewer. At this point, individual studies became a unified data set and our goal as research synthesists was to look for patterns across the studies. There was a familiarity with some of the research. Indeed, we had read some of the articles previously but not necessarily with specific questions in mind. We knew we wanted to extract basic categories from the literature so we could provide a survey of the kinds of articles (empirical or theoretical), the publication years, the rate of collaborative authorship, and the geographical setting of the study. We were also interested in more interpretive questions (e.g., role of the researcher and how learning is addressed).

The code book for the 2005 literature review developed semi-inductively from the research team's reading of the primary research and from our reading of the field (including critiques). We used sample studies to refine the coding scheme and developed inter-rater reliability. In the article, we wrote, "[w]e developed a codebook to *standardize our reviews*" (p. 373). In my handwritten notes of this process, I wrote that the "[o]ne of the goals of the coding sheet is to develop descriptive statistics of the CDA articles." Appendix D shows the 2005 codebook used to enter data into the spreadsheet. It takes a great deal of effort and insight to extract useful comparisons and contrasts of literature. When there is a large data set of research to review, having a research team is very important and some quality standards should be in place. Ultimately, as the lead researcher in the research team, I read all of the articles and cross-checked each person's code book.

The different kinds of categories in the codebook allow for different kinds of analysis. Descriptive statistics can be generated from categorical data that can be quantified (e.g., the number of empirical articles and the number of articles that focus on elementary level learners, etc.). There were other categories that lend themselves to thematic and critically oriented analyses. The point is that the research framing was built into this code book. This is an interpretive process, not simply a procedural one. Table 3.6 includes questions that synthesists might ask themselves as they develop a code book.

In retrospect, I grappled with the tension in efforts to "standardize" readings of critically oriented scholarship which may run counter to the epistemological

TABLE 3.6 Researcher Questions

Questions Researchers Might Ask When Developing a Code Book to Review Literature
- Does my code book address the conceptual categories that are driving the research?
- Will the categories help me/my research team move beyond descriptive statistics?
- What kinds of interpretations will be mined from the code books?
- What level of data will be necessary for analysis within and across categories?
- Are there debates or critiques in the field that might become part of the code book and analysis of the data set?

---

84 Traditional Literature Reviews and Follow Up Reviews

and ontological tenets of a critical tradition. Yet, it was necessary to extract pieces of each of the primary studies in order to synthesize across studies. We handled this tension by bringing a critical lens to the cross-study synthesis where we put the trends we were seeing across the studies into dialogue with larger critiques and debates in the field. We might think of the code book for research synthesists as a tool that functions similarly to the interview protocol. Rather than interviewing people, the research synthesist is "interviewing" each empirical study, recognizing there will be descriptive and interpretive slippage.

When we embarked on the follow up review, we used all of the categories from the 2005 code book and added categories based on conceptual and empirical developments in the field. By this point, I referred to it as an Analytic Review Template (ART), a term introduced by Compton-Lilly, Rogers, and Lewis (2012). The purpose of the synthesis tool was meant to offer some structure to our reading of individual studies with the unified data set in mind.

The field had grown substantially, as had our understanding of the field, and we found it important to integrate additional categories. We were quite interested in looking more deeply at how scholars in the field enacted constructs, such as reflexivity, social action, deconstructive–reconstructive stance, and context. Appendix E displays the 2016 ART which is substantially longer and more in-depth than the original code book.

Because of the expansion of the field and the enhanced complexity of our ART, the coding of the 2016 study was much more detailed and complex. We had turned certain qualitative features into categorical data that could be quantified. Appendix F is the coding sheet we developed whereas the general categories feature from the ART (e.g., article type, disciplinary field, and study design) was designed as a code book for data entry. For example, looking in the third column, you can see that AT-EMP was the code for an empirical article. DF-TCHED was the code for articles that were in the field of teacher education. By this time, we had developed a "schemata" for the qualities of studies (e.g., social action, reflexivity, deconstructive/reconstructive, and context) and each study was given a score from one to three in the spreadsheet. These data could then be sorted by time, geographical period, data sources of research design, participants, etc.

The spreadsheet we used to enter data from the codebook is illustrated in Figures 3.1 and 3.2. From this, you can see all of the categories from the codebook in Row 1. Part 1 includes roughly half of the entries and Part 2 includes the rest of the entries. Data from each codebook was entered into this spreadsheet for ease of management, sorting, and analysis. The spreadsheet allowed us to manipulate and analyze the data in different ways. In addition to the figures, examples from the spreadsheet can be found here:

tinyurl.com/92sdef3r

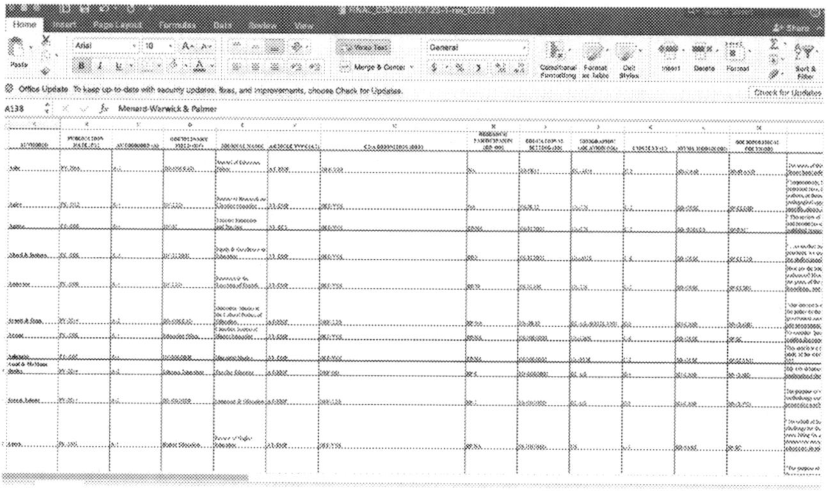

Traditional Literature Reviews and Follow Up Reviews **85**

FIGURE 3.1 Part 1 of the Spreadsheet

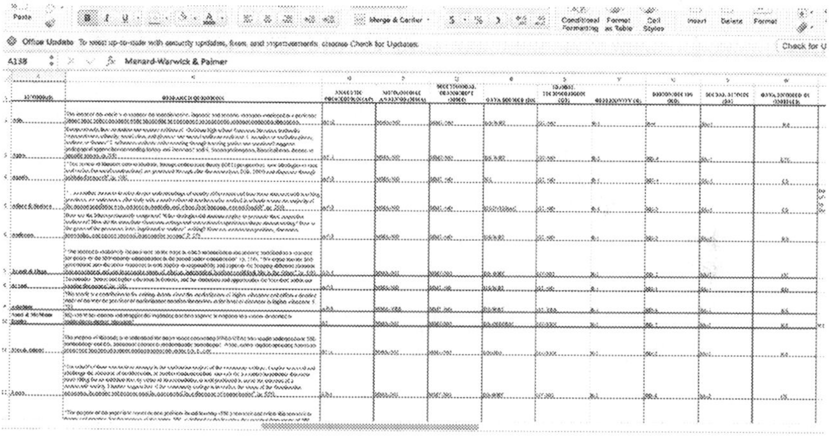

FIGURE 3.2 Part 2 of the Spreadsheet

Analysis of Primary Studies

The analysis process of both reviews was very similar. We developed descriptive statistics of the categories and then inductively and cross-comparatively analyzed categories. Other categories, such as the "Findings" of each study needed to be analyzed thematically. Figure 3.3 is a sample of a working document that I created to synthesize the key findings of each study into groups. In the left-hand margin, you can see the numbers "1," "2," "3," and so forth. These represented

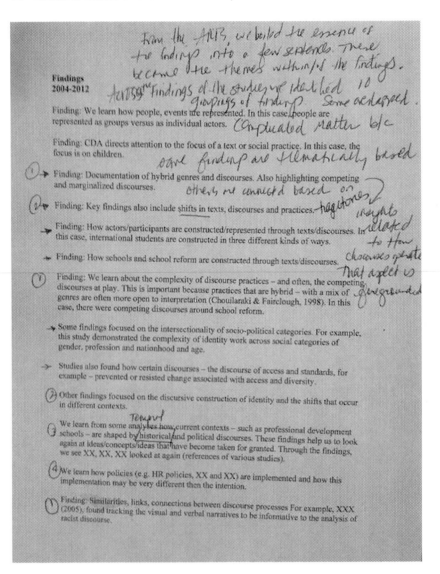

FIGURE 3.3 Thematic Analysis of the Findings

similar findings which were then grouped into categories. The analytic memo that is written along the top right-hand corner of the paper reads,

> From the ARTs, we boiled the essence of the findings into a few sentences. These became the themes from the findings. Across the findings of the studies we identified 10 groupings of findings. Some overlapped. Some

Traditional Literature Reviews and Follow Up Reviews **87**

findings are thematically based and others are connected based on insights related to how discourses operate.

This analytic memo (Figure 3.4) is an example of just one page in several notebooks devoted to analyzing the data set. With the research questions in mind, I looked across the studies to compare, contrast, and give examples. This example demonstrates how the process of writing helped me to synthesize findings across the studies. In the middle of the page, you can see how I began to make sense of how each author represented their findings (e.g., through tables, themes, and movement across constructs). The bottom of the page are early notes about the category of social action and reflexivity and what I noticed in one of the studies.

The big difference between the two reviews was the development of schemata to assess important qualities of the scholarship that had remained constant over time. Our goal with this analysis was to see how studies were generally grouped in each of these areas for the purpose of illuminating the field, not to "score" people. Our purpose was to help indicate the trends and patterns, not to be normative and determinative. Jumping ahead to representation of findings, we provided one illustrative study for each tier, in each of the four qualities. Our analysis in the follow up review also included a citation count of most cited CDA theorists to make claims about the scholarship drawn on with frequency in educational research.

Creating tables helped with the interpretive process and also the representation. We created many tables to help organize, analyze, and represent the findings across the data set. For example, we created a separate spreadsheet and table just by authors and findings. This helped us to make sense out of what collective findings had been generated from this corpus of scholarship.

Representing the Synthesis

Questions of representation are always at stake for research synthesists. We need to provide enough context for individual studies (or representative studies) within the body of the article while also demonstrating the themes and patterns across the collection of studies. This is a frame issue. Here, I give a few examples from the literature reviews that display different representational choices. In general, both reviews took on the structure and organization of an empirical article. This felt like a good choice given the journal *Review of Educational Research* and also highlighted that research syntheses are, indeed, knowledge generation. Of course, as we discussed in Chapter 1, there is variety in how research reviews are represented, not all of which use the structure of an empirical article. Some readers find that structure off-putting. For example, one reviewer of the 2005 literature review wrote, "I find the framing of the article as an empirical study with references to 'primary investigator,' 'modes of analysis,' 'findings,' etc., irritating and a bit arrogant. This is a review article, for heaven's sakes, not an empirical study." Even

88 Traditional Literature Reviews and Follow Up Reviews

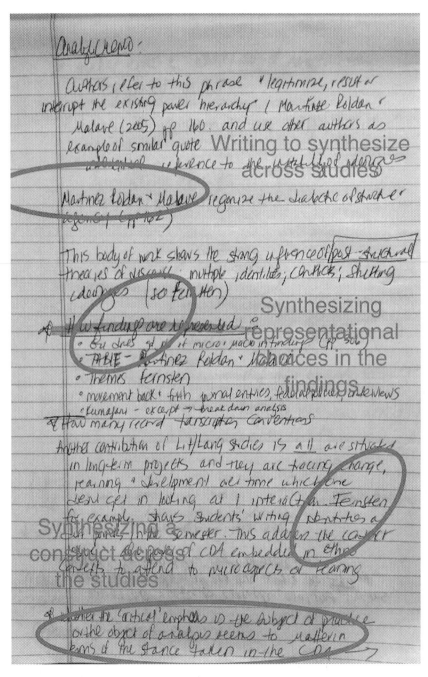

FIGURE 3.4 Analytic Memo: Synthesis Across Studies

with this criticism of the organization of the review, we decided to stick with the format of an empirical article, keeping in mind that there are other choices (see Appendix G for a sampling of feedback we got from the journal reviewers).

Beyond the structure of the paper are choices of representing the new knowledge generated from the synthesis itself. What has been learned from looking at the studies as a unified data set? The 2005 review included a section called "Organization of the Review" which was a paragraph or two long and provided a road map for the reader. The findings in the follow up paper were organized by research questions. Many reviewers use their research questions as headings within the findings section. The trick as writers of a research synthesis is to capture the complexities of individual studies while representing the synthetic themes across the data set. Suri (2014) puts it this way "a careful balance must be maintained between immersing in sufficient detail to maintain integrity of each study while refraining from drawing in so much detail that it interferes with identification of overarching themes" (p. 137).

Here, I provide a few examples of representational choices made in each of these literature reviews. Both reviews included a table of descriptive statistics which illustrated the breadth and depth of the field over time. This helps the reader get a sense of the "big picture" of the field. In the 2005 review, we chose to use conceptual categories that represented debate and tension in the field as an organizing structure for the findings. In the follow up review, we chose to organize the findings by research question. In each section, we shared representative studies and various ways that scholars represented their CDA. This helps to give the reader a sense of the details of particular studies and how they fit into the scope of the review. Table 3.7 includes ideas for research synthesists to keep in mind when representing the findings of their literature reviews.

TABLE 3.7 Ideas for Research Synthesists to Keep in Mind when Representing Findings

- The importance of thinking synthetically across the articles;
- Decisions will need to be made about where interpretations are made; that is, are interpretations of descriptive statistics made in the findings section? Or, does the synthesist wait until the Discussion section to interpret and discuss these findings?
- Provide the reader with a "road map" of how to read the findings. The section might be called "Organization of the Review";
- Avoid long quotations from articles/other scholars without synthesis;
- The findings should not simply be a description or summary of other studies and their findings. It should be a synthesis;
- Avoid strings of in-text references;
- Attempt to integrate conceptual work and critiques into the synthesis; and
- Coverage of various research studies should be relatively balanced. Based on the feedback from a reviewer, we wanted to avoid some studies getting more coverage than other studies.

Discussion: Limits, Possibilities, and Reflections

The 2005 literature review established a call for research in Critical Discourse Studies (CDS) – CDA in early grades, a focus on race, more attention to theories of learning and CDA, and integration of multimodality into CDA frameworks. In retrospect, this call directed my own line of scholarship for the next ten years. Indeed, the empirical studies I conducted focused on racial literacy at different points across the lifespan. Always in my mind were the findings from this review. In this way, literature reviews can direct the synthesists' line of scholarship in very personal and meaningful ways. Writing literature reviews is not only a contribution to the field but also, in very real ways, provides a very solid foundation for the synthesist to create an intellectual lineage for themselves, buttressed by a case that has been made with the literature review.

To summarize, the follow up review engaged with many of the same search procedures, coding techniques, and framing in critiques and debates in the field as the original review. However, we added some analytic features, such as additional categories to the ART, using a digital spreadsheet to quantify frequencies across categories, the development of a schemata for analyzing four constructs (reflexivity, social action, deconstructive–reconstructive stance, and context), and additional calls for CDA research. A big difference was the development of the schemata for the four constructs. The salience of the four constructs emerged in the 2005 article and because of the six-fold increase of scholarship in just 8 years (from 46 articles in 2005 to 257 articles in 2016), we decided to tighten up our criteria for evaluating these important constructs. This was important in terms of tracing and adding to theoretical developments in this area.

In this way, educational researchers are positioned to elevate scholarship in a field – that is, to address critiques – especially, as we pointed out in our review of the separation of CDA from social contexts. Indeed, one of the main contributions of educational researchers has been the integration of CDA in contexts of educational literacies. This realization from this literature review simultaneously signaled the presence of educational researchers in the landscape of CDA and pushed educational researchers to strengthen this approach. It was also personal in the sense that this review provided some direction – and a foundation on which to stand to justify that direction – in a published review.

Each of these literature reviews was useful because they performed two complementary critical roles simultaneously, in addition to its role of reviewing the field. First, we used work in educational CDA to contest popular critiques of CDA. From this standpoint, the review provides a valuable service to fellow researchers working in the area. Second, at the same time the paper subjects the articles under review to critique in their own right. This double edged critique – combined with a review of scholarship spans new and established researchers.

One of the points I make in this chapter is that literature reviews can help push lines of inquiry forward. This kind of "push" happens across subfields of literacy research. About this dialogue between reviews and empirical research, Suri (2014) writes, "methodological developments in either mode influence methodological developments in the other mode" (p. 28). Ultimately, we made the point that current education research 'is informed by and informs CDA' (p. 374). It is this dialogue between educational researchers and the larger field of discourse studies that is one of the main contributions of this article. In effect, we argued that educational researchers have brought novel and important insights to CDA work. For example, after the publication of the 2016 review, I felt adequately prepared to make a case for positive approaches to discourse analysis which became the subject of my 2018 book "*Reclaiming Powerful Literacies: New Horizons for Critical Discourse Analysis*." It was clear from this longitudinal synthesis of scholarship that deconstructive analyses were common in literacy studies and educational research. However, there was an emerging variety of CDA that specifically focused on discourses of hope, liberation, and transformation. My research imagination began to wander. I wondered, what would happen if I brought a shift in focus to the design and analysis of discourse practices? What if we became better at understanding the discursive contours of love, solidarity, and social transformation? What if we brought our understanding of discourses and discourse analysis to the educational contexts and conditions we wished to see?

Going Public with Literature Reviews – Audience, Purpose, and Uptake

Understanding the ever-changing state of CDA in educational research has been an ongoing scholarly project for me. I interact with the scholarship as a researcher, a reviewer for journals, a research methodologist, and an educator. I routinely teach doctoral seminars in critical discourse analysis which keeps me grounded not only in research but in how to make this research accessible to educators, counselors, social workers, and future researchers. For this reason, issues of access and accessibility often crop up.

To serve as a resource for the second edition of "An Introduction to CDA in Education," I created a companion website for CDA practitioners (2004/2011). The website is intended to extend inquiry, exploration, and dialogue amongst CDA practitioners. The organization and the content of the website is directly linked to my work in the literature reviews. My hope is that the website could be used as a teaching tool and make some of the theories and methods of CDA available to a wider audience. The site can be found here:

http://cw.routledge.com/textbooks/9780415874298/.

This is just one example of how scholars might go public with the findings of literature reviews. Indeed, our literature reviews can and should inform public sphere decisions. The text box at the start of the chapter includes a sample of how the research undertaken for these two reviews laid the foundation for a network

92 Traditional Literature Reviews and Follow Up Reviews

of scholarship. Each of these pieces engages with a different audience – reviewers, researchers, and educators. I should also comment on the "uptake" of the literature reviews. Both reviews have been well cited. As of September 2020, the 2005 review has been cited 803 times and the 2016 review has been cited 49 times.

Decolonizing Literature Reviews

In 2009, I completed a Fulbright at the Universidad de San Martín in Argentina (UNSAM). As I prepared for a course I was teaching on CDA, I found some CDA work by Norman Fairclough, Gunther Kress, and James Gee that had been translated into Spanish. However, I was uneasy simply importing these North Atlantic frameworks into a Latin American context. Yet, I did not have access to some of the CDA works available in Latin America. Teun van Dijk's enormous contribution of *Discurso y Sociedad* was a monumental resource for me and students at UNSAM. Through this journal, critically oriented scholarship was made accessible to the Spanish speaking world and could serve as a place for Latin American scholars to publish their work. Through the work of students in my class I became aware of the traditions of indigenous education, digital literacy, and popular education in Latin America. I also learned more about Latin American databases, research collaborations, and the geo-politics of publishing. The important CDA work of Latin American scholars came into focus (e.g., Bolivar, 2010; López-Bonilla, 2011; Pardo, 2010; Pini, 2009; Resende, 2010). It was also within this time period that I sought out opportunities to have my CDA research translated into Spanish for *Discurso & Socieded* (Rogers, 2009, 2010). It became visible to me that the work of translation has historically been shouldered by Latin American scholars not by those in the global North and this has resulted in inequitable flows of knowledge. Open access databases such as Redalyc and SciELO can be helpful to counter the biases around language, accessibility, and geographic locale which are always already built into reviews of literacy research. These insights traveled with me as I continued to synthesize family literacy studies reported on in the next chapters.

Related Appendices

Appendix D: Code Book from the 2005

Appendix E: Code Book for the 2016 Literature Review

Appendix F: Coding Chart for Spreadsheet

Appendix G: Sample Response Letter to Editors and Reviewers

References

Bolivar, A. (2010). A change in focus: From texts in contexts to people in events. *Journal of Multicultural Discourses*, 5(3), 213–225.

Blommaert, J., & Bulcaen, C. (2000). Critical discourse analysis. *Annual Review of Anthropology*, 29, 447–466.

Compton-Lilly, C., Rogers, R., & Lewis, T. (2012). Analyzing epistemological considerations related to diversity: An integrative critical literature review of family literacy scholarship. *Reading Research Quarterly*, 47(1), 31–58.

Eisenhart, M. (1998). On the subject of interpretive reviews. *Review of Educational Research*, 68(4), 391–399.

Gee, J. & Green, J. (1998). Chapter 4: Discourse analysis, learning, and social practice: A methodological study. *Review of Research in Education*, 23(1), 119–169.

Hart, C. (1998). *Doing a literature review: Releasing the social science research imagination.* London: SAGE.

López-Bonilla, G. (2011). Narratives of exclusion and the construction of the self. In R. Rogers (Ed). *An introduction to critical discourse analysis in education* (2nd ed., pp. 46–67). NY: Routledge.

Luke, A. (1995). Text and discourse in education: An introduction to critical discourse analysis. *Review of Research in Education*, 21, 3–48. doi:10.2307/1167278

Luke, A. (2002). Beyond science and ideology critique: Developments in critical discourse analysis. *Annual Review of Applied Linguistics*, 22, 96–110. doi:10.1017/S0267190502000053

Mora, R. (2012). Literacidad y el aprendizaje de lenguas: Nuevas formas de entender los mundo y las palabras de nuestros estudiantes. *Revista Internacional Magisterio*, 58, 52–56.

Pardo, L. (2010). Latin American discourse studies: State of the art and new perspectives. *Journal of Multicultural Discourses*, 5(3), 183–192.

Pini, M. (2009). *Discurso y educación: Herramientas para el análisis crítico.* San Martin, Argentina: UNSAM Edita.

Resende, V. (2010). Between the European legacy and critical daring: Epistemological reflections for critical discourse analysis. *Journal of Multicultural Discourses*, 5(3), 193–212.

Rogers, R. (2009). Alfabetización racial en una clase de segundo grado: Teoría crítica de raza, estudios de blancura, e investigación de alfabetización. *Discurso & Sociedad*, 3(3) (reprint)

Rogers, R. (2010). Entre contextos: Un analisis crítico del discurso de la alfabetizacion familiar, practicas discursivas y subjetividades en los procesos educativos. *Revista LatinoAmericana de Estudios del Discurso (Journal of the Latin American Association of Discourse Studies)*, 7(2). (reprint)

Santos, B. (2014). *Epistemologies of the South: Justice against Epistemicide.* Boulder, CO: Paradigm Publishers.

Suri, H. (2014). *Towards methodologically inclusive research syntheses: Expanding possibilities.* New York: Routledge.

Trigos-Carrillo, L. & Rogers, R. (2017). Latin American influences on multiliteracies: From epistemological diversity to cognitive justice. *Literacy Research: Theory, Method, and Practice*, 66, 373–388.

4

INTEGRATIVE CRITICAL LITERATURE REVIEWS

Introduction

In this chapter, I (Catherine) describe our process of writing an **integrative critical literature review** (see Table 4.1). Integrative literature reviews investigate a body of research through a particular lens or terms of particular questions or perspectives (Thorne et al., 2004). Unlike **traditional reviews** (see Chapter 3), integrative reviews do not aspire to establish the breadth and depth of a field of scholarship. Integrative critical literature reviews focus on a particular issue, question, or impose a particular lens or perspective on the field. Identifying integrative critical literature reviews in our sample was challenging because most authors did not use the term "integrative" to identify their work. As synthesists, we needed to carefully read each research synthesis to identify whether the review focused on a particular issue or question or imposed a particular lens or perspective on the field. We learned that integrative literature reviews are far less common than traditional literature reviews. While several integrative literature reviews have been published in literacy studies, in contrast to the 76 traditional literature reviews we identified, we located only 28 integrative critical literature reviews (see Table 4.2).

We describe our integrative review as *critical* because we apply a perspective that reveals how ideology, power, and privilege operate in family literacy scholarship. Specifically, we analyzed family literacy scholarship with a focus on equity, representation, and bias to discern how family literacy research treated diversity. Attention to diversity is a significant consideration for family literacy scholars since family literacy research and initiatives are generally designed to serve families of color from historically underserved communities. A well-designed integrative review focuses on an issue or question that is particularly salient to the body of scholarship being analyzed.

Integrative Critical Literature Reviews **95**

TABLE 4.1 Our Integrative Critical Literature and Related Scholarship

Compton-Lilly, C., Rogers, R., & Lewis, T. (2012). Analyzing epistemological considerations related to diversity: An integrative critical literature review of family literacy scholarship. *Reading Research Quarterly, 47*(1), 31–58.

Networked/Related Scholarship
Compton-Lilly, C. (2011). Family literacy across time: The field, families, and Bradford Holt. In P. Dunston, L. Gambrell, K. Headley, S. Fullerton, P. Stecker, V. Gillis, C.C. Bates (Eds.), *Proceedings of the 60th Literacy Research Association Yearbook* (pp. 45–61). Oak Creek, Wisconsin: Literacy Research Association.

Compton-Lilly, C. & B. Graue with Rebecca Rogers and Tisha Y. Lewis. (2013). Agency, authority, and action in family literacy scholarship: An analysis of the epistemological assumptions operating in family literacy scholarship. In J. Larson & J. Marsh (Eds.) *Handbook of Early Childhood Literacy* (2nd ed., pp. 368–402). London: Sage Publications.

Compton-Lilly, C., Lewis Ellison, T. & Rogers, R. (invited column; 2019). The promise of family literacy: Possibilities and practices for educators. *Language Arts, 97*(1), 25–35.

TABLE 4.2 Integrative Reviews Related to Literacy

	Topic Addressed	*Focus: Issue, question, or perspective*
Mosenthal (1983)	Classroom writing competence	"This paper argues the need to consider the sociopolitical dimension of this construct [classroom writing competence], in addition to the conceptual and design criteria dimensions" (p. 217).
Erickson (1984)	School literacy, reasoning, and civility	"This paper takes a perspective on schools, teaching, and learning that places in the foreground the social organization and cultural patterning of people's work in everyday life" (p. 525).
Lipson and Wixson (1986)	Reading disability research	"In this paper, we examine reading (dis)ability from an interactionist perspective, and discuss the implications of this view for research on reading disability" (p. 111).
DiPardo and Freedman (1988)	Peer response groups in the writing classroom	"Our intention is not to provide an exhaustive critical review of the literature on small-group learning, but to examine that work which contributes to a theoretic frame for organizing issues important to pedagogy and research on response groups in the writing classroom" (p. 122).

(Continued)

96 Integrative Critical Literature Reviews

TABLE 4.2 Continued

	Topic Addressed	*Focus: Issue, question, or perspective*
Durst and Newell (1989)	James Britton's category system and research on writing	"This paper critically reviews Britton's discourse system in terms of the system's uses in writing research and what this research has found about the ways writing is employed and conceived of, particularly in schools; major areas of critical debate over the system's contributions; and the current status of the system and how it might be refined through further research" (p. 376).
Sperling (1996)	The writing-speaking connection	This review makes sense of "assumptions by critically examining research on the teaching and learning of writing, focusing specifically on the literature in which relating writing and speaking is implicated" (pp. 53–54).
Kucan and Beck (1997)	Thinking aloud and reading comprehension	"This is a review of research on thinking aloud in reading comprehension that considers thinking aloud as a method of inquiry, a mode of instruction, and a means for encouraging social interactions" (p. 271).
Brantlinger (1997)	Nonrecognition of the politics in special education	"This article challenges the supposed neutrality of the special education status quo and the moral grounding of the reviewed authors 'position'" (p. 425).
Fabos and Young (1999)	Telecommunication in the classroom	"This paper analyzes the educational discourse surrounding telecommunication exchanges, and argues that much of the current research is contradictory, inconclusive, and possibly misleading" (p. 217).
Roskos and Christie (2001)	The play–literacy interface	"In this article, we review the recent empirical research that assumes an emergent literacy stance in examining relationships between play and literacy" (p. 60).
Smagorinsky (2001)	Meaning construction	"In this article, I aim to propose what is involved when readers engage with texts in such a way as to produce these transactions and transformations" (p. 134).

Integrative Critical Literature Reviews **97**

	Topic Addressed	*Focus: Issue, question, or perspective*
Commeyras and Inyega (2007)	Teaching reading in Kenyan primary	"This integrative review on the teaching of reading in Kenyan primary schools provides a foundation for the growing movement there to improve reading education" (p. 259).
Carlisle (2010)	Effects of instruction in morphological awareness	"This review was undertaken to integrate findings of studies that sought to determine whether such instruction contributed to improvement in literacy" (p. 464).
Greene and Ackerman (1995)	Expanding the constructivist metaphor	"In this review we summarize some of the accomplishments and shortcomings of constructivist accounts of reading and writing activity as part of our argument for social and textual views of literacy. literacy. Arguing that reading and writing are inseparable from each other and from other modes of meaning making, we aim to foreground studies and theories that depict the rhetorical dimensions of literacy" (p. 383).
McVee, Dunsmore, and Gavelek (2005)	Schema theory	"The authors review various conceptions of schema theory to consider how recent social and cultural perspectives might prompt reconsideration of schemas as transactional and embodied constructs. Concomitantly, they explore how earlier conceptions of schema theory may assist researchers in their articulation of concepts such as ideal and material tools and the role of activity in Vygotsky's work" (p. 531).
Petchauer (2009)	Hip-hop educational research	The review "critically reviews three major strands of selected literature across these categories that are relevant to educational research" (p. 946).
Newell, Beach, Smith, and VanDerHeide (2011)	Teaching and learning argumentative reading and writing	"[W]e use this critical review to make the case for more research on teaching and learning argumentative reading and writing that integrates a range of research perspectives for how and why to conduct studies of this important aspect of academic learning" (p. 274).

(Continued)

98 Integrative Critical Literature Reviews

TABLE 4.2 Continued

	Topic Addressed	Focus: Issue, question, or perspective
Compton-Lilly, Rogers, and Lewis (2012)	Epistemological considerations related to diversity in family literacy scholarship	"The purpose of this review of family literacy scholarship was to examine the epistemologies underlying both family studies and reviews of family literacy studies. We were especially concerned with those epistemological issues related to the cultural, class, racial, gender, ethnic, and linguistic diversity of people served by family literacy programs" (p. 33).
Juzwik (2014)	American evangelical Biblicism as literate practice	"Critically reviewing scholarship across history, anthropology, religious studies, and sociology, I characterize evangelical Biblicism as an interpretive tradition mediated by a complex set of sociocultural practices and textual ideologies" (p. 335).
Reed, Cummings, Schaper, and Biancarosa (2014)	Assessment fidelity in reading intervention research	"We conducted a systematic review of studies to address the question: To what extent is assessment fidelity reported in reading intervention research conducted in elementary and middle schools?" (p. 278).
Hadley and Dickinson (2020)	Measuring young children's word knowledge	"This conceptual review works towards a more robust theoretical framework for vocabulary knowledge, focusing especially on the understudied dimension of vocabulary depth, which can be used to evaluate and design measures for early childhood learners" (p. 1).
Kucirkova (2019)	Empirical research on children's e-reading	"The paper aims to exemplify an integrated approach to the examination of children's reading on screen with a literature review that is theorised and applies rigorous review techniques" (p. 6).
Bomer, Land, Rubin, and Dike (2019)	Preparation of writing teachers	"This review of empirical research focused on the preparation of writing teachers" (p. 198).
Flores, Vlach, and Lammert (2019)	Children's literature and teacher preparation	"This review of literacy education scholarship examines the ways children's literature is used as a resource within literacy methods classes in the preparation of preservice teachers" (p. 215).

	Topic Addressed	Focus: Issue, question, or perspective
Fowler-Amato, Keenan, Warrington, Nash, and Brady (2019)	Teacher education and social justice	"This review of literature highlights the efforts teacher educators and researchers have made over the past 18 years to work toward social justice in secondary English language arts (ELA) preservice teacher (PT) education" (p. 158).
Hoffman et al. (2019)	Literacy tutoring and mentoring	"The goal of this research is to report and synthesize the findings from research into literacy tutoring and literacy mentoring in initial teacher preparation" (p. 233).
Wetzel et al. (2019)	Teacher education and sociocultural knowledge	This analysis examines the "connections that pre-service teachers make as a result of experiences focused on sociocultural knowledge and literacy and barriers they face in building these connections." (p. 138).

Thus, for family literacy, we focused on diversity. For other bodies of scholarship, the lens or focus will reflect the field, the people involved, and the political, institutional, and cultural spaces that influence that body of scholarship. If a review focuses on scholarship related to standardized curricula, an integrative critical review might examine how teachers are positioned and assessed. If a review focuses on scholarship related to special education, an integrative critical review might examine how differently abled children are described and served. Integrative reviews contribute to our understanding of particular bodies of scholarship and reveal trends and patterns that scholars might find confirming, provocative, or troubling.

Integrative critical reviews can identify gaps and/or propel scholars to consider the scope of a body of scholarship, consider the lenses that have been used and not used, and inspire renewed personal and professional commitments to new questions, novel types of analyses, and revised research trajectories. Integrative critical literature reviews might focus on people whose voices and perspectives have been under recognized and underappreciated. As Suri (2013) writes, "sometimes synthesists can strategically highlight the reports by authors who are from relatively silenced groups in the field" (p. 82).

Establishing an Inquiry Team and Identifying Purpose

In many ways, this book is the culmination of 15 years of our collaboration as research synthesists. When we met in 2004, we were not sure what type of writing we wanted to do. We knew that we had a shared interest in the literacy

100 Integrative Critical Literature Reviews

practices within families, but remained open to a range of possibilities. It was at that time that I became aware of the power and usefulness of quantitative meta-analyses. It was when I (Compton-Lilly) was working with Reading Recovery© that I became aware of how quantitative researchers used effect sizes to look across studies to identify instructional methods that positively affect student learning. While I knew that many scholars had conducted important studies on literacy in families, many of the family literacy studies that I found most compelling were qualitative and ethnographic. Thus, they were not candidates for meta-analyses that were based on effect sizes. As qualitative researchers are often reminded – qualitative research is not generalizable in a traditional sense. However, Rogers, Lewis, and myself believed that there were points of alignment across family literacy scholarship and claims that could be made that transcend individual pieces of scholarship.

I began asking colleagues at my university about systematic methods for looking across qualitative research and was introduced to meta-ethnography. As a result, we each read Noblit and Hare's (1988) classic discussion of meta-ethnography. We collectively found the focus on language, the power of metaphor, and attention to both context and researcher reflexivity compelling. Thus, we agreed that meta-ethnography provided a promising methodology for looking across qualitative family literacy scholarship. Our goal was to seek ways to make sense of qualitative studies related to literacy in families. However, as described below, this plan was soon postponed.

Designing an Integrative Critical Literature Review

As we embarked on our project and began to conceptualize how we might conduct a meta-ethnography of family literacy scholarship (see Chapter 5), we soon recognized that we needed to know more about the range of scholarship available and the relative impact of that research. We had several false starts as we proposed various ways to get a sense of available scholarship and select the studies that would constitute the data for our meta-ethnography. Because meta-ethnography draws on a small set of studies, we recognized that the selection process for choosing studies was important. After playing with various lists of criteria and conceptualizing possible categories that might help us to negotiate the morass of qualitative, ethnographic research related to family literacy, we realized that prior to conducting a meta-ethnography we needed a better sense of the field. Thus, we began to read a vast range of family literacy scholarship creating organizational and analytic tools to capture our thinking as we read.

Ultimately, we decided to write two papers and created a one-page document describing each paper. Paper one was designed as an integrative critical literature review focused on "race, language, and silences in family literacy" and is described in this chapter. A second paper – which is described in detail in Chapter 5 – was our "meta-ethnography of family literacy studies." Both papers drew on the

Integrative Critical Literature Reviews **101**

same basic data set comprised of published articles, books, and book chapters. However, these data were subjected to different analyses for each paper.

In revisiting digital records and hard copies from this project, I am struck by the number of lists, outlines, and charts that we created as we searched for ways to look across an intimidating mound of scholarship. For example, an early document presented a plan that entailed sorting the stacks of data based on the type of texts (i.e., position papers, stand-alone reviews, or research reports), the methodologies used (i.e., qualitative, quantitative, or mixed methods), or the theories applied (i.e., emergent literacy, Bronfenbrenner, Bourdieu, or causal theories related to literacy). These plans were ultimately rejected because they merely created smaller stacks of data and did little to grapple with the themes, patterns, and collective meaning-making across family literacy scholarship. Over time, some plans were merged and others were discarded as we drafted the following research questions for the integrative critical literature review:

> What questions have defined the field of family literacy and how has family literacy been constructed as a 'field of study?'

We also asked the following sub-questions:

1. What trends and patterns have emerged and what changes are evident over time in the field?
2. Who has researched and reported on family literacy and whose research has been most readily cited? What implications might these researcher patterns have on the field of family literacy?
3. Whose literacies have been silenced, privileged, marginalized, normalized, and/or misrepresented?

As I reflect on these questions, it is interesting that the third sub-question is the one that most directly drove our collaboration, while questions one and two operated in service of the third. However, even question three evolved. While we may have intended to focus on "whose literacies" were silenced, privileged, marginalized, normalized, and/or misrepresented, we actually addressed the ways in which family literacy scholars attended to the diverse cultures, languages, and economic situations experienced by their participants.

Early in the project we were neither aware of various types of research syntheses, nor were we clear about what type of literature review we would conduct. However, even as we conceptualized the project, we thought about how our research synthesis differed from traditional literature reviews. We noted three differences that distinguished our review from many of the literature reviews that we had read:

- We conceptualized a review that was explicitly and consciously grounded in sociocultural understanding about race, language differences, and accompanying macro social and political contexts.

102 Integrative Critical Literature Reviews

- Our analysis of family literacy explicitly addressed race in relation to researchers, research participants, and findings.
- Finally, our review involved a multi-layered analysis in which primary studies were examined in relation to citation patterns, a qualitative analysis of attention to diversity.

Thus, we explicitly and intentionally assumed a sociopolitical stance, attended to race, and sought to situate sociopolitical issues in conversation with citation patterns. In short, we focused on a particular set of issues and imposed a critical lens, which qualified our review as an integrative critical review. However, it was not until we were deep in the project and became more aware of various forms of research syntheses that we adopted this label.

Transparency related to who conducts research and who is researched highlights the need for a reflexive stance on the part of research synthesists. Thus, as discussed later in this chapter, we briefly named positionalities and experiences that may have affected how we read and analyzed the primary studies. We then compared our professional autobiographies and collectively identified and articulated the shared values and beliefs that we brought to family literacy. We agreed on four theoretical premises:

- Conceptualizations of literacy practices as multiple and local (Barton & Hamilton, 1998; Gee, 1990; Heath, 1983; Street, 1984, 2014);
- Critical constructs related to voice, access, and privilege (Bakhtin, 1981, 1986; Bourdieu, 1977; Delpit, 1988; Gee, 1990);
- Constructs about language difference and literacy learning (Baugh, 1999; LeMoine, 2001; Purcell-Gates, 2002); and
- Constructs associated with critical race theory (Ladson-Billings, 2003; Ladson-Billings & Tate, 1995; Parker & Lynn, 2002).

As I describe the conceptual decisions we made in the writing of the review, they may seem linear, neat, and logical. However, as noted above, these decisions and plans evolved from a series of false starts, discarded ideas, and reiterative attempts to make sense of what was a daunting stack of scholarship. As we began this journey, we briefly considered using Google Scholar or another online search engine to identify highly cited studies. We decided against this strategy for two reasons. First, we came to recognize the limits of these search engines; in particular, the fact that these tools are limited by the journals that happen to be searched by that particular tool. These limits are discussed further in Chapter 7. Second, we soon recognized that tools like Google scholar searched all citations for each scholar we were tracking – including citations in publications that were not related to family literacy. These were formidable challenges that necessitated hand-searching citations across our data set. Only tenacity and a shared commitment to the project moved us beyond these early challenges.

Searching and Sampling Family Literacy Scholarship

In order to locate primary studies, we oscillated between searching particular journals and using databases that included multiple journals. We ultimately opted for using databases as they were more efficient and comprehensive in their ability to search the field. However, as described in other sections of this volume, databases bring their own limitations related to incomplete sampling and international/multilingual representation. While these limits are to some degree addressed by our use of multiple databases – as well as university library holdings and Amazon, which was searched with the hope of ensuring that we had adequately identified relevant books. These are very real limitations that inevitably affected our findings.

While searching of databases and file cabinets started during the earliest phases of the project, the process evolved over time and entailed reiterative and often duplicitous processes, since we had located some prior studies prior to identifying a working system for searching databases and library collections. Thus, we often found duplicate copies of the same primary study in our data set and had to constantly monitor our expanding corpus.

Our search was also complicated by the various terms that scholars interested in literacy in families used to describe their work. As we began to locate articles, we began listing the terms scholars used. It soon became apparent, that not only were different terms used (i.e., family literacy, family as educator, home literacy environment, literacy funds of knowledge, and reading/writing experiences at home), but these terms also indicated different relationships surrounding literacy including differing degrees of agency, types of activities, home/school partnerships, and social/literacy practices. While we attempted to track the use of these terms and relationships across time, we found no definitive pattern and settled on a workable set of search terms, despite the differences in how these terms are used. Thus, our search elicited many studies that were ultimately rejected when viewed in relation to our selection criteria.

We systematically applied the following search terms in various combinations: literacy/ies, family/ies, handbook, bibliographies, reference(s), "family literacy/ies," and "home literacy/ies." We searched four databases: *Academic Search, Education Full Text, ProQuest*, and *JSTOR: The Scholarly Journal Archive*. Because we noted that these search engines were better at locating articles than books, we also searched the collection of a major university and Amazon to ensure that we had located all relevant books.

Locating Primary Studies and Ending the Search

Once we identified potential texts for our review, we focused on texts that included scholarly reviews of family literacy scholarship. We analyzed those studies to identify selection criteria that we would use to select primary studies.

104 Integrative Critical Literature Reviews

In the process, we located many texts that did not review family literacy scholarship. We systematically rejected book reviews and articles that presented only tips for teachers or parents unless they also included a review of relevant scholarship. We did not include secondary/journalistic reports on research such as articles published in newspapers or newsletters (i.e., *Reading Today*) as they generally synthesized information from empirical research that was already represented in the data set. We did not include research on instruments designed to "measure" family literacy or reports on particular family literacy programs. Research on particular measurement instruments and programs often over-represented scholarship by the scholar(s) who contributed to the creation of these measures and programs. We also excluded grant notices and announcements about family literacy programs and projects. A summary of our selection/rejection criteria is presented in Table 4.3. The outcome of this process is presented in Table 4.4.

Results from database searches, which primarily indexed journal articles and book chapters, were combined with searches of the university library and Amazon, which indexed books. In particular, we sought book chapters that reviewed family literacy and placed particular effort into locating handbooks that might include reviews of family literacy. Once we established that a text included a review that met our criteria, we added that review to an evolving list of studies, and analyzed it using the *analytical review template*, described below.

A contingency of the review process is the passing of time. In particular, between the time we analyzed our data, drafted the original paper, submitted it to a journal, and had responded to the first set of reviews, 3 years had passed. Thus,

TABLE 4.3 Summary of Selection/Rejection Criteria

Rejection Criteria	*Rationale for Rejection*
• Book reviews and articles without a scholarly review of relevant scholarship.	• No review of family literacy scholarship.
• Secondary/journalistic reports on research (e.g., newspapers and newsletters without a scholarly review of relevant scholarship).	• Syntheses of empirical research that was already represented in the data set and no review of family literacy scholarship.
• Research on instruments designed to "measure" the effects of family literacy programs.	• Over-representation of scholarship based on particular methodological procedures.
• Reports on the effectiveness of practices used in particular family literacy programs.	• Over-representation of scholarship by the scholar(s) who contributed to the creation of these programs.
• Grant notices and announcements about family literacy programs and projects.	• No review of family literacy scholarship; over-representation of scholarship by the scholar(s) who contributed to the creation of these programs or projects.

Integrative Critical Literature Reviews **105**

TABLE 4.4 Included and Rejected Studies

Total Search	490 Potential Articles, Book Chapters, and Books	
Rejected Studies	218 articles, book chapters, and books were rejected	No review of family literacy and/or did not meet our selection criteria
Included Brief Reviews of Family literacy	60 articles, book chapters, and books included brief reviews of family literacy	Included in the citation coding analysis but not the ART analysis
Included Substantive Reviews of Family literacy	213 book chapters and books included substantive reviews of family literacy	Included in the citation coding analysis and the ART analysis

our literature review was significantly out-of-date and needed to be updated. Thus, in the midst of responding to the second round of reviewer's comments we were simultaneously updating our data set by using search engines to locate reviews that had been published during recent years, counting the citations in these new reviews, and crafting ART's for the new reviews. As we completed the final search, fewer and fewer novel texts were identified. We ended with a search of JSTOR which elicited only six previously unidentified studies. Thus, we ended our search with faith that we had elicited a viable sample of studies.

Reading as a Reviewer: Describing, Analyzing, and Sorting the Studies

Our integrative critical review entailed three analyses. First, a citation-coding scheme was created to identify the major citations in each review and across the sample of brief and substantive reviews. Second, we identified and analyzed nine comprehensive, edited volumes that were dedicated to family literacy scholarship. These volumes were analyzed in terms of content and contributors, including particularly close readings of editorial introductions which generally included statements of purpose. Finally, an analytic review template was created to qualitatively analyze substantive reviews of family literacy in relation to diversity.

Our initial attempts to review the selected texts were disappointing in terms of efficiency and results. We started by each writing narrative reflections of the primary studies. This proved to be highly time consuming and cumbersome. Each researcher brought a different stance and set of experiences to each text which resulted in a set of unwieldy analyses that did not help us to make connections, see patterns, or draw conclusions. Table 4.5 presents a sampling of a text reviewed through that process.

As a result, we sought a more systematic and collaborative process of describing and analyzing the selected studies. The process we ultimately agreed upon

106 Integrative Critical Literature Reviews

TABLE 4.5 An Early Attempt at Analysis

Heath, S. B. (1983). Ways with Words. New York: Cambridge University Press.

Compton-Lilly	I remember being fascinated by *Ways with Words*. The book was full of the voices of people, people who acted and interacted in the familiar space of classrooms. Heath made powerful links between language and literacy and applied her evolving understandings to attempts to design classroom practices that would acknowledge and develop the ways of knowing that children brought to classrooms. Her stories of children were played out in particular contexts and language became the tool for understanding how these contexts were different and what effect that difference had on children and their learning in school.
Rogers	In this ethnography, Heath is critical of social policies that further disadvantage African American families economically. She refers to how the AFDC created "absentee" fathers through wages that were much lower than the previous decades. She also refers to "economic upheaval" and "cultural clashes" but does not address institutionalized racism in the name of red-lining, zoning, affordable housing, and residential segregation practices to name a few.
Lewis Ellison	I appreciated Heath's (1983) study from *Ways with Words*. Her analysis examined and traced the naturalistic occurrences at home within the Roadville and Trackton community in how children learned how to use language at home and at school. More specifically, oral language use in Trackton and Roadville was very different and reflected how these families structured their linguistic lives. This study has significant implications for preparing young children for school.

involved creating and applying an *analytical review template* (ART). The ART, presented in Appendix H, identifies the focus, methods, data sources, and findings for each study that met our inclusion criteria. All three authors of the integrative critical review and some of our graduate students participated in completing these ARTs. These descriptive analyses allowed us to quickly search the data set in relation to methodology, theoretical framing, population, and findings. The methodology used and the foci of each study were particularly salient as we analyzed and sorted the studies. As we commenced this search, the three co-authors participated in an inter-rater reliability process. Specifically, we randomly chose ten articles from our data set and used an inter-rater reliability checklist (Appendix I) to ensure that our characterization of each primary study was consistent across the team.

Citation Coding Scheme

We soon noticed that some studies were cited over and over again, while others were rarely cited in our data set. Thus, in order to get a sense of the field, we noted which scholars were significant citations across multiple primary studies.

Integrative Critical Literature Reviews **107**

We defined significant citations as those that were cited across three or more sentences. We then counted the number of significant citations for each highly cited scholar and listed those scholars in order from most to the least cited based on the number of significant citations. We discovered that the top four cited scholars were all qualitative researchers (Heath, 1983; Taylor, 1983; Purcell-Gates, 2002; Moll et al., 1992). This analysis revealed whose voices that had significantly impacted the field; we then examined the backgrounds of these scholars (e.g., race, nationality, and gender) and the attention they paid to diversity in their research.

Analysis of Comprehensive Edited Volumes

Our search process identified several comprehensive, edited volumes related to family literacy. These volumes included at least ten chapters, focused on family literacy, and addressed a wide range of related issues. We applied critically oriented discourse analysis to the tables of contents and introductory materials of these volumes. We examined content, contributors, and references to diversity. Procedurally, we photocopied the tables of contents and introductory materials from each comprehensive volume and arranged these text sets in chronological order. We used critical discourse analysis techniques to attend to the treatment of diversity and the epistemological stances presented. For example, we attended to strong language (e.g., crime, homelessness, and teenage pregnancy), the words used to refer to diverse families (e.g., ESOL families and Cantonese-speaking peers), and terms that referenced literacy (e.g., literacy and literacies). We used these analyses to craft general summative statements for each edited volume. Tables of contents were analyzed in regard to the topics addressed, organization, length, and contributors. Figure 4.1 presents the review process for comprehensive, edited volumes.

Review Process for Comprehensive, Edited Volumes

Questions

- How has diversity been addressed and treated in family literacy scholarship?
- What epistemological stances are discernible in family literacy scholarship?

Steps

1. Locate comprehensive, edited volumes that meet the selection criteria.
2. Photocopy each book's table of contents and introductory materials.
3. Create a statement about each book based on analysis of the table of contents and introductory materials.

4. Compile the tables of contents in chronological order.
5. Place the books with bibliographic information on a chart in chronological order.
6. Analyze patterns, including critical discourse analysis, of the following over time:

- Topics addressed (e.g., family literacy programs, family literacy practices)
- Length
- Editorial statements of purpose and perspective
- Changes in terminology (e.g., first time certain words appear)
- Contributors

FIGURE 4.1 Review Process for Comprehensive, Edited Volumes

108 Integrative Critical Literature Reviews

ART Analysis Related to Diversity

The analyses described above helped us to recognize whose literacies have been silenced, privileged, marginalized, normalized, and/or misrepresented and how diversity has been treated in family literacy scholarship. However, in order to fully address whose literacies had been silenced, privileged, marginalized, normalized, and/or misrepresented, an additional level of analysis was needed. In this final analysis, we distinguished between family literacy studies that did not explicitly name or address the diversity of the communities, studies that generally referenced dimensions of diversity, studies that treated differences solely as research variables, and studies that explicitly and intentionally attended to diversity in regard to race, ethnicity, language, social class, or other dimensions. We then focused on the later set of studies to explore how they attended to diversity and to assess the contribution of these studies to family literacy scholarship.

Representing the Synthesis

Representing our synthesis involved a set of collaborative decisions. Some of these decisions involved consistency in terminology and stylistic features. It was through conversations throughout the drafting process that we came to recognize and agree that we were drafting an "integrative" review and that we would use the word "critical" to describe our work. We also agreed to the use of certain terms across our review (i.e., scholarship, exploration, and examinations of the literature) and avoidance of others (i.e., family literacy initiatives). We agreed to the use of the pronoun "we" to present our methodology.

While these decisions were significant, perhaps more critical and less intentional were the conversations we had about the organization and content of our integrative critical review. As a review with a complicated and multi-tiered methodology that led to multiple sets of findings, we drafted, revised, and re-revised how we organized the paper. This process started very early during the conceptualization of the review and was continuously revisited. There were several sections that were drafted and eventually rejected. For example, early drafts included a detailed section that described how we used the term "field" in relation to family literacy and in response to what we thought would be an essential research question, we began to explore how fields – including family literacy – emerged and became a field of study. These sections were minimized or dropped as we increasingly refined the research questions presented above.

Findings from the Citation Counting Analysis

As we completed the citation coding, three patterns became particularly clear. First, we noted that some scholars were cited much more regularly than others and that there was a significant break between the top four cited scholars, who were

Integrative Critical Literature Reviews **109**

cited between 33 and 46 times in our data set and those cited less often – less than 25 times. Second, we noted that all four of these top-cited scholars were qualitative researchers whose work focused on family practices in localized communities. Finally, we noted that the cited work of these scholars was published between 1981 and 2005; thus, the contribution of these highly cited scholars did not fully reflect more current family literacy scholarship. When we revisited and extended this data for the meta-ethnography described in Chapter 5, we purposely sought the most cited scholars whose first publications appeared after 1996, in order to address this omission. Table 4.6 presents the 28 most cited scholars in our data set.

TABLE 4.6 Twenty-Eight Most Cited Scholars in Reviews of Family Literacy

Number of Citations	Dates of Works Cited	Name	Methods/Theory	Focus
46	1982–1995	Shirley Brice Heath	Qualitative ethnography	Language and literacy practices
41	1981–1997	Denny Taylor	Qualitative ethnography	Literacy practices
34	1988–2000	Victoria Purcell-Gates	Qualitative ethnography	Literacy practices
33	1990–2005	Luis Moll	Qualitative ethnography	ELL community practices
24	1977–2001	Catherine Snow	Quantitative causal/ predictive	School literacy success
23	1992–1998	Trevor Cairney	Family literacy theory	Field of family literacy
21	1987–1997	Elsa Auerbach	Family literacy theory	Family strengths
22	1992–2003	Vivian Gadsden	Qualitative narrative analysis	Generational literacy, race, and gender
			Family literacy theory	Field of family literacy
18	1996–2002	Monique Sénéchal	Quantitative causal/ predictive	Storybook reading
17	1987–2001	Concha Delgado-Gaitan	qualitative	Home literacy practices
17	1988–2001	Grover Whitehurst	Quantitative causal/ predictive	Storybook reading
15	1978–1987	Lev Vygotsky	Language and thought theory	Culture, thought, and language

(*Continued*)

110 Integrative Critical Literature Reviews

TABLE 4.6 Continued

Number of Citations	Dates of Works Cited	Name	Methods/Theory	Focus
13	1974–1995	Uri Bronfenbrenner	Ecological theory	Families as ecological systems
12	1970–2005	Paulo Freire	Liberation theory and pedagogy	Literacy and cultural action
12	1991–2004	Robert St. Pierre	Quantitative program effects	Family literacy programs
11	1994–2003	Linda Baker	Qualitative program development	Home/school partnerships
11	1991–2000	Barbara DeBaryshe	Quantitative causal/ predictive	Parent beliefs
10	1988–2001	Adriana Bus	Quantitative causal/ predictive	Storybook reading
10	1987–1999	Peter Hannon	Qualitative reviews	Home school partnerships
10	1990–1999	Jeanne Paratore	Family literacy theory	Family literacy and literacy learning
10	1984–2005	Brian Street	Qualitative observational	Literacy and schooling; New literacy studies
10	1978–1986	William Teale	Qualitative observational	Emergent literacy
9	1977–2002	Pierre Bourdieu	Sociological theory	Social class, schooling
9	1966–1982	Delores Durkin	Qualitative ethnography	Successful readers
9	1989–1994	Annette Lareau	Qualitative observational	Social class, schooling
9	1993–1997	Christine Marvin	Quantitative causal/ predictive	Speech and language impaired children
9	1981–1987	Sarah Michaels	Qualitative narrative analysis	Children's narratives
9	1985–1991	Elizabeth Sulzby	Qualitative observational	Emergent literacy

Findings from Review of Comprehensive Edited Volumes

Critical discourse analysis was applied to the comprehensive edited volumes to attend to content, contributors, and attention to diversity. Early volumes – published between 1995 and 1996 – were generally framed with causal discourses of intervention and remediation revealing modernist assumptions and presenting family literacy as a means to social change. However, some of these early edited books were inconsistent and some chapters addressed continuing controversies including the need to attend to the strengths and abilities of families and the importance of true collaboration. Rather than presenting a field that has moved from ignorance to enlightenment, these texts suggest that some family literacy researchers have historically problematized their work and insisted on the importance of attending to ongoing epistemological and ethical tensions in family literacy scholarship.

Volumes published between 2003 and 2005 are less focused on family literacy as a means to cure poverty and a means for social change. These comprehensive edited volumes describe family literacy as an intellectual right. There is a mixed emphasis on traditional family literacy programs, and new types of programs that merge traditional linear notions of literacy with accounts that highlight multiple, dynamic, and situated literacy practices. More chapters reference "literacies" rather than "literacy," address a broader range of local and international contexts, and include discussions of multimodal and technological practices. Diverse and situated literacies were highlighted.

Later volumes, published between 2009 and 2010, focused on relationships between home and school literacies and the diversity of literacy practices found in homes and – with the exception of the volume edited by Dunsmore and Fisher (2010), increasingly focused on international and transnational contexts as well as literacy within specific local communities. Reflecting postmodern perspectives, references to literacy were increasingly situated within local communities rather referencing general and universal notions of literacy. In these more recent volumes, family literacy scholars attended more to technological media practices, research that focused on white families; these volumes began to address *Whiteness*. Despite these changes, more recent comprehensive edited volumes also narrowed the scope of diversity to reference primarily culture, race, ethnicity, and/or language. While earlier texts referenced adolescent mothers, fathers, and children with disabilities, these groups are not addressed in more recent volumes.

Findings Related to the Analysis of the Article Review Templates

The analyses identify literacies that have been silenced, privileged, marginalized, normalized, and/or misrepresented. In order to fully address whose literacies had been silenced, privileged, marginalized, normalized, and/or misrepresented, we drew on our analysis of the analytical research templates (ARTs). Based on a

112 Integrative Critical Literature Reviews

grounded sorting of the 213 studies, we identified the following ways in which researchers attended to the diversity of their participants:

- Family literacy studies that did not explicitly name or address the diversity,
- Studies that generally reference dimensions of diversity,
- Studies that treat differences solely as research variables, and
- Studies that explicitly and intentionally attend to diversity in race, ethnicity, language, social class, or other dimensions.

Table 4.7 illustrates the number of studies that fit into each of these categories.

TABLE 4.7 Numbers of Studies and the Degree of Attention to Diversity

Attention to Diversity	Number of Studies	Patterns across the Studies
Family literacy studies that did not explicitly name or address the diversity.	31 of 213 studies 15% of the sample	Culture, social class, race, gender, ethnicity, and language differences were neither mentioned nor discussed.
Studies that generally reference dimensions of diversity.	58 of 213 studies 27% of the sample	Diversity was alluded to but only in general terms. These studies used terms such as nonmainstream, multiple perspectives, and language differences to refer to diversity but did not discuss specific literacy practices in diverse communities nor what these practices meant in terms of schooling, access to resources, or educational trajectories.
Studies that treat differences solely as research variables.	36 of 213 studies 17% of the sample	These quantitative studies treated differences as methodological variables that correlated with specific literacy practices and eventual school success or failure. These predictive and causal studies focused on family literacy in diverse populations of students, including children from low-income families or children from particular racial, ethnic, or linguistic groups.
Studies that explicitly and intentionally attend to diversity in race, ethnicity, language, social class, or other dimensions.	88 of 213 studies 41% of the sample	These studies identified culture, social class, race, gender, ethnicity, and language as central to their analyses. Many researchers noted inextricable connections between literacy and diversity. For example, Wasik and Hendrickson (2004) noted, "any serious study of literacy development must include an examination of family culture and beliefs" (p. 158).

Integrative Critical Literature Reviews **113**

We then focused on the primary studies that intentionally attended to diversity to explore who was included, how diversity and what dimensions of diversity were addressed.

Going Public and Publishing Our Integrative Literature Review

While the complete integrative literature review was eventually published in the *Reading Research Quarterly* (2012), various versions of this integrative critical literature were presented at conferences and various universities. In our presentations, we often used images alongside figures and text to present our findings and experimented with various images – including word or tag clouds. Figure 4.2 displays the frequency of words occurring in the titles of the primary studies in our sample. Various versions of this evolving integrative review were presented at the *Literacy Research Association*, the *Discourse Analysis Working Conference*, the *American Educational Research Conference*, and the *European Conference on Educational Research*.

FIGURE 4.2 A Word Cloud Based on Titles of Papers in Our Sample

114 Integrative Critical Literature Reviews

Our presentations culminated with an invitation to present the annual research review at the Literacy Research Association in 2010; Cathy drew on this integrative literature review as part of that presentation. The presentation was later published as part of the *60th Yearbook of the Literacy Research Association* (Compton-Lilly, 2011). Soon after, Cathy was invited to contribute a handbook chapter to the second edition of the *Handbook of Early Childhood Literacy* (Larson & Marsh, 2013). A chapter that drew on this same data set and explored the epistemologies operating in family literacy scholarship was crafted based on this same data set. Finally, because we believed that our integrative review included important information for educators, we submitted a version of our review to two teacher-oriented journals. Both rejected our submission. However, a few years later, Cathy was invited to submit a review related to family literacy to *Language Arts*. Thrilled to have finally found a practitioner audience, the paper was revised and updated for publication as an invited column (Compton-Lilly, Lewis Ellison, & Rogers, 2019). Thus, what started out as a meta-ethnography, which would not be completed and published for another seven years (see Chapter 5), had various inculcations, and has been revised and rewritten for multiple audiences.

As might be expected, our biggest challenge was preparing our integrative critical research review for publication in the *Reading Research Quarterly*, the internationally top-ranked literacy journal. We submitted our manuscript in *Fall* of 2010. By mid-January, we had our first set of reviews and an invitation to *revise and resubmit*. The manuscript had been sent out to four reviewers and their comments and those of the editors spanned 12 single-spaced pages. The editorial synthesis of the reviews focused on our framing of the review, concerns about the systematicity, and transparency of our analytic processes, our conclusions, and the contribution of the review. A set of miscellaneous concerns were also raised. In regard to our framing of the study, reviewers and editors asked us to clarify our "purpose for conducting the review" and to be clear on how the field of family literacy is currently and historically defined. While clarifying our purpose was a fairly simple revision, providing a sense of what the field of family literacy entailed required careful rethinking of what we were referring to as the field of family literacy. We eventually decided that defining *the field* was problematic and chose instead to focus on family literacy scholarship, which we described as a:

> loosely defined group of scholars, researchers, and educators who have attended to literacy-related beliefs and practices in families. In our analysis, we examine existing reviews that focus on literacy in homes – most use the term *family literacy*; many do not.
>
> (Compton-Lilly, Rogers, & Lewis, 2012, p. 34)

Integrative Critical Literature Reviews **115**

This allowed us to present this body of scholarship as relatively fluid while related to the use of literacies in home spaces, despite variations in terms and accompanying academic boundaries. Reviewers also asked us to expand our discussions of liberatory pedagogies and critical race theory.

In the original manuscript, we wanted to be certain to highlight how our respective positionalities affected our reading of the primary reviews. Thus, we presented our scholarly trajectories prior to presenting the research methodologies. Our reviewers read this as problematic, worrying that "the positionalities of the researchers/authors appear to be used as a framing for the manuscript." While this was not our intent, we understood this concern and moved the discussion of our own positionalities to the methodology section, a more traditional location.

To respond to questions raised about the systematicity and transparency of our review process, we carefully described our selection processes for primary texts. Finally, we addressed a set of "miscellaneous concerns" and worked to problematize dichotomies that we had inadvertently presented and addressed an unintended privileging of our own epistemologies and thus a corresponding negation of the work of others.

We re-submitted our integrative critical review in September of 2009 and received an invitation to *revise and resubmit* in January of 2010. We were granted four months to make the required revisions. We received the next set of reviews in August of 2010; the reviews extended across 11 pages. A frustration with the next set of reviews was that even though we had conscientiously attempted to address the reviewers' and editors' prior comments and suggestions, some of the same concerns continued to be voiced. For example, reviewers asked for additional clarity on the contribution of our review for the family literacy scholarship and requested that we provide a more coherent theoretical framework for the paper. These comments were frustrating because we had already tried to do these tasks and were disheartened that our efforts were not sufficient. In addition, reviewers continued to raise important questions about the systematicity and transparency of our methodological processes. Table 4.8 illustrates the publication timeline for this integrative critical literature review.

Alongside these ongoing concerns, we also noted increased attention to the nuances of our argument. Reviewers and editors asked for a clearer connection between our theoretical frame and our analytical processes, and justification for the framework used to analyze primary studies. While we recognized these revisions as significant, we also believed that these specific and nuanced suggestions indicated an interest in our work and commitment to helping us figure out how to present the integrative review in a way that presented its full potential. Other comments included making our chain of reasoning more coherent, revisiting our title by aligning it more closely with the content of our paper, and tempering language that overstated tends across family literacy scholarship. By this time, we were concerned about the timeliness of our data set and we conducted a second search of primary scholarship to locate studies

116 Integrative Critical Literature Reviews

TABLE 4.8 Timeline for the Publication of our Integrative Critical Literature Review

September 20, 2009	Submission of the Integrative Critical Literature Review to the *Reading Research Quarterly*
Reviews received mid-January 2010	R1 – Revise and resubmit Four-month deadline Revisions due mid-May, 2010
Reviews received mid-August 2010	R2 – Revise and resubmit Six-month deadline Revisions due mid-February, 2011
February 14, 2011	Final revision received
May 13, 2011	Accepted for publication in the *Reading Research Quarterly*
January, 2012	Publication in the *Reading Research Quarterly*

that had been published since 2009. Our response letter to the second round of reviews is presented in Appendix J. Finally, in May of 2011, we received a letter of acceptance from the *Reading Research Quarterly*. That letter included requests for a few final revisions.

Decolonizing Integrative Literature Reviews

As with all reviews, our work was limited by the methods we chose, the search engines we used, our selection criteria, and our own positionality as researchers. Thus, despite the integrative critical review being published in a major journal we had some concerns about our process and the finished product. Specifically, we were very aware that our published paper does not do enough to decolonize family literacy scholarship. In other words, did our review challenge existing hegemonic structures and disrupt the privileging of white, male, English-speaking, and financially comfortable perspectives and experiences. We remain concerned that our focus on citation rates fixated on scholars who – with exception of Moll and his colleagues (1992) – were white, English-speaking women. This use of citation rate obfuscated the contributions of many accomplished scholars of color whose work has significantly informed our thinking (e.g., Nieto, 1996; Edwards et al., 1999; Gadsden, 1994).

We are also concerned that white English-speaking countries – particularly the United States – are over-represented. Thus, as we continued our journey toward crafting a meta-ethnography, we tried to remain focused on the limits and silences that permeated our integrative critical review. There were points in our analytical and writing process where we specifically sought to globalize our review. For example, we added a long paragraph (Compton-Lilly et al., 2012, p. 35) that not only recognized the contributions of international scholars, but also presented some of the critiques that they had raised about how family literacy was discussed and addressed in the United States. However, these efforts are

Discussion: Limits, Possibilities, and Reflections

While we believe that our integrative critical review has clear limitations related to the representation of diverse voices and the limits of our own perspectives, we believe that highlighting the degree and the ways in which various forms of diversity have been addressed in family literacy scholarship is an important contribution of our work. We are particularly interested in the possibility of a dedicated integrative review that would highlight the voices of well-cited scholars of color and their respective contributions to the field. We recognize an enduring problem with both our stance and the current state of family literacy scholarship. Specifically, we note that attention to voice, equity, and opportunities for families and children have been problematically slow leaving many children to move through childhood, youth, and young adulthood without educational experiences that honor who they are, the strengths they bring, and how they might be best served. While slow and continual change might be encouraging, it is not sufficient for the children and families that we aspire to serve. We hope that this integrative critical review reminds us of the serious limitations of current scholarship.

Related Appendices

Appendix H: Final Analytic Review Template (ART)

Appendix I: Inter-Rater Reliability Check

Appendix J: Response Letter to Editors for Our Critical Integrative Literature Review

References

Bakhtin, M. M. (1981). *The dialogic imagination: Four essays by M. M. Bakhtin* (M. Holquist, editor). University of Texas Press.

Bakhtin, M. M. (1986). *Speech genres and other late essays.* (C. Emerson & M. Holquist editors). University of Texas Press.

Barton, D. & Hamilton, M. (1998). *Local literacies: Reading and writing in one community.* Routledge.

Baugh, J. (1999). *Out of the mouths of slaves: African American language and educational malpractice.* University of Texas Press.

Bomer, R., Land, C. L., Rubin, J. C., & Van Dike, L. M. (2019). Constructs of teaching writing in research about literacy teacher education. *Journal of Literacy Research*, 51(2), 196–213.

Bourdieu, P. (1977). *Outline of a theory of practice.* Cambridge University Press.

Brantlinger, E. (1997). Using ideology: Cases of nonrecognition of the politics of research and practice in special education. *Review of Educational Research*, 67(4), 425–459.

118 Integrative Critical Literature Reviews

Carlisle, J. F. (2010). Effects of instruction in morphological awareness on literacy achievement: An integrative review. *Reading Research Quarterly*, 45(4), 464–487.

Conmeyras, M., & Inyega, H. N. (2007). An integrative review of teaching reading in Kenyan primary schools. *Reading Research Quarterly*, 42(2), 258–281.

Compton-Lilly, C. (2011). Family literacy across time: The field, families, and Bradford Holt. In P. Dunston, L. Gambrell, K. Headley, S. Fullerton, P. Stecker, V. Gillis, & C.C. Bates (Eds.), *Proceedings of the 60th Literacy Research Association yearbook* (pp. 45–61). Literacy Research Association.

Compton-Lilly, C., Rogers, R., & Lewis, T. (2012). Analyzing epistemological considerations related to diversity: An integrative critical literature review of family literacy scholarship. *Reading Research Quarterly*, 47(1), 31–58.

Compton-Lilly, C., & M. E. Graue with Rebecca Rogers and Tisha Y. Lewis. (2013). Agency, authority, and action in family literacy scholarship: An analysis of the epistemological assumptions operating in family literacy scholarship. In J. Larson & J. Marsh (Eds.), *Handbook of early childhood literacy* (2nd ed., pp. 368–402). Sage.

Compton-Lilly, C., Lewis Ellison, T., & Rogers, R. (invited column; 2019). The promise of family literacy: Possibilities and practices for educators. *Language Arts*, 97(1), 25–35.

Delpit, L. (1988). The silenced dialogue: Power and pedagogy in educating other people's children. *Harvard Educational Review*, 58(3), 280–299.

DiPardo, A., & Freedman, S. W. (1988). Peer response groups in the writing classroom: Theoretic foundations and new directions. *Review of Educational Research*, 58(2), 119–149.

Durst, R. K. & Newell, G. E. (1989). The uses of function: James Britton's category system and research on writing. *Review of Educational Research*, 59(4), 375–394.

Dunsmore, K., & Fisher, D. (Eds.). (2010). *Bringing literacy home*. International Reading Association.

Edwards, P. A., Pleasants, H. M., & Franklin, S. H. (1999). *A path to follow: Learning to listen to parents.* Heinemann.

Erickson, F. (1984). School literacy, reasoning, and civility: An anthropologist's perspective. *Review of Educational Research*, 54(4), 525–546.

Fabos, B., & Young, M. D. (1999). Telecommunication in the classroom: Rhetoric versus reality. *Review of Educational Research*, 69(3), 217–259.

Flores, T., Vlach, S. K., & Lammert, C. (2019). The role of children's literature in cultivating preservice teachers as transformative intellectuals: A literature review. *Journal of Literacy Research*, 51(2), 214–232.

Fowler-Amato, M., LeeKeenan, K., Warrington, A., Nash, B. L., & Brady, R. B. (2019). Working toward a socially just future in the ELA methods class. *Journal of Literacy Research*, 51(2), 158–176.

Gadsden, V. L. (1994). Understanding family literacy: Conceptual issues facing the field. *Teachers College Record*, 96(1), 58–66.

Gee, J. P. (1990). *Social linguistics and literacies: Ideologies in discourses.* Falmer Press.

Greene, S., & Ackerman, J. M. (1995). Expanding the constructivist metaphor: A rhetorical perspective on literacy research and practice. *Review of Educational Research*, 65(4), 383–420.

Hadley, E. B., & Dickinson, D. K. (2020). Measuring young children's word knowledge: A conceptual review. *Journal of Early Childhood Literacy*, 20(2), 223–251.

Heath, S. B. (1983). *Ways with words: Language, life and work in communities and classrooms.* Cambridge University Press.

Hoffman, J. V., Svrcek, N., Lammert, C., Daly-Lesh, A., Steinitz, E., Greeter, E., & DeJulio, S. (2019). A research review of literacy tutoring and mentoring in initial teacher preparation: Toward practices that can transform teaching. *Journal of Literacy Research*, 51(2), 233–251.

Juzwik, M. M. (2014). American evangelical Biblicism as literate practice: A critical review. *Reading Research Quarterly*, 49(3), 335–349.

Kucan, L., & Beck, I. L. (1997). Thinking aloud and reading comprehension research: Inquiry, instruction, and social interaction. *Review of Educational Research*, 67(3), 271–299.

Kucirkova, N. (2019). Socio-material directions for developing empirical research on children's e-reading: A systematic review and thematic synthesis of the literature across disciplines. *Journal of Early Childhood Literacy*. doi:10.1177/1468798418824364

Ladson-Billings, G. (2003). It's your world, I'm just trying to explain it: Understanding our epistemological and methodological challenges. *Qualitative Inquiry*, 9(1), 5–12.

Ladson-Billings, G., & Tate, W. F. (1995). Toward a critical race theory of education. *Teachers College Record*, 97(1), 47–68.

Larson, J., & Marsh, J. (eds.) (2013). *Handbook of early childhood literacy* (2nd ed.). Sage Publications.

LeMoine, N. R. (2001). Language variation and literacy acquisition in African American students. In J. L. Harris, A. G. Kamhi, & K. E. Pollock (Eds.), *Literacy in African American communities* (pp. 169–194). Lawrence Erlbaum.

Lipson, M. Y., & Wixson, K. K. (1986). Reading disability research: An interactionist perspective. *Review of Educational Research*, 56(1), 111–136.

McVee, M. B., Dunsmore, K., & Gavelek, J. R. (2005). Schema theory revisited. *Review of Educational Research*, 75(4), 531–566.

Moll, L. C., Amanti, C., Neff, D., & Gonzalez, N. (1992). Funds of knowledge for teaching: Using a qualitative approach to connect homes and classrooms. *Theory into Practice*, 31(1), 132–141.

Mosenthal, P. (1983). Defining classroom writing competence: A paradigmatic perspective. *Review of Educational Research*, 53(2), 217–251.

Newell, G. E., Beach, R., Smith, J., & VanDerHeide, J. (2011). Teaching and learning argumentative reading and writing: A review of research. *Reading Research Quarterly*, 46(3), 273–304.

Nieto, S. (1996). *Affirming diversity: The sociopolitical context of multicultural education* (2nd ed.). Longman.

Noblit, G. W., & Hare, R. D. (1988). *Meta-ethnography: Synthesizing qualitative studies*. Sage.

Parker, L., & Lynn, M. (2002). What's race got to do with it? Critical race theory's conflicts with and connections to qualitative research methodology and epistemology. *Qualitative Inquiry*, 8(1), 7–22.

Petchauer, E. (2009). Framing and reviewing hip-hop educational research. *Review of Educational Research*, 79(2), 946–978.

Purcell-Gates, V. (1995). *Other people's words: The cycle of low literacy*. Harvard University Press.

Purcell-Gates, V. (2002). "As soon as she opened her mouth!": Issues of language, literacy, and power. In L. Delpit & J. K. Dowdy (Eds.), *The skin that we speak: Thoughts on language and culture in the classroom* (pp. 121–141). The New Press.

Reed, D. K., Cummings, K. D., Schaper, A., & Biancarosa, G. (2014). Assessment fidelity in reading intervention research: A synthesis of the literature. *Review of Educational Research*, 84(2), 275–321.

Roskos, K., & Christie, J. (2001). Examining the play–literacy interface: A critical review and future directions. *Journal of Early Childhood Literacy*, 1(1), 59–89.

120 Integrative Critical Literature Reviews

Smagorinsky, P. (2001). If meaning is constructed, what is it made from? Toward a cultural theory of reading. *Review of Educational Research*, 71(1), 133–169.

Sperling, M. (1996). Revisiting the writing-speaking connection: Challenges for research on writing and writing instruction. *Review of Educational Research*, 66(1), 53–86.

Street, B. (1984). *Literacy in theory and practice*. Cambridge University Press.

Street, B. (2014). *Social literacies: Critical approaches to literacy in development, ethnography, and education*. Longman Publisher.

Suri, H. (2013). *Towards methodologically inclusive research syntheses: Expanding possibilities*. Routledge.

Taylor, D. (1983). *Family literacy: Young children learning to read and write*. Heinemann.

Thorne, S., Louise J., Kearney, M. H., Noblit, G., & Sandelowski, M. (2004). Qualitative metasynthesis: Reflections on methodological orientation and ideological agenda. *Qualitative Health Research*, 14(10), 1342–1365.

Wasik, B. H., & Hendrickson, J. S. (2004). Family literacy practices. In C. A. Stone, E. R. Silliman, B. J. Ehren, & K. Apel (Eds.), *Handbook of language and literacy: Development and disorders*. Guilford Press.

Wetzel, M., Vlach, S. K., Svrcek, N., Steinitz, E., Omogun, L., Salmerón, C., & Villarreal, D. (2019). Preparing teaches with sociocultural knowledge in literacy: A literature review. *Journal of Literacy Research*, 51(2), 138–157.

5
META-ETHNOGRAPHIES

Like other review designs we have discussed so far in this book, our **meta-ethnography** drew on methodological practices across a range of ethnographic research designs (e.g., case studies and ethnographies). In short, we synthesized ethnographic studies to identify gaps and silences alongside recurring metaphors in family literacy scholarship. Thus, our 2020 *Reading Research Quarterly* article might be thought of as both meta-ethnography and as a critical research synthesis – or as a critical meta-ethnography. Scholarship related to our meta-ethnography is presented in Table 5.1.

Family literacy entails a unique body of scholarship for meta-ethnographic analysis. While research that addressed literacy practices in families existed prior to the early 1980s (i.e., Durkin, 1961, 1963, 1966), the studies that established family literacy as a field of study appeared in the 1980s and early 1990s. This is not true for all sub-fields of literacy research; for example, research that focuses on recitation or phonemic analysis have been published for decades.

Ethnographies of family literacy practices (e.g., Heath, 1983; Taylor, 1983) contributed to the "ethnographic turn" (Street, 1984, 1995) in literacy studies. As family literacy scholars, we were fortunate to learn from and have our own

TABLE 5.1 Our Meta-ethnography and Related Scholarship

Compton-Lilly, C., Rogers, R., & Lewis Ellison, T. (2020). A meta-ethnography of family literacy scholarship: Ways with metaphors: *Reading Research Quarterly, 55*(2), 271–289.

Networked/Related Scholarship
Compton-Lilly, C. (in press). Meanings and metaphors: What do they tell us about silence? A special issue on silence, *Linguistics, and Education*.

122 Meta-Ethnographies

work informed by these ethnographies. In part, research with a focus on families and communities, contributed to the rise in ethnography as a viable and accepted research methodology. That is, understanding of "naturally occurring" (Taylor, 1983) literacy practices in families meant observing families in action as they negotiated children's reading and writing at home and at school, alongside their own literacy practices. This complexity extended the knowledge that could be gained through surveys, short-term observational studies, experimental work, or short-term interview studies. Researchers adopted ethnographic procedures in order to be sensitive to time, culture, relationships, and ethics. Thus, due to their emergence over the past 40 years, family literacy studies provide a unique opportunity to focus on the emergence and the establishment of a novel body of scholarship. Thus, meta-ethnography has been a response to the increasing numbers of ethnographies and ethnographic research. As Urrieta and Noblit (2018) explained, "[i] n place of generalization, meta-ethnography seeks a *specification* of what the studies as a whole are about and then goes deeper into the meanings evident in this specified realm" (p. 36).

Meta-ethnography is both a theory and method that was developed to study the metaphors used in qualitative and ethnographic research. As Major and Savin-Baden (2010) point out, the use of qualitative studies has exploded across the past 30 years; this explosion has inspired the development of meta-analytical procedures for synthesizing qualitative research. Some scholars make distinctions between "meta-ethnographic" approaches and "meta-ethnography"; this distinction is similar to the distinction made between studies that draw on ethnographic methods and those that are ethnographies. In other words, metaphorical analysis – the definitive analytic process used in meta-ethnography can be applied to research studies that are not ethnographies. Savin-Baden, McFarland, and Savin-Baden (2008) describe meta-ethnography as: a

> qualitative approach to managing a large range of literature from the interpretivist tradition in a way that presents an analysis of the findings across studies and then interprets them in relation to further themes that emerge across studies. Interpretive meta-ethnography is a systematic approach that enables comparison, analysis and interpretations to be made that can inform theorising and practice (p. 213).

Some meta-ethnographies include only ethnographies that meet stringent criteria and address closely related topics. Other meta-ethnographies include studies that use ethnographic methods to various degrees, but might be better characterized as qualitative studies (Savin-Baden, MacFarlane, & Savin-Baden, 2008) or ethnographic case studies (Compton-Lilly, Rogers, & Lewis Ellison, 2020; Doyle, 2003).

Early meta-ethnographies in education include research syntheses conducted by Pielstick (1998) and Rice (2002). Pielstick (1998) conducted what he described as a "meta-ethnography" related to scholarly literature on educational leadership. Specifically, he focused on "themes, patterns, and connections that define transformational leadership" (p. 15). While his report fails to comment on several aspects of his methodological process (e.g., search and selection processes and the number of studies included), he does present an analysis that attends to "keywords, concepts, and impressions" (p. 18) revealed through open coding, which were then submitted to constant comparison techniques and axial coding revealing seven themes that are then reported and discussed. While he describes his review as a meta-ethnography, little attention is paid to the contexts of the primary studies and/or his own positionality as a research synthesis.

Focusing on studies published between 1990 and 1998, Rice (2002) used meta-ethnography to explore characteristics of the collaborative processes occurring in professional development schools. They used coding to analyze 20 case studies and identified 12 themes related to collaboration. These themes addressed situational, structural, procedural, and relational aspects of collaboration processes. Their work highlights the significance of relationships across multiple dimensions of school/university collaborations. Like Pielstick (1998), Rice (2002) pays little attention to the contexts in which the primary studies were conducted and her own positionality as a research synthesist.

Savin-Baden, MacFarlane, and Savin-Baden (2008) conducted what they described as an "interpretive meta-ethnography" of 83 primary studies that addressed learning and teaching in higher education. They argued that analysis of "pedagogical stance, disjunction, learning spaces, agency, notions of improvement and communities of interest can help to locate overarching themes and hidden subtexts that are strong influences on areas of practice, transfer and community" (p. 211). Specifically, their comparison of data across the studies included revisiting "metaphors, ideas, concepts and contexts… to review how the initial findings had been contextualised and presented" (p. 215). They used annotations, maps, tables, and grids to identify and connect studies with the key themes. Their analysis identified both tensions and understandings as well as "areas that are sometimes ignored, marginalised or dislocated from the central arguments about teaching and learning thinking and practices in higher education" (p. 211).

As meta-ethnography has gained attention in recent years, Noblit and his colleagues have revisited the methodology. For example, Hughes and Noblit (2017) describe their process for conducting a meta-ethnography of autoethnographies, which they refer to as *meta-autoethnography* (p. 211). Specifically, they focused on teacher educators who had carried out autoethnographies of their processes of centering race in teacher education. Echoing the original description of meta-ethnography (Noblit & Hare, 1988), Hughes and Noblit presented the six phases of a meta-ethnography – from "getting started," determining inclusion criteria, reading the studies, determining how the studies are related, and synthesizing translations, to expressing the synthesis. As they explained, "[t]he meta-ethnography of autoethnographies produces analogies that allow readers to anticipate possibilities rather than predict the meanings of lives lived in certain contexts and under certain conditions" (p. 224). While highlighting the uniqueness of each autoethnography, meta-ethnography poses invites reflection on patterns within and across bodies of scholarship and sets of findings.

In a recently published book, Urrieta and Noblit (2018) assemble eight chapters to explore relationships between meta-ethnography and identity studies. While each chapter's author addresses a particular body of scholarship related to identity, they all bring explicitly critical perspectives to their analyses. This edited text not only provides important insight into various areas of identity studies, but also demonstrates the potential of meta-ethnography to move toward deeper and more critical readings of bodies of scholarship.

Meta-ethnography relies on the close analysis of a small set of ethnographic studies. Thus, the selection of studies is key to appreciating the significance and contribution of the resulting analysis. Noblit and Hare (1988) remind researchers that "translations of studies will vary with the translators" (p. 31) in the same way that two ethnographers working with the same data set might produce different sets of findings. As Noblit and Hare explain, meta-ethnography is best regarded as presenting "interpretations of interpretations of interpretations" (p. 35) that allow researchers to focus on broad cultural phenomena operating in and across target studies.

Ethnographies have played an important role in the field of literacy studies over the past 30 years. Situating language and literacy practices in the complexity of everyday families and communities and schools has broadened the field's understanding of literacy acquisition and learning and the sociopolitical contexts in which this work happens. Yet, there has been unrealized potential in this rich body of work due to the lack of systematic syntheses across studies. Meta-ethnography holds great potential to provide insight about phenomenon across ethnographies and ethnographic accounts.

Significantly, meta-ethnography requires researchers to preserve the context and specificities of ethnographies while, at the same time, examining their shared and unique features. Urrieta and Noblit (2018) identify a "tension between identifying the salient themes/concepts/metaphors that can reduce the account to a manageable level and preserving the specific contexts in which these themes/concepts/metaphors make sense" (p. 37). In short, meta-ethnographies extend insights across time, space, contexts, and people in ways that would be impossible for individual ethnographers.

Attending to the unique social and cultural contexts that surround the primary studies help to establish epistemological alignment between original studies and the analytical processes that was brought to those texts. In other words, an interpretive paradigm is needed to synthesize interpretive work. Thus, it is essential that research synthesists contextualize the interpretations made in primary studies.

Once metaphors have been identified in and across the primary studies, researchers generate a new set of interpretations based on the themes/metaphors that operate across the corpus of primary studies. As Suri (2013) discusses, there are varying levels of interpretation and abstraction that happens across these levels of interpretation. Taken together, translations can provide deeper insights into a body of scholarship, which in turn inform interpretations of individual studies. Eisenhart (2017) states that an ethnography's "authority" is strengthened "with the support of multiple studies rather than only one" (p. 141).

Like ethnographers, meta-ethnographers grapple with the notion of generalizability. If, as researchers, we value the complexity that is found through qualitative research, what does it mean to synthesize findings across studies? Are we admitting that a degree of positivism is useful or necessary? If positivism is necessary, is it sufficient? Are findings transferable or translatable versus being aggregated or generalizable? Is transferability and translation sufficient for guiding educational policy and practice?

Finally, we must reflect on the concept of translation, a key element in meta-ethnographic analyses. Asad (1986) writes that "all good translation seeks to reproduce the structure of an alien discourse within the translator's own language" (p. 156). What does it mean for cultural beings to translate meanings? As Asad writes, "the process of 'cultural translation' is inevitably enmeshed in conditions of power – professional, national and international. And among these conditions is the authority of ethnographers to uncover the implicit meanings of subordinate societies" (p. 163). In our work as meta-ethnographers, we worked with studies published by peers. Yet, we are part of the scholarship we seek to synthesize. This demands that we critically examine the assumptions operating in our own work, which we consider below as we describe our process of conducting our meta-ethnography.

In the original description of meta-ethnography (Noblit & Hare, 1988), and in more recent inculcations (Hughes & Noblit, 2017; Urrieta & Noblit, 2018), meta-ethnography is described as involving six steps which are described below.

Working as a Research Team to Craft a Meta-Ethnography

Research syntheses are often collaborative endeavors (Lee, Hart, Watson, & Rapley, 2015). Indeed, in our review of research syntheses in literacy studies, 97 of the 144 published syntheses were conducted by collaborative teams of scholars. Notable, most of the sole-authored reviews were published before 2000 when bodies of scholarship were smaller and fewer journals were operating. Furthermore, only 18 of the 47 sole-authored syntheses were published in the current century. Our work is no exception and conducting our meta-synthesis entailed joint reading and discussion, collaborative dialogue and analysis, creation of composite documents, and more. We have many artifacts from this collaborative activity. For example, as we commenced our analysis, each member of the research synthesis team reviewed three studies including (Purcell-Gates, 1996) using our recently refined analytic review template. We ultimately created a composite document for each study that combined our individual ART responses (see Table 5.2).

TABLE 5.2 A Sampling of our Collaborative Analysis of Purcell-Gates (1996)

	Becky	Cathy	Tisha
Is this qualitative research?	Yes, Purcell Gates describes it as a descriptive study (p. 410). "The design of the study is best termed descriptive because the field researchers were instructed to focus exclusively on literacy events occurring in the home."	Yes. It is described as a "descriptive study" (p. 410).	Yes.
What is the purpose of the study?	"The present study was designed to provide the piece of the picture missing from Purcell-Gates & Dahl (1991) and Taylor & Dorsey-Gaines (1988) and Teale & Sulzby (1986) studies: the relationships between types of home literacy practices and the different written language knowledges brought to school by young children" (p. 409).	"The purpose of this study was to document and describe the ways in which print is used in the homes of low-income U.S. families and to explore the relationships between these uses of print and the emergent literacy knowledges held by the young children in these homes" (p. 406).	"The purpose of this study was to document and describe the ways in which print is used in the homes of low-income U.S. families and to explore the relationships between these uses of print and the emergent literacy knowledges held by the young children in these homes" (p. 406).
What theoretical perspective was used?	Literacy learning as a situated, cultural practice (Gee, Bakhtin, Vygotsky).	"The situated, dialogic nature of language learning implies that literacy needs to be viewed as a cultural practice (Gee, 1992) and that literacy development occurs wherever literacy practices are occurring" (p. 406).	"Theory of language learning resulting from a construction of knowledge within instances of situated dialogue" (p. 406).

While conducting a meta-ethnography had been our goal since we met in 2004 in St. Louis, we discovered the need to first conduct a more traditional review of family literacy studies to gain a better understanding of the field. As part of that critical integrative review (described in Chapter 4), we hand-searched family literacy studies to identify the most cited scholars in the field and comment on how family literacy scholars attended to diversity.

When we eventually turned our attention back to our original goal of conducting a meta-ethnography, we began by re-reading Noblit and Hare's (1988) monograph: *Meta-Ethnography: Synthesizing Qualitative Studies*. In addition to using their procedures, we drew important conceptual understandings from this classic text that greatly informed how we conducted our meta-ethnography.

Designing a Critical Meta-Ethnography

We were eager to dive in to the ethnographies to explore metaphors but we found ourselves pushing the pause button yet again. Indeed, we found that we needed to explore the field of metaphor studies in order to gain a sense of how language operated metaphorically, what metaphors revealed about thought, and how metaphorical analysis contributed to meaning construction across texts. This entailed reading about metaphors in linguistic studies (Charteris-Black, 2004; Lakoff & Johnson, 2008; Lakoff & Turner, 1989), literacy studies (e.g., Scribner, 1984; Reinking, 2011) and critical discourse studies (e.g., Van Dijk, 2014). Through this process of reading, writing, and generating analytic memos, we began to envision the role metaphorical analysis might play in our review of family literacy.

The following analytic memo illustrates the kind of contextual thinking that we engaged in as we considered how individual ethnographies contributed to family literacy scholarship across time. Becky wrote this analytical memo on October 30, 2011 as we were generating an outline for our meta-ethnography. Speaking about the contribution of our meta-ethnography (Compton-Lilly et al., 2020), Becky wrote:

> Our meta-ethnography picks up where Savin-Baden and her colleagues argue that many meta-analyses fall short. They write: 'There are degrees of transparency and points beyond which it is not possible to go when undertaking such reviews. The difficulty with **meta-analysis** that it is not located in an interpretive tradition with the propensity to decontextualise material, thin descriptions and ignore methodological difference' (p. 214). By way of contrast, our meta-ethnography examines the contextual detail surrounding language and literacy interactions within families. Further, our design includes a more detailed approach to metaphor analysis that we have been able to locate in published meta-ethnographies. Thus, our analytic framework might help refine future meta-ethnographies.

128 Meta-Ethnographies

Searching Family Literacy Scholarship

As done in our 2012 review (Compton-Lilly, Rogers, & Lewis, 2012), we systematically applied search terms in various combinations: literacy/ies, family/ies, handbook, bibliographies, reference(s), "family literacy/ies," and "home literacy/ies." We searched four databases: *Academic Search, Education Full Text, ProQuest*, and *JSTOR: The Scholarly Journal Archive*. Because we noted that these search engines were more inclined to locate articles rather than books, we also searched the collection of a major university and Amazon.

As we had in our integrative critical integrative review of family literacy scholarship, we sought to identify texts that had significantly impacted family literacy scholarship. We agreed that by focusing on highly cited and highly influential texts we would obtain a unique and compelling view of the field. Thus, we built on the citation-coding scheme created as we conducted our 2012 integrative critical review (Compton-Lilly et al., 2012) to identify researchers who were cited as major references in reviews of family literacy. This analytic process was developed and refined early in our initial literature retrieval process, as we collaboratively analyzed reviews of family literacy to identify major citations. The following codes were entered on the citation list for each article, chapter, and report.

- L—The study was referred to only on a list with other references.
- S—The study was discussed in one to three sentences and was not a major reference.
- P—The study was discussed in one or two paragraphs or four or more sentences.
- C—The study was discussed in one or two paragraphs and was central to the paper and its argument.

Results for each scholar were then tabulated across the emerging sample. We updated our existing data set of primary studies, and eventually analyzed 377 reviews of family literacy scholarship to identify highly cited scholars. Our process approximated the centrality of citations related to family literacy in each article or chapter and across the field.

Locating the Research and Ending the Search

Noblit and Hare (1988) recommend maximum variation as a principle for sampling. However, our selection criteria were derived from an earlier analysis of most frequently cited scholarships (Compton-Lilly et al., 2012). Thus, our meta-ethnography focused on a partially bounded sample, and existing set of procedures (Noblit & Hare, 1988). As a result, our meta-ethnography can be considered an example of what Doyle (2003) refers to as an "enhancement" of the meta-ethnographic approach. We began the meta-ethnography described in this chapter only after we had completed our critical integrative literature review (Compton-Lilly et al., 2012). We started with a set of articles that had been analyzed using the citation counting method described above. We then applied this same citation counting process to the new studies that were eventually added to our data set. Because the critical integrative literature review was published in 2012 and the meta-ethnography was published eight years later, it was necessary to update the existing data set of 213 texts that reviewed family literacy scholarship; we added 164 more reviews bringing our corpus to 377 studies. Searching and adding studies to this corpus continued through the review process, as we continued to identify additional studies.

Early in our citation counting process, we noticed that a few classic studies were extensively and consistently cited across multiple reviews. We created a chart of all the studies that were coded at the paragraph or central level and through our analysis of more than 2,300 citations, we identified authors whose work was cited extensively in reviews of family literacy.

Four of the articles that we selected for our meta-ethnography were the most cited studies on our master list. However, we soon realized that all of these highly cited studies were published in or before 1991, providing little information about recent trends in the field. Thus, we also crafted a list of the most-cited contemporary scholars whose work first appeared as major citations in 2000 or later; we refer to these more recent articles as *influential contemporary scholars* and argue that their inclusion is essential if we want to consider the current state family literacy scholarship. The articles included in our meta-analysis are peer reviewed, examples of empirical research that primarily used ethnographic qualitative methods, directly address literacy in families, included the voices of participants, and included a description of the methodologies used and description of the research contexts. While the quality, focus, and methods used in each study varied, we reasoned that because these scholars were amongst the most-cited that their work had particular impact on the field of family literacy.

Because meta-ethnographers deal with a small sample of studies, issues related to study selection are particularly salient. For example, in an analytic memo dated October 30, 2011, we reflected on our process and rationale:

> Controversy exists amongst meta-ethnographers about the process for including studies to review. Are studies chosen purposefully? Should quality be a factor when synthesizing studies? We decided to include the most referenced studies in the field.

Some research synthesis scholars discuss the importance of congruence in epistemological tradition, review design, methods, and modes of representation between the synthesis approach used and the primary studies. That is, meta-ethnography must be aligned with the spirit of the methodological approach(es)

130 Meta-Ethnographies

used in the original study. While the studies included in our synthesis were all ethnographic, variations across the studies complicated our analysis process. Moll et al. (1992), for example, report on a community-based ethnography and a teacher inquiry project and was more action oriented than the other ethnographies we reviewed.

Reading as a Reviewer: Describing, Analyzing, and Sorting the Studies

In meta-ethnography, Noblit and Hare (1988) propose the synthesis of metaphors across studies. Thus, the first step in analyzing studies is to identify the metaphors used in each study. Identifying metaphors meant that we needed to read and reread each study with a metaphoric lens. Table 5.3 illustrates some of the metaphors that we identified in the article by Purcell-Gates (1996).

We started by having all three of us – Cathy, Becky, and Tisha – list the metaphors found in three of the most highly cited studies. We then discussed, vetted, and combined these lists to create master lists of metaphors that we agreed upon for each study. We used these lists to refine our understanding of what counted as a metaphor. Eventually, we agreed on a broad definition for metaphorical language that included not only direct metaphors (i.e., resources as funds of knowledge

TABLE 5.3 Metaphors Identified in Purcell-Gates (1996)

	Metaphors at the Lexical Level / Metaphorical Expressions		
	Becky	*Cathy*	*Tisha*
Metaphors that present space as being readily inhabited by literacy	"The data collected on the literacy-related activities **contained** in the school curricula" (p. 421) (metaphor relating to space/ being contained)	"The home was **filled with** posters with print" (p. 423) "**surrounded by written materials** in every room in the apartment" (p. 424) "**ecologically valid** a manner" (p. 425) "texts used for **purposes of daily living**" (p. 419) "challenges the notion that literacy is literally **interwoven into** all people's lives in a literate society" (p. 425)	"**surrounded by written materials** in every room in the apartment" (p. 424) "This information has been gathered in as **ecologically valid**" (p. 425) "**print embedded** activities" (p. 426) "literacy is **literally interwoven** into all people's lives in a literate society" (p. 425)

and children as consumers) but also less direct metaphors (i.e., the presentation of boundaries between home and school; presenting a parent as the child's first teacher). Once we had established clear agreement on what constituted metaphorical language, two members of the research team worked together to identify the metaphors operating in each of the four remaining studies.

We identified and sorted the metaphors operating in each of the studies and noted the location of these metaphors in each article using page numbers. We intentionally used the author's language rather than rewording their metaphors. Like Doyle (2003), we felt this choice preserved "the particulars of each study

TABLE 5.4 Sampling of Metaphors in Taylor (1983)

Categories of Metaphors	Examples of Metaphors Taylor (1983)
Parents as teachers	"family as educator" (p. 93)
	"the family is an arena" (p. 93)
	"sensitize parents to their role as teachers of reading" (p. 93)
	"parents are a child's first reading teachers" (p. 94)
	"Parents and teachers are partners" (p. 94)
Family literacy, both established and evolving	"evolving ways of working with children" (p. 98)
	"already an established facet of family life" (p. 99)
Parent Biographies	"interplay of individual biographies and educative styles" (p. 98)
	[learned to read] "in spite of the teachers" (p. 99)
	"he was not a 'reader'" (p. 100)
Styles of Reading	"the child's development of an individual educative style" (p. 92)
	"interplay of biographies and individual styles within each family" (p. 92)
	"conceptual frameworks that are sensitive to the unique complexities of the institution that we call the family" (p. 94)
	"the child's development of an individual educative style" (p. 94)
	"interplay of individual biographies and educative styles" (p. 98)
	"parent's and child's explorations of approaches to learning" (p. 99)
	"these styles have evolved" (p. 101)
	"individual needs and interests of their children have been accommodated" (p. 101)
	"difficulties in 'sitting still' for extended periods of time" (p. 101)

TABLE 5.5 Major Translations across Time

	Taylor (1981)	Heath (1983)	Moll et al. (1992)	Purcell-Gates (1996)	Marsh and Thompson (2001)	Li (2003)	Pahl (2004)
Over Time	"repetition of experiences" across generations	Implied generational continuity in language, cultural practices, and, literacy interactions	Cultural funds of knowledge of families		Popular culture media boxes as a way to mediate home and school differences	Language and literacy learning as central to children's futures	Narratives with communicative landscapes
	Reciprocal: Culture/literacy practices as generally stable and as continuous across generations.				**Refutational:** Culture/literacy practices as culturally emergent; parents and children as active.		
Home and School	Transition to school as a "period of adjustment."	Transition as particularly difficult for children from Roadville and Trackton.	Teachers as mediators who must engage in authentic collaboration with families.	Home read/writing "scribbles" versus "literacy knowledge" acquired in school.	Popular culture media boxes as a way to mediate home and school differences.	Home and school as discontinuous and antithetical and parents as agential but not always successful.	Web of possibility involving interwoven home and school literacy practices.
	Reciprocal: Home and school as distinctly different literacy spaces; children are [generally] responsible for making this transition.						
			Line of argument: Increased nuancing of home and school differences – teachers as mediators (Moll et al.), media boxes as mediational (Marsh & Thompson), and home and school as interwoven webs of possibility (Pahl).				

Natural & Everyday	Literacy activity as conservation, "rooted in the past" and occurring within an environment	Maintown: taking meaning from the environment	Teachers as having natural entrée and funds of knowledge as "seeds"	"Naturally occurring instances of literacy use"	Children as "avid consumers" of literacy texts and popular culture	Literacy practices as connected to social realities (e.g., race, privilege, and language) that define everyday life	Artifacts and experiences as conduits for narrative that sediment over time
		Roadville and Trackton: Literacy learning as more/less available to some children					

Reciprocal: Children naturally learn literacy from their cultural and lived experiences within families.

Refutational: Some children do not learn literacy naturally; other opportunities are needed.

Line of Argument: Nuances are identified in what is defined as natural and the recognition of the range of experiences that inform literacy learning.

Light Gray: Reciprocal translations; Medium Gray: Line of argument translations; Dark Gray: Refutational translations; Black: No clear pattern of metaphors related to this topic.

134 Meta-Ethnographies

longer allowing them [authors] to speak more directly to readers of the synthesis" (p. 333). These metaphors became the basis for the descriptive analysis of the metaphors operating in each article and for the translations that we conducted across the articles.

Our lists of metaphors addressed a vast range of issues related to literacy and families including parents as teachers, the role of parental biographies, interactions with print, and references to agency by various actors. Table 5.4 illustrates a sampling of the categories of metaphors we identified in the article by Taylor (1983).

Once metaphorical themes were identified, we looked across the studies to see which metaphors were reciprocal or consistent across the studies, which were refuted or challenged, and which metaphorical themes constituted a line of argument with later studies building on and extending the insights/metaphors presented in earlier studies.

At this point, we created a table (Table 5.5) to compare major metaphors operating across the three studies. We explored how metaphors presented in each study were related to the metaphors presented in other studies. Comparative analyses of metaphors provide insight into how the primary researchers understood various issues. Specifically, we explored how primary researchers conceptualized literacy practices over time, home/school relations, and literacy practices as natural and everyday ones. Eisenhart (2017) explains that

> the point of meta-ethnography is not to collapse the insights of one study into another or to gloss over important differences with general summaries; the point is to integrate or coordinate nuanced interpretations or explanations from individual ethnographic studies so as to develop a more generalizable understanding of what individual studies collectively reveal (p. 140).

In addition to translations across the seven studies, we also noted a critical silence. Specifically, we noted and interrogated an almost complete silence related to racism and its effects on the experiences of children and their families. This silence was particularly significant because family literacy research and programs generally focus on raced and classed families who have been historically underserved in schools. Thus, silences around racism are particularly salient given the families and communities served.

Representing the Synthesis

In our meta-ethnography, we attended to the metaphors used and the metaphorical relationships that operated across family literacy studies. At the same time, we were mindful of the broader social, cultural, economic, and historical contexts in which the participants in these studies lived and operated. Thus, prior to identifying and analyzing metaphors, we presented a gloss of each study. Our goal was to retain a sense of the context and focus of each study – a mainstay of qualitative and ethnographic traditions. On the one hand, as synthesists, we

Meta-Ethnographies **135**

needed to preserve the context of the original ethnographic studies so that they were recognizable and accurately represented. We provided summaries of each ethnographic study, which were admittedly whittled down with each revision of the paper due to space limitations. Hughes and Noblit (2017) underscore the significance of context when interpreting primary interpretations explaining, "the meanings of life experiences of different authors in relation to other people, conditions and in various contexts are what we are trying to understand" (p. 223).

TABLE 5.6 Early and Later Drafts of our Metaphor Analysis of Pahl's (2004) Ethnography

Our Early Draft of Metaphor Analysis for Pahl (2004)	*Final Draft of Metaphor Analysis for Pahl (2004)*
Family narratives as embedded in everyday artifacts and experiences. For Pahl (2004), literacy in families is enacted through the emergence of narratives that are expressed through metaphors of *doing* alongside the artifacts that accompany that *doing*. Participants are positioned as capable text makers through scanned photography, retold stories, and other resources being shaped. As Pahl reports, family narratives "reside in oral accounts, visual phenomena, and artifacts" (p. 339). Artifacts served as "conduits" and were "inscribed" (p. 339) with family's narratives. For Pahl's families, these artifacts embodied narratives of "loss, displacement, and migration" (p. 357) that were "shaped and re-told" to form "wider, longer-running" narratives (p. 344) that were continuously shaped and reshaped through ongoing iteration. For Pahl's families, multimodal artifacts and texts involve "visual images and written images as well as oral conversation" that are "expressed across a multimodal landscape of communication, in which meaning jumped across modes" (p. 347). For Pahl, literacy practices are recognized as emerging from contexts and lives that are fundamentally structured through historically constructed waves of privilege and oppression.	*Family narratives as embedded in everyday artifacts and experiences.* Pahl (2004) positioned participants as text makers through their creation and use of photography, retelling stories, and drawing. For Pahl's families, multimodal artifacts involved "visual images and written images as well as oral conversation" that were "expressed across a multimodal landscape of communication, in which meaning jumped across modes" (p. 347). Artifacts, in particular, served as "conduits" that were "inscribed" (p. 339) with family's narratives. For Pahl's families, artifacts embodied narratives of "loss, displacement, and migration" (p. 357) that were "shaped and re-told" to form "wider, longer-running" narratives (p. 344).

136 Meta-Ethnographies

They note that meta–ethnography only "produces analogies that allow readers to anticipate possibilities rather than predict the meanings of lives lived in certain contexts and under certain conditions" (p. 224).

In our original version of the paper, rich narratives were presented describing the types of metaphors used by each scholar; illustrative quotes were used to substantiate our claims. Ultimately, large chunks of these narratives were cut from the final version of our *RRQ* article. For example, Table 5.6 presents paragraphs we wrote to represent our metaphor analysis of Pahl's (2004) study in an earlier and later form.

In addition to our intentional efforts to contextualize the studies, we were also highly aware of our own positionality as metasynthesists. Despite challenges related to word count, we included a section of the paper dedicated to our own positionality as family literacy scholars, although the published version is much shorter than the original.

As Suri (2013) argues, our synthesis includes triple layers of interpretation: participants' interpretations of their experiences, the interpretations of primary researchers, and the interpretations of metasynthesists. Regardless of our efforts to contextualize, honor, and preserve the nature of the original studies and our efforts to reflexively grapple with our own positionalities, "high degrees of interpretation, bordering on transformation, are required in a synthesis that addresses a question different from the focus of the included primary research studies" (Suri, 2013, p. 116).

Finally, our analysis, as outlined above, included varying levels of abstraction. As we described in the analysis section, we relied heavily on quotations of the primary researchers and used their words – as much as possible – to present the metaphors discussed in our meta–ethnography. We also created visual maps to reveal how metaphors were related within a particular study. See Figure 5.1 for an example of a metaphorical map related to the metaphors we identified in Heath (1983). These maps were not included in our published article due to space limits.

Throughout the process, we reflected on our procedures and presentation of the analysis across a vast set of emailed memos. Some of these memos were about our search and sampling.

CATHY We are also (regretfully) taking out Edwards (1995) and Delgado–Gaitan (1992) as they only have 4 & 8 citations respectively. This simplifies our selection argument as we now have a clear split between researchers that are highly cited (24+ citations) and those that are less cited among the historical researchers (first appearing before 1996). We grappled with this decision for two reasons: (1) we have all completed the ART for Edwards (1995) and Delgado-Gaitan (1992), and (2) these are both minority scholars.

Others were conceptual:

BECKY I am interested not only in interpreting the themes from the study to ask and answer: What has been learned? But also, to look at how concepts of

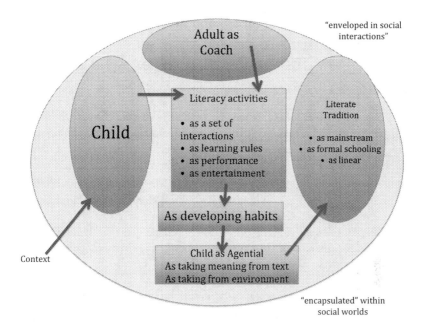

FIGURE 5.1 A Metaphor Map for Heath (1983)

family literacies, identities, practices have changed over time. Also of interest to me is looking closely at the studies' methodologies and what we learn when we look across time. If we choose studies from before 1997 and those after, we can also re-interpret some of the older data in light of what is known about family literacy practices now.

Still others were methodological:

CATHY We have now all completed the revised ART for the first three articles for the meta-ethnography project. From here on, only one of us will complete the full ART for each article. BUT we will all continue to identify the metaphors for all of the articles. It is clear from what we have completed that most of the questions on the revised ART are non-controversial (we all came up with the same/very similar responses). However, with the metaphors, having more eyes on the data seems to be a really good thing as metaphors can be slippery.

Together, these memos tracked our progress, our revisions, and changes in direction. Despite hours of initial planning and relying on a clear description of the meta-ethnography process (Noblit & Hare, 1988), our journey was neither linear nor efficient. Crafting our meta-ethnography required redirection, reorganization, and reiteration.

Discussion: Possibilities, Limits, and Reflections

In this section, we share possibilities, reflections, and limits for meta-ethnography in literacy studies. Addressing possibilities, Doyle (2003) argues that meta-ethnography holds the possibility to democratize research methodologies and to present analyses that "are not only rich in detail, but also tell stories that make them [the analyses] believable and useful for readers" (p. 332). First, meta-ethnography can amplify the voices of participants. Second, meta-ethnographic studies – like other forms of literature review – are often referenced by policy makers and educational leaders. Thus, the design and associated methodology may support changes in practice in ways that other forms of published research may not. Third, the "data" that meta-ethnographers use are published studies. Thus, these primary data are available for others to investigate, replicate, or challenge themes and translations. It is essential that synthesists reveal their "place in the text" (Doyle, 2003, p. 340) – their positionality and stance – as they work across published studies. Fourth, meta-ethnography holds the potential to extend borders because "meta-ethnography does not conceptually dismiss single case studies as locally bound. By reconceptualizing and synthesizing case studies, meta-ethnography compels us to acknowledge the importance of not only the uniqueness of individual cases, but also the uniqueness of collectives" (p. 340).

It is also possible for meta-ethnographers to explore themes operating across primary ethnographic studies. For example, a researcher might use meta-ethnography to analyze primary studies related to bilingual teaching and learning: What themes and metaphors exist across studies? How do they represent the people, spaces, and activities that are part of bilingual learning? Whose voices are heard and how do participants represent their worlds? Metaphors can reveal thinking on the part of both participants and the researchers who select and curate participants' words.

Meta-ethnographies also have discernable limits. They consistently reflect the positionalities and biases of synthesists. The questions brought to a corpus of studies, the search methods used, and the primary studies that can or cannot be located affects what is learned or not learned through the synthesis. Limits also relate to the power of meta-ethnography to comment upon a body of scholarship. As Noblit and Hare (1988) argue, translations of accounts are "interpretations of interpretations of interpretations" and the "person conducting the synthesis is intimately involved in the synthesis that results" (p. 35). Thus, the findings of meta-ethnographies should be recognized as interpretations based on scholarly evidence and limited by the knowledge, experiences and perspectives of participants, primary researchers, and the synthesists.

As we reflect on our experiences as meta-ethnographers, we are particularly aware of the time and care needed to make meaning across ethnographic studies. Our process involved the need to spend significant time reviewing a large body of literature and conducting a critical integrative review of family literacy,

Meta-Ethnographies **139**

multiple dead ends, extensive revision, and an emergent methodology that was both time-consuming and humbling. Finally, as we approached the publication of our synthesis, we faced the particular challenge of word count and producing a concise presentation of what we found to be a complex and daunting corpus of studies.

Going Public and Publication of Our Meta-Ethnography

We have presented the findings from our meta-ethnography in various forums. Cathy presented this work in progress on multiple occasions at a working conference on Discourse Analysis hosted at the Ohio State University. In these informal presentations/conversations, she used a combination of words and images to present the metaphors operating in the texts. For example, various images featuring birds were used to present differences on how literacy learning was metaphorically discussed as taking, providing, or grasping literacy (see Figure 5.2). These visual metaphors worked particularly well for PowerPoint presentations, but were less efficient in journal articles where space is limited.

While drawing on a very different set of primary studies, Cathy found meta-ethnography to be a unique and useful method for responding to a set of articles related to silence published in a forthcoming special issue of *Linguistics and Education*. In this meta-ethnography, she analyzed the metaphorical language used to discuss silence in five articles and the editorial introduction to this special issue. While the search and selection processes were prescribed by the articles included in the volume, other aspects of the meta-ethnography process were consistent with Noblit and Hare's (1988) description. Meta-ethnography provided a particularly useful tool as the articles featured in this special issue all addressed silence,

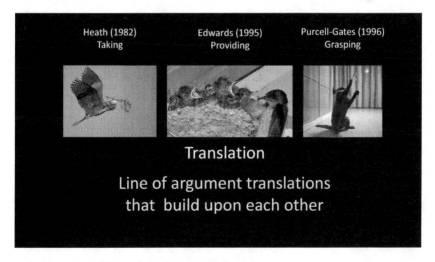

FIGURE 5.2 Visual Metaphors for Literacy Learning

140 Meta-Ethnographies

how silence operated, and the effects of silence across a vast range of educational contexts. Meta-ethnography and the translation of metaphorical meanings across the articles, provided powerful means of moving beyond summary to explore the ways silence was treated and operationalized across the volume.

In journal articles, charts were particularly helpful as they could succinctly capture large amounts of information in relatively small spaces. In addition, these visual representations can spatially represent metaphors from one study in relation to metaphors from another as illustrated in Figure 5.2.

Because our integrative critical was published in the *Reading Research Quarterly,* we were hopeful that our meta-ethnography might be published in this same highly ranked journal. We submitted the paper in August of 2018. By October, we had our first round of reviews. Important questions were raised about whether or not the metaphors we identified represented the full scope of each scholar's work. Based on these responses, we were careful to clarify across the article that one article does not represent the full body of any scholar's work and this was a limitation of the current research. Reviewers also suggested that attend to race across the paper and more systematically and consider the possibility that "the metaphors employed by researchers crowd out substantive discussion of racism or that structural issues." Reviewers also requested a visual depiction of our findings which was added and presented here as Figure 5.2. Other challenges included a more explicit articulation of research questions, the purpose of the synthesis, and a discussion of the types of studies that we believed were warranted. Finally, reviewers suggest that we shorten the manuscript and work toward a "tightened and sharpened" argument. Table 5.7 illustrates the timeline for publishing our meta-ethnography.

We resubmitted the manuscript in January 2019 and were again told that the manuscript was too long. Helpful suggestions were included, which identified places where the piece could be shortened. Reviewers also asked us to refine our critique of the highly cited scholars and to include scholarship that critiqued

TABLE 5.7 Timeline for the Publication of our Meta-Ethnography

August 22, 2018	*Submission of the Meta-Ethnography to the Reading Research Quarterly*
October 2018	R1 – Revise and resubmit
	Revisions due in mid-April 2019
January 12, 2019	R2 – Revise and resubmit
	Revisions due February 26, 2019
February 26, 2019	R3 – Submitted
April 9, 2019	Article is provisionally accepted
May 10, 2019	Final revision received
May 23, 2019	Accepted for publication in the *Reading Research Quarterly*
Spring 2020	Publication in the *Reading Research Quarterly*

research on family literacy. We resubmitted the revised meta-ethnography at the end of February and it was provisionally accepted on April 9, 2019. Our response to those reviews is presented in Appendix K. The meta-ethnography was finally accepted in May of 2019 and appeared in Spring 2020.

Going Critical: Decolonizing Meta-Ethnography

One dilemma we discussed extensively in designing our meta-ethnography was the potential constraints of our sampling procedures. Because we established a cut-off number of citations to define the most *highly cited scholars,* we unintentionally excluded Scholars of Color, who were not cited as readily. An alternative means of sampling would have been to focus on Scholars of Color who had authored highly cited family literacy scholars. This may have tempered our critique that racism is generally invisible and unacknowledged in the field of family literacy studies. In particular, by limiting our analysis to highly cited scholars, we struggled to find a way to include the voices of diverse scholars – specifically Edwards (1995), an African American family literacy scholar, and Delgado-Gaitan (1992), a Latina family literacy scholar. While we recognized the citation rates might be biased in favor of white scholars, we recognized that if our goal was to identify scholars who had a strong influence on the field, we could not justify including these less-cited scholars despite our personal and professional respect for the contributions of Edwards (1995) and Delgado-Gaitan (1992). However, not including them in the corpus of highly cited studies did contribute to our identification of silences related to racism within primary scholarship. In short, while several researchers mentioned race and some even considered how cultural dimensions of race operated within literacy contexts (Heath, 1983; Moll et al., 1992), with the exception of Li (2003), racism was not named in these highly cited primary studies.

Discussion: Limits, Possibilities, and Reflections

We believe that this meta-ethnography, like all research syntheses, have clear limitations. In particular, because we relied heavily on citation rates, there are significant limitations related to the representation of diverse voices. However, we believe that attending to who has been highly cited and how power, racism, and equity are addressed in those studies reveal a significant silence within the field of family literacy. We also contend that by attending to metaphors in the findings of each focal study, we have revealed consistent, conflicting, and emerging ways of thinking about literacy in families and the opportunities provided to children. We are particularly interested in the possibility of a dedicated meta-ethnography that would highlight the metaphors used by well-cited scholars of color and suspect that reciprocal, refutational, and lines argument will be apparent across those texts and that this analysis will provide significant lessons for

142 Meta-Ethnographies

family literacy scholars. As Doyle (2003) suggests "[m]eta-ethnography expands the conversation about qualitative synthesis as methodology to one that furthers the cause of democratic principles because it offers new conceptualizations of how knowledge and power may be transgressed" (p. 339). It is our hope that our methodology has contributed to the recognition of both claims and silences operating in the field. While our focus has been on family literacy research, meta-ethnographies as theory and method, transcend disciplinary boundaries.

Relevant Appendix

Appendix K: Response Letter to Editors for Our Meta-Ethnography

References

Asad, T. (1986). The concept of cultural translation in British social anthropology. In J. Clifford & G. E. Marcus (Eds.), *Writing culture: The poetics and politics of ethnography* (pp. 141–164). University of California Press.

Charteris-Black, J. (2004). *Corpus approaches to critical metaphor analysis.* Springer.

Compton-Lilly, C., Rogers, R., & Lewis, T. Y. (2012). Analyzing epistemological considerations related to diversity: An integrative critical literature review of family literacy scholarship. *Reading Research Quarterly, 47*(1), 33–60.

Compton-Lilly, C., Rogers, R., & Lewis Ellison, T. (2020). A meta-ethnography of family literacy scholarship: Ways with metaphors: *Reading Research Quarterly, 55*(2), 271–289.

Delgado-Gaitan, C. (1992). School matters in the Mexican-American home: Socializing children to education. *American Educational Research Journal, 29*(3), 495–513.

Doyle, L. (2003). Synthesis through meta-ethnography: Paradoxes, enhancements, and possibilities. *Qualitative Research, 3*(3), 321–344.

Durkin, D. (1961). Children who read before grade one. *The Reading Teacher, 14*(3), 163–166.

Durkin, D. (1963). Children who read before grade one: A second study. *The Elementary School Journal, 64*(3), 143–148.

Durkin, D. (1966). *Children who read early.* Teachers College Press.

Edwards, P. A. (1995). Empowering low-income mothers and fathers to share books with young children. *The Reading Teacher, 48*(7), 558–564.

Eisenhart, M. (2017). A matter of scale: Multi-scale ethnographic research on education in the United States. *Ethnography and Education, 12*(2), 134–147.

Gee, J. P. (1992). *The social mind: Language, ideology and social practice.* New York: Bergin and Garvey.

Heath, S. B. (1983). *Ways with words: Language, life and work in communities and classrooms.* Cambridge University Press.

Hughes, S., & Noblit, G. (2017). Meta-ethnography of autoethnographies: A worked example of the method using educational studies. *Ethnography and Education, 12*(2), 211–227.

Lakoff, G., & Johnson, M. (2008). *Metaphors we live by.* University of Chicago Press.

Lakoff, G., & Turner, M. (1989). *More than cool reason: A field guide to poetic metaphor.* University of Chicago Press.

Lee, R. P., Hart, R. I., Watson, R. M., & Rapley, T. (2015). Qualitative synthesis in practice: Some pragmatics of meta-ethnography. *Qualitative Research*, 15(3), 334–350.

Li, G. (2003). Literacy, culture, and politics of schooling: Counternarratives of a Chinese Canadian family. *Anthropology & Education Quarterly*, 34(2), 182–204.

Major, C. H., & Savin-Baden, M. (2010). New approaches to qualitative research. *British Journal of Educational Technology*, 42(1), 16–17.

Marsh, J., & Thompson, P. (2001). Parental involvement in literacy development: Using media texts. *Journal of Research in Reading*, 24(3), 266–278.

Moll, L. C., Amanti, C., Neff, D., & Gonzalez, N. (1992). Funds of knowledge for teaching: Using a qualitative approach to connect homes and classrooms. *Theory into Practice*, 31(2), 132–141.

Noblit, G. W., & Hare, R. D. (1988). *Meta-ethnography: Synthesizing qualitative studies*. Sage.

Pahl, K. (2004). Narratives, artifacts and cultural identities: An ethnographic study of communicative practices in homes. *Linguistics and Education*, 15(4), 339–358.

Pielstick, C. D. (1998). The transforming leader: A meta-ethnographic analysis. *Community College Review*, 26(3), 15–34.

Purcell-Gates, V. (1996). Stories, coupons, and the TV Guide: Relationships between home literacy experiences and emergent literacy knowledge. *Reading Research Quarterly*, 31(4), 406–428.

Purcell-Gates, V., & Dahl, K. L. (1991). Low-SES children's success and failure at early literacy learning in skills-based classrooms. *Journal of Reading Behavior*, 23(1), 1–34.

Rice, E. H. (2002). The collaboration process in professional development schools: Results of a meta-ethnography, 1990–1998. *Journal of Teacher Education*, 53(1), 55–67.

Reinking, D. (2011). Beyond the laboratory and lens: New metaphors for literacy research. In P. J. Dunston, V. R. Gillis, & C. C. Bates (Eds.), *60th yearbook of the literacy research association* (pp. 1–17). Literacy Research Association.

Savin-Baden, M., MacFarlane, L., & Savin-Baden, J. (2008). Learning spaces, agency, and notions of improvement: Influencing thinking and practices about teaching and learning in higher education: An interpretive meta-ethnography. *London Review of Education*, 6(3), 211–229.

Scribner, S. (1984). Literacy in three metaphors. *American Journal of Education*, 93(1), 6–21.

Street, B. (1984). *Literacy in theory and practice*. Cambridge University Press.

Street, B. (1995). *Social literacies: Critical approaches to literacy in development, ethnography, and education*. Longman Publisher.

Suri, H. (2013). *Towards methodologically inclusive research syntheses: Expanding possibilities*. Routledge.

Taylor, D. (1981). The family and the development of literacy skills and values. *Journal of Research in Reading*, 4(2), 92–103.

Taylor, D. (1983). *Family literacy: Young children learning to read and write*. Heinemann.

Taylor, D., & Dorsey-Gaines, C. (1988). *Growing up literate: Learning from inner-city families*. Heinemann.

Teale, W. H., & Sulzby, E. (1986). *Emergent literacy: Writing and reading*. Sage.

Urrieta L., & Noblit, G. W. (Eds.). (2018). *Cultural constructions of identity: Meta-ethnography and theory*. Oxford University Press.

Van Dijk, T. A. (2014). *Discourse and knowledge: A sociocognitive approach*. Cambridge University Press.

6

A METASYNTHESIS OF SCHOLARSHIP BY BLACK, INDIGENOUS PEOPLE OF COLOR

We learned important lessons as we completed the **meta-ethnography** described in Chapter 5. As we analyzed the metaphors used by scholars with an interest in families and literacy, we noted a deafening silence related to racism and how it operated for communities served by family literacy initiatives. Thus, in this chapter, we describe our ongoing efforts to address this silence. We collaboratively decided that one way to do this would be to study and synthesize the findings from family literacy scholarship written by scholars who identify as Black, Indigenous, or as People of Color (BIPOC). As we pointed out in both our critical integrative synthesis (Compton-Lilly, Rogers, & Lewis, 2012) and our meta-ethnography (Compton-Lilly, Rogers, & Lewis Ellison, 2020), studies conducted by BIPOC scholars and their perspectives, are generally underrepresented in our data set. The data set referenced in Chapters 4 and 5 relied on citation-counting to identify the studies related to family literacy that were included in our analyses and were accessed using major search engines used primarily in the United States. We recognize this selection process as a critical limitation to the syntheses that we have crafted and more generally to scholarly reviews and syntheses that draw on similar methods.

In this chapter, we share the methodological and theoretical pathways we took in crafting a **metasynthesis** of this scholarship. As we shifted our sampling criteria to highlight BIPOC scholars, we intentionally broadened the boundaries of our search to include voices and perspectives that are not be well represented in current scholarship. This meant moving beyond simple citation counting. Specifically, we recognized that with very few exceptions (Luis Moll, Guofang Li), BIPOC scholars were not cited enough to meet our inclusion criteria and be included our lists of the most-cited historical or contemporary scholars. As we conducted these research syntheses, we continuously named BIPOC scholars who were missing from our analysis. We regretted their exclusion and noted the significant impact they had had on our own research and thinking about literacy in families.

In this chapter, we described our two-tiered approach for identifying BIPOC scholars for the specific purpose of centering diverse epistemic claims within family literacy scholarship. While we grappled with the term we would use to reference Scholars of Color, we decided on BIPOC scholars as it clearly names the range of scholars we intentionally reference. We define BIPOC scholars as researchers and educators who identify as BIPOC and who bring racial, linguistic and/or cultural differences to their work with families and literacy. We believe that including BIPOC scholars into conversations about family literacy is particularly critical as Families of Color are generally the recipients of family literacy initiatives and programs.

Over the past 40 years, there has been an avalanche of family literacy scholarship including the publication of definitive family literacy studies (e.g., Heath, 1983; Taylor, 1983; Taylor & Dorsey-Gaines, 1988). These studies established literacy in families as an important field of study within education. Research related to families and literacy has also been published in allied fields including anthropology, learning sciences, media studies, critical race studies/whiteness studies, and gender studies. Likewise, our understandings of literacies have expanded to include the diverse and complex ways in which meanings are made across modes for different purposes (e.g., building racial awareness, sustaining intergenerational connections, promoting academic advancement, pleasure, and recreation, and advocating for change). We have consistently defined family literacy practices as *naturally occurring within families*, while recognizing that families travel in and out of homes, communities, and institutions. We recognize that scholarship in allied fields that has also produced important knowledge that can inform family literacy scholarship. For example, studies of immigrant and refugee families have revealed the complex ways families use digital literacies and multimedia in a globalized world (Compton-Lilly et al., 2019). CHAT theorists and others have explored families learning together in museums, communities, and natural settings (Marin & Bang, 2018; Pahl & Pollard, 2010; Rowe et al., 2002). Educational researchers have advanced our understanding of the family literacy practices of first generation college students (Trigos-Carrillo, 2016). Anthropologists have expanded our understanding of the naturally occurring translingual and multilingual practices that flow within and beyond families (e.g., González, 2006; Orellana, 2009). We are also starting to understand more about the deliberate ways in which families socialize members into racially encoded worlds (e.g. Evans-Winters & Esposito, 2010; Yosso, 2005). Thus, the boundaries of family literacy practices have extended beyond print literacies, beyond the home, beyond the nuclear family to include fictive kinships, extended families, communities, and ancestors, and beyond synchronous times and spaces.

We define qualitative **metasynthesis** as a form of systematic review that integrates findings from across various primary qualitative research studies that

146 A Metasynthesis of Scholarship

focus on a particular issue or body of scholarship. The current metasynthesis targets family literacy studies conducted by BIPOC scholars. The primary studies included in our metasynthesis applied a wide range of qualitative methodologies.

Some scholars have compared qualitative metasyntheses to quantitative meta-analyses. Both processes focus on findings related to particular issue from across studies. However, we recognize that qualitative metasynthesis and quantitative **meta-analysis** involve very different epistemological assumptions. In short, quantitative meta-analysis approaches focus on measurable effect sizes of particular variables while qualitative metasynthesis methods deal with the nuances of understanding and insights learned from and across various studies.

As Sandelowski and Barroso (2003) report, qualitative metasyntheses include methodological approaches that are sometimes referred to as qualitative meta-data-analysis, qualitative meta-analysis, qualitative metasynthesis, or meta-ethnography. In a review of various types of metasynthesis approaches, Thorne, Jensen, Kearney, Noblit, and Sandelowski (2004) describe qualitative metasynthesis as "a family of methodological approaches for developing new research based on rigorous analysis of existing qualitative findings" (p. 1343). Sandelowski and Barroso (2003) describe metasynthesis as "a form of systematic review or integration of qualitative research findings in a targeted domain that are themselves interpretative syntheses of data, including phenomenologies, ethnographies, grounded theories, and other integrated and coherent descriptions or explanations of phenomena, events, or cases" (p. 227). Other researchers describe metasynthesis as "The theories, grand narratives, generalizations, or interpretive translations produced from the integration or comparison of findings from qualitative studies" (Sandelowski et al., 1997, p. 366). Or, as an attempt to "[c]reate overarching or synoptic claims on the basis of various analytic and synthetic strategies applied to the bodies of extant qualitative research" (Thorne et al., 2004, p. 1342).

Conceptualizations of metasynthesis also differ in regard to expressed goals. McCormick, Rodney, and Varcoe (2003) describe qualitative metasynthesis as "another 'reading' of the data, an opportunity to reflect on the data in new ways" (p. 936) while Beck (2009) highlights the opportunity to "delve deeper into the research to reveal some new information that may increase our understanding" (p. 702). Despite variation in definitions and expressed goals, the scholars cited above agree on the significance and power of qualitative metasynthesis. Sandelowski and her colleagues (1997) maintain:

> Qualitative metasynthesis is not a trivial pursuit, but rather a complex exercise in interpretation: Carefully peeling away the surface layers of studies to find their hearts and souls in a way that does the least damage to them. (p. 370)

Despite this potential, attempts at metasynthesis have been plagued with difficulties. McCormick et al. (2003) worried that the techniques for conducting metasyntheses were new and poorly developed; they noted that conducting metasynthesis was complex and time-consuming, which they believed contributed to a lack of practical examples (McCormick et al., 2003).

A Metasynthesis of the Family Literacy Scholarship by BIPOC Scholars

Designing a Critical Metasynthesis

In order to address silences related to racism and include the voices of BIPOC scholars we recognized that we needed to move beyond simple citation-counting to identify the primary studies for our metasynthesis. One of our first challenges was to identify a set of criteria that would help us to identify and select the primary research studies to include in that synthesis. Controversy exists amongst metasynthesists about the criteria that should be used for primary study selection. While quantitative meta-analyses often apply stringent criteria related to the use of control groups, sample size, internal validity, and replicability, qualitative studies take many forms and reviewers must always remain sensitive to local research contexts and the people involved as well as the quality of the studies. Thus, applying lists of established criteria to select primary studies for a metasynthesis is problematic since narrow definitions of quality could easily exclude important studies.

Hoon (2013) argued that "a metasynthesis needs to incorporate a broad yet still manageable set of studies in which sensitivity toward the analysis and synthesis of other researchers' findings can be maintained" (p. 527). Thus, Hoon attends to the need for research synthesists to be accountable to the claims and contexts of the scholars who designed and conducted the primary studies. Cooper (2010) noted that the justification for a metasynthesis should not only reflect the number of studies reviewed but also the selection of studies must offer new insights to the field. Thus, in our metasynthesis, we have attempted to identify and analyze not only findings from several high-quality studies, but we also aspired to address silences related to racism revealed in our previous work as we synthesize findings reported by BIPOC scholars. We view our synthesis as a form of counter-story (Solórzano & Yosso, 2002) that challenges and complicates dominant reading of the field. As Hoon (2013) maintained, "[the] variety inherent in the primary studies can lead to the identification of contradictions and deviating evidence that yield counter instances of an existing theory" (p. 527).

Searching Family Literacy Scholarship

While we recognized the limits of citation counting, we also felt strongly that the BIPOC scholars whose work emerged through the citation counting process, should be included in our analysis. Thus, we adopted a two-tiered search and selection process for our metasynthesis project. The first tier involved identifying

148 A Metasynthesis of Scholarship

highly cited BIPOC scholars. The second tier involved collaboratively identifying BIPOC scholars who had influenced our own work and/or represented voices that were under-represented in the field. Thus, our analysis allowed us to both consider scholars whose work was relatively well cited and thus assumedly influential, alongside scholarship that might be less recognized yet presents important findings and conclusions.

Highly Cited BIPOC Scholars

In order to identify highly cited BIPOC scholars, we revisited our existing data set of family literacy scholarship, spanning 1981 through 2018. While BIPOC scholars are present in that data set, with the exception of Luis Moll and his colleagues (1992), and Guofang Li (2000), these scholars did not appear among the highly cited primary studies included in our earlier research syntheses (Compton-Lilly et al., 2012, 2020). This list is presented in Figure 6.2 (BIPOC scholars, List #1), and does not include highly cited theorists (e.g., Freire) whose work did not directly address literacy in families.

As we considered this list of scholars, we became critically aware of the limitations of our past work. Once again, we noted the dominance of white women, not only in our review, but also in citation patterns across published work related to families and literacy. This dominance exists despite the propensity for family literacy research to be conducted with historically underserved families, families who speak languages other than English, and families from a range of different racial backgrounds. This is significant due to the tangible effects of racism, linguistic biases, and classism on families and in communities.

For each highly cited BIPOC scholar, we noted when that scholar's research first appeared as a major citation in one of the 377 primary studies that we reviewed (details on the methodology used to compile the master list are presented in Chapters 4 and 5). The BIPOC scholar included in List #1 had ten or more total citations based on our hand-search of family literacy scholarship. In Table 6.1, we include Google Scholar Search numbers for the purposes of comparison. However, we warn readers to view the Google Scholar numbers critically:

- The Google Scholar numbers for BIPOC scholars reflect not only citations by scholars interested in family literacy, but also citations across disciplines; thus, these numbers do not reflect citation rates in family literacy.
- In many cases, Google Scholar lists the total number of citations for a particular scholar in other cases these numbers are not available. The reason for this is not clear.

TABLE 6.1 Our Emerging Metasynthesis

Compton-Lilly, C., Rogers, R., & Lewis Ellison, T. (in preparation). A metasynthesis of family literacy scholarship produced by Black Indigenous Scholars of Color [working title].

A Metasynthesis of Scholarship **149**

- In some cases, Google Scholar citation rates involve obvious errors; for example, Guofang Li's scholarship is conflated with the work of a highly cited geneticist. In fact, the first 16 articles listed on her citation page address genetics research.

While in this chapter we draw on our existing data set, our data set is currently being updated for a peer-reviewed research synthesis article that will be submitted to a major journal in 2021. Our manuscript will not enter the review process until after this book is *in press*. Once we update our data set, it is very possible that the scholars and articles listed in Table 6.2 and included in our sample will change.

In addition to the limits presented by Google Scholar and our data set, we must recognize an additional limitation which was also present in our past

TABLE 6.2 BIPOC scholars in our 1981–2018 Data Set (List #1)

Criteria: Article length text; authored, co-authored by BIPOC scholars who had ten or more total citations in our data set; the study is related to literacy in families with findings that speak directly to family literacy practices and policies.

	Scholar	First appeared in our data set	Most cited article in our data set	Cites in our Analysis This Article/This Scholar	Google cites for Article/ Scholar
#1	Luis Moll	1992	Moll, L., Amanti, C. Neff, D., & Gonzalez, N. (1992). Funds of knowledge for teaching: Using a qualitative approach to connect homes and classrooms, Theory into practice, *31*(2), 132–41.	10/42	7963/NA
#2	Vivian Gadsden	1992	Gadsden, V. L. (1995). Literacy, education, and identity among African-Americans: The communal nature of learning. *Urban Education*, *27*(4), 352–369.	2/23	57/NA*

(Continued)

150 A Metasynthesis of Scholarship

TABLE 6.2 Continued

Criteria: Article length text; authored, co-authored by BIPOC scholars who had ten or more total citations in our data set; the study is related to literacy in families with findings that speak directly to family literacy practices and policies.

	Scholar	First appeared in our data set	Most cited article in our data set	Cites in our Analysis This Article/This Scholar	Google cites for Article/ Scholar
#3	Concha Delgado-Gaitan	1992	Delgado-Gaitan, C. (1992). School matters in the Mexican American home. *American Educational Research Journal, 29*(3), 495–513.	2/19	842/NA★
#4	Guofang Li	2003	Li, G. (2003). Literacy, culture, and politics of schooling: Counternarratives of a Chinese Canadian family. *Anthropology & Education Quarterly, 34*(2), 182–204.	1/11	108/24,033 Dr. Li's citations are conflated with a geneticist
#5	Norma Gonzalez	1995	Gonzalez, N., Moll, L. C., Tenery, M. F., Rivera, A., Rendon, P., Gonzales, R., & Amanti, C. (1995). Funds of knowledge for teaching in Latino households. *Urban Education, 29*(4), 443–470.	0/10	596/NA★

★ Some scholars do not have a Google page that shows the compilation of all their publications.

research syntheses (Compton-Lilly et al., 2012, 2020). In short, by focusing on citation rates, we privilege texts and scholars that were published in the past and downplay the contribution and impact of more recent scholars and their work. We have attempted to address this issue in the second tier of our selection process.

Inviting a Counter-Story: Engaging with BIPOC Scholars

As we considered the list of BIPOC scholars presented in Table 6.2 alongside our own trajectories of becoming family literacy scholars, we noted missing voices, perspectives, and contributions to family literacy scholarship, particularly from BIPOC scholars whose work has emerged since 2000. Thus, in our metasynthesis, we supplemented our list of highly cited BIPOC scholars with a personal and professional review of recent scholarship produced by BIPOC scholars whose work we have found inspiring, important, and potentially essential as we consider literacy learning and practices in families.

In order to address the shortcomings of this data set and to address the deafening silence related to racism that was revealed through our previous review (Compton-Lilly et al., 2020), we implemented an alternative – and admittedly more subjective – process for identifying scholarship related to families and conducted by BIPOC scholars. In our earlier work:

> We not only considered the metaphors used but also became aware of silences related to racism and structural inequities across the articles. Like Prendergast (2003), we worried that although family literacy research focused on racially diverse families, highly cited studies, with the exception of Li (2003), remained silent in regard to racism.
>
> (Compton-Lilly et al., 2020, p. 275)

After reviewing the texts listed in Table 6.2, we individually asked ourselves, "Who is missing?" and "As a field, whose voices do we need to hear?" Next, we each crafted a list of 5–8 scholars and identified one research article by each scholar, whose work spoke back to the silence we had identified. Once we had assembled our personal/professional lists of BIPOC scholars, we met to identify a final list that was comprehensive in terms of the voices we believed needed to be represented, yet manageable in size for a team of three scholars to thoughtfully analyze. We sought to include BIPOC scholars who addressed a range of families and communities, including LGBTQ scholars.

Our criteria for List #2 emerged as we identified Scholars and representative articles. First, we discussed each article speaking to why and how it contributed to family literacy studies. Some of the scholarship in this area was from outside of literacy research. We noted the importance of recognizing scholarship conducted in allied fields (e.g., learning sciences, bilingual education). For example, Marin and Bang's (2018) article, *"Look It, This is how You Know" Family Forest Walks as a Context for Knowledge-Building About the Natural World* is probably more aptly located in scholarship related to indigenous knowledge than family literacy. However, the authors note how they "theoretically develop walking, reading, and storying land" as a lens on meaning making within families. Thus, articles were chosen based on their relevance to literacy in families rather than a stated

152 A Metasynthesis of Scholarship

focus on family literacy practices, programs, or initiatives. To keep our focus on the voices of BIPOC scholars, we excluded scholarship if it did not meet our emerging inclusion criteria. For example, Becky used search terms "race" and "family literacy" and found Carmen Luke's scholarship related to literacy practices in multiracial families. Recognizing her discontent with the dominant field of family literacy studies that do not center race, even when racial, linguistic and cultural diversity were acknowledged, Luke was placed on our list. However, we excluded Luke's (2003) research on interracial families for two reasons. First, she is not a BIPOC scholar and second, she did not explicitly address "literacy" and "literacies," instead the focus was on "how couples cope with racializing practices within immediate and extended families and the local community" (p. 379).

This collaborative process required significant deliberation. As with Luke (2003), we encountered several white scholars whose work we found valuable. For example, Becky wanted to include scholarship that illustrated how family literacy practices are racialized, including scholarship that draws on Critical Race Theory and sociological theories; thus, we considered including Margaret Hagerman (2014) and her research related to white families and children. However, for this review, we felt the need to stay true to our intent to highlight BIPOC scholars. We also considered France Winddance Twine's work (1996) on race negotiations in families. As a scholar of British, Caribbean, and African heritages, she is BIPOC scholar, however, literacy practices and learning are not central to her work and her work lingers at the very fringe of what might be considered family literacy scholarship. As we developed List #2 (Table 6.3), we kept track of articles that were excluded and why; we expect to revisit to these articles as we frame our metasynthetic analysis conceptualize future projects.

During our research meetings, we deliberated definitions of families, literacy, and considered the spaces within which literacy practices occurred. Indeed, the notion of family is a cultural construct, enacted through people's literacy practices. Whereas we might have excluded some studies because of their focus on discrete adolescent literacy practices, we intentionally centered the researchers' understandings of families as embodied, distributed, and extending across fictive kinships and communities.

List #2 includes our preliminary list of fourteen BIPOC scholars whose research we collectively agreed to include in our initial sample for our metasynthesis.

As we selected the specific articles from each BIPOC scholar to include in our analysis, some articles were rejected and replaced by other articles written by the target scholar. In some cases, we had initially identified a position paper or scholarly review rather than a report on qualitative empirical study. Focusing on empirical studies was critical given the focus of metasynthesis on research findings. In addition, we intentionally sought articles that reported on communities that were under-represented in our sample. Finally, we favored articles that directly attended to both literacy and communities/families/extended families.

TABLE 6.3 BIPOC scholars from the Second Analysis (List #2)

Criteria: Article-length text; authored and/or co-authored by Scholars of Color; not represented in list one; related to literacy in families with findings that speak to family literacy practices and policies; fills a gap related to representation in terms of author's racial position(s), the geographic location of the study; and/or the ways in which "families" and "literacies" were conceptualized and enacted.

Scholars	References/Abstract/Keywords Scholars' Research Focus	Domains	Research Design
G. Campano & M. Ghiso	Campano, G., Ghiso, M., Yee, M., & Pantoja, A. (2013). Toward community research and coalitional literacy practices for educational justice. *Language Arts, 90*(5), 314–326	Family Literacy as Activism	Practitioner research and participatory action research
Flores, Tracy	Flores, T.T. (2018). Chicas fuertes: Counterstories of Latinx parents raising strong girls. *Bilingual Research Journal, 41*(3), 329–348.	Intergenerational Storytelling & Activism	Qualitative case study
Jan Hare	Hare, J. (2012). 'They tell a story and there's meaning behind that story': Indigenous knowledge and young indigenous children's literacy learning. *Journal of Early Childhood Literacy, 12*(4), 389–414.	Narrative, Indigenous Knowledge	Focal groups and interviews
Bobbie Kabuto	Kabuto, B. (2010). Code-switching during parent—child reading interactions: Taking multiple theoretical perspectives. *Journal of Early Childhood Literacy, 10*(2), 131–157.	Trans/Bilingual Literacy in Families	Collective case study
Judy Kalman	Kalman, J. (2001). Everyday paperwork: Literacy practices in the daily life of unschooled and underschooled women in a semiurban community of Mexico City. *Linguistics & Education, 54*, 523–538.	Community, Adult, and Family Literacies	Ethnography
Jungmin Kwon	Kwon, J. (2019). Parent–Child translanguaging among transnational immigrant families in museums. *International Journal of Bilingual Education and Bilingualism*, 1–16.	Translanguaging and Transnational Practices	Multisite ethnographic study
Tisha Lewis (Ellison)	Lewis, T.Y. (2013). "We txt 2 sty cnnectd": An African American mother and son communicate: Digital literacies, meaning-making, and activity theory systems. *Journal of Education, 193*(2), 1–13.	Digital Literacies in Families	Ethnographic case study

(Continued)

TABLE 6.3 Continued

Criteria: Article-length text; authored and/or co-authored by Scholars of Color; not represented in list one; related to literacy in families with findings that speak to family literacy practices and policies; fills a gap related to representation in terms of author's racial position(s), the geographic location of the study, and/or the ways in which "families" and "literacies" were conceptualized and enacted.

Scholars	References/Abstract/Keywords Scholars' Research Focus	Domains	Research Design
Marin, A. & Bang, M.	Marin, A., & Bang, M. (2018). "Look It, This is how You Know:" Family forest walks as a context for knowledge-building about the natural world, *Cognition and Instruction, 36*(2), 89–118.	Intergenerational Literacies in Informal Spaces	Family case study
Maria Teresa de la Piedra	de la Piedra, T. (2009). Hybrid literacies: The case of a Quechua community in the Andes. *Anthropology & Education Quarterly, 40*(2) 100–128.	Immigrant & Multilingual Family Resources	Ethnographic case study
Prichard, Eric Darnell	Pritchard, E. D. (2014). 'Like signposts on the road': The function of literacy in constructing Black Queer Ancestors. *Literacy in Composition Studies, 2*(1), 29–56.	Black Queer, LGBTQ Literacies & Ancestorship	Life story, narrative
Loukia Sarroub	Sarroub, L. K. (2002). In-betweenness: Religion and conflicting visions of literacy. *Reading Research Quarterly, 37*(2), 130–148.	Transnational Family Literacy	Ethnography and discourse analysis
Kwangok Song	Song, K. (2016). "Okay, I will say in Korean and then in American": Translanguaging practices in bilingual homes. *Journal of Early Childhood Literacy, 16*(1), 84–106.	Immigrant & Multilingual Families	Qualitative case study
Mariana Souto-Manning	Souto-Manning, M. (2018). Disrupting Eurocentric epistemologies: Remediating transitions to centre intersectionally minoritised immigrant children, families and communities. *European Journal of Education, 53*(4), 456–468.	Teacher Beliefs about Parents and Families	Case study
Lina Trigos-Carrillo	Trigos-Carrillo, L. (2019). Community cultural wealth and literacy capital in Latin American communities. *English Teaching: Practice & Critique, 19*(1), 3–19.	Family Literacy as Activism	Transnational ethnography

A Metasynthesis of Scholarship **155**

We ultimately chose the 14 of studies presented in List #2 (Table 6.3). We acknowledge that this list is not an exhaustive and does not fully represent historically silenced voices in the field. We agreed that to be included, the scholarship should be an empirical study, written by a BIPOC scholars, and represent diversity in the field. In sum, the following criteria was used to vet these scholars and each representative article:

- Each article was authored by a BIPOC scholar whose voice/perspective has informed our own work as literacy scholars.
- The BIPOC scholars included in List #2 are not represented in List #1 of highly cited scholars.
- We chose collaboratively journal articles for which the targeted BIPOC scholar served as first author.
- We selected articles that reported on a qualitative research studies that were relevant to literacy research in families and communities.

As we deliberated our sample, we considered each author's racial position(s), the geographic location of each study, and the ways in which "families" and "literacies" were conceptualized and treated in the research design. We then crafted a descriptive table that summarized important study elements across each primary study. We believe that synthesizing findings from these inspiring and important studies has the potential to provide important insights for our work as family literacy scholars and will ultimately serve children and families.

Reading as a Reviewer: Describing, Analyzing, and Sorting the Studies

Once we identified this second list of BIPOC scholars, we each assumed responsibility for locating and uploading articles from Lists #1 and #2 to a shared webspace. The first step in the process entailed locating a digital version of each text, preferably a PDF that would allow us to cut and paste the findings and other information into our Analytic Review Template (ART) (see Appendix L).

The ART used for the metasynthesis was adapted from our critical integrative review and our meta-ethnography. For the metasynthesis, we paid particular attention to identifying the research findings presented in each article. We recognized that extracting findings is an interpretative process that involves encounters among synthesists, the primary researchers, and their participants. Suri (2014) captured the complexity of this process when she wrote, "research synthesis can be a triple hermeneutic process. A synthesis report is often the synthesist's interpretation of the primary researcher's interpretation of the interpretations of the participants in the primary research study" (p. 115). Because our goal was to learn from the findings of BIPOC scholars who studied literacy in families, it was important to us to stay close to the researcher's interpretations. To complete the

156 A Metasynthesis of Scholarship

findings section of the ART, we quoted directly from the articles and were careful to note page numbers for each quote. This allowed us to easily recontextualize information pulled from the original article as we moved through our synthesis and writing processes.

To refine the adapted ART and pilot our process, we each read the study and completed the ART for one study from List #2: Tracey Flores (2018) (see Appendix L for Lewis Ellison's completed ART for Flores). We then reconvened to discuss, compare, and analyze our completed ARTs. As we looked across our ARTs, we realized that we had each approached the task differently. Cathy attended to the sections of the article where findings were reported and identified those section in parenthesis (introduction, theoretical frameworks, findings). Tisha noted the importance of researcher's positionality and identified sections in the paper where Flores disclosed her vulnerability and relationship with participants. Tisha also noted the implications Flores that had identified and highlighted the contribution this work could make for future scholars and educators. Becky highlighted Flores' attention to participants' voices and she quoted portions of the findings written in the families' primary language (Spanish). This led to a discussion about the nature of representational claims and how we might capture findings that were implied by the decision that researchers made but were not stated directly.

Through this process, we refined the ART to include attention to participants' voices, researcher positionality, note section of the article where findings were presented, and implications of the study. Our completed ARTs, along with the selected articles, were uploaded to a shared online space.

Extracting and Synthesizing Findings

While we were clear that attending to findings was a major step in completing our metasynthesis, we soon realized that listing the findings was complicated and involved attending to findings that were often not stated directly. For example, when we individually identified the findings presented by Flores (2018), our collective breath was taken away by how stories told and written by family members across generations served as vehicles that enabled ancestral knowledge to travel across space and time. Flores brought fresh insights to family literacy studies not only in her explicit claims presented in the "findings" section of the article but also in her theoretical framing and representational choices. As we sifted through our three ARTs, we identified different types of findings: explicit, implicit, and representational.

Explicit Findings: Explicit claims were stated directly. For example, Flores wrote, "Parents support their daughters in navigating borders, real and imagined, and institutions in order to ensure that they can benefit from the many opportunities that are offered to them" (p. 344). In these examples, BIPOC

Scholars explicitly state what they learned and point to the significance of the findings – in this case, the agency of the parents to help their daughters benefit from opportunities.

Implicit Findings: In other cases, the findings are presented less directly, such as when Flores writes, "Samuel shared with his daughter that as a teenager he was concerned about 'doing good' in school and he wants to let 'my daughter know I am here for her 100%. She [will] never disappoint me'" (p. 342). In this example, a similar claim is made about parents and their support for their daughters, but it is presented through the example of school support and using the words of participants.

Representational Findings: Finally, we noted a set of findings that were not stated directly. We call these "representational claims" because they are represented or evidenced by what the scholar does or how the scholar presents information. For example, Flores never tells us that the parents' use of Spanish is an important vehicle for presenting their stories. Instead of telling us, she shows us by including numerous quotes in Spanish and inviting her readers to hear participants' language and words, and voices.

As we continued to identify findings across the data set of primary studies (List #1 and List #2), we struggled to differentiate between explicit and implicit claims with the recognition that the degree of explicitness exists on a continuum. We eventually decided that our focus was on the claims themselves rather than how they are stated; we did not perseverate on these distinctions. However, we agreed that it was essential to remain alert to representational claims, as they reflect what BIPOC scholars have learned and what they view as significant.

As we collectively analyzed Flores' (2018) article, we clarified in our own minds what qualified as a *finding* and were collectively moved forward. Since we all completed ARTs for Flores' article (2018), our next step was to look across the findings we had identified. An example of that analysis is presented in Table 6.4, where we have noted merged columns when multiple researchers identified the same finding/quote. We added our initials for further clarity. As is evident, we did not always capture the exact same text segments; thus, this chart became the subject of the lengthy conversation described above. Our next step was to conduct a grounded analysis of the findings, color-code findings that suggested themes, and then identify themes based on these clusters of findings. Figure 6.1 depicts a sample of our coded findings. In this example, pink references stories from the past, purple highlights stories of resistance, green references family stories, and orange references the future. As we analyzed these coded findings, we developed a codebook that identified the stated and representational findings for each study (see Table 6.5).

As we completed this process for Flores (2018), we soon realized that this process was time-intensive and probably redundant. While we agreed that individually completing the ART and identifying findings for Flores was an essential

158 A Metasynthesis of Scholarship

TABLE 6.4 A Sampling of Findings Identified by Each Synthesist

Cathy (CCL) *Becky (BR)*	*Tisha (TLE)*

CCL, BR, & TLE: Stories of Family: "Family is the most important thing."
[BR: REPRESENTATIONAL – She uses the participants' words in the sub-headings of her findings]

CCL & BR: Valente, Samuel, Alma, and Rose "reflected on their lived experiences from their childhood and teen years to write and share memories about their own parents, lessons learns from their families, and cuentos ('stories') shared with them by their own abuelitos, tias, and tios."

CCL, BR, & TLE: The stories that parents shared with their daughters illustrate the cultural and familial resources of their homes and communities, their "funds of knowledge" (Moll et al., 1992) and "pedagogies of home" (Bernal, 2001) that are embedded in the narratives they shared with their daughters" (p. 341).

> **TLE:** "These family stories that parents shared with their daughters illustrate the cultural strength (Delgado-Gaitan, 1992; Valdés, 1996), love, and support of the generations that came before them. Most importantly, these stories highlight the deep love of family and provide their daughters with the lesson that "family is the most important thing" (p. 342).

> **BR & TLE:** Stories for the future: "I want her to be happy."

CCL & BR: "At workshops, Valente, Samuel, Alma, and Rose shared with their daughters and with each other stories that illustrated their love for their daughters and the deep desire for them to be happy in their current and future lives. For example, during the fifth workshop, parents and their daughters reflected and wrote a personal letter to one another in which they shared what it is/was like being a teenager, who they are, who they are becoming, and important advice they wish to share with each other" (p. 342).

A Metasynthesis of Scholarship **159**

	BR: "I found that embedded in the stories shared at the workshops, recounted in interviews, and recalled during discussion, parent's stories and consejos were based upon their experiential knowledge, in which they shared stories that had been silenced hidden, lost, or forgotten over time and space" (p. 338)	
CCL, BR, & TLE: Three categories emerged: stories of resistance, stories of family, and stories for the future.(p. 338)		
CCL: "parents are raising their daughters to be chicas fuertes ("strong girls")."		
	BR & TLE: Stories of resistance: "I write to let my daughter know that I am here" [BR: She uses the participants' words in the sub-headings of her findings]	
	BR: "I made this intentional decision to categorize their stories as resistance rather than struggle to foreground the strength and dignity of each parent in the face of challenging and life-changing events (Villenas, 2005). Although many of their	

FIGURE 6.1   A Sample of Coded Findings Identified by Each Synthesist

step as we designed our analysis and clarified how we would identify findings, we agreed to move forward with just two members of the team analyzing each of the remaining 18 articles. Thus, we identified one team member to complete the ART and identify the initial set of findings from across the article. Then, a second team member carefully read the ART, added any additional findings, conducted a grounded coding of the findings, and crafted definitions for each code. At every step of this process, we remained alert to representational findings that were not explicitly stated.

Our final task was to look across the articles to identify patterns in the types of findings that were presented across the studies. We conducted a separate cross primary study analyses for Lists #1 and #2 for two reasons. First, the articles in List #1 were articles that were relatively highly cited and we wondered if their citation rate might reflect different types of findings, perhaps those that better resonated with the family literacy community. Second, the articles in List #1 are over 20 years old, while most of the articles in List #2 – with the exceptions of Kalman (2001) and Sarroub (2002) – are less than 10 years old. In order to identify patterns across each data set, we created a master chart that clustered similarly coded findings from across each list. Table 6.6 presents a sampling of the sorted code definitions for the five articles presented in List #1.

Representing the Synthesis

While there is not space in this chapter to report on all the findings of our ongoing Metasynthesis, we share one preliminary set of findings from List #1. Specifically, we focus on a cluster of findings related to how the *past and the future affect the opportunities children encounter in schools*. This finding is addressed by four of the five highly cited BIPOC scholars included in List #1. However, these scholars address these temporal constructs differently.

160 A Metasynthesis of Scholarship

TABLE 6.5 A Sampling of Grounded Code Definitions for Flores (2018)

Flores (2018) Findings (Across three analyses)
A Sampling of Code Definitions and Illustrative Examples

Finding Code	Definition	Illustrative Examples
Navigate	This set of findings speaks to the "tools" – including "stories" – that parents use to prepare children to "navigate" their daily lives, including real and imagined "borders" and "institutions"	CCL & BR: "Through the sharing of consejos, stories, and experiences – their 'pedagogies of the home,' (Bernal, 2001), these parents provide their daughters with strategies and tools to navigate their daily lives, including their personal, social, and academic worlds, while ensuring that they stay connected to their familial, cultural and linguistic roots" (p. 329).
		CCL & BR: "Parents support their daughters in navigating borders, real and imagined, and institutions in order to ensure that they can benefit from the many opportunities that are offered to them." (p. 344)
Roots/Past	This set of findings speaks to how parents draw on stories of the past draw on "cultural and familial resources" of homes and communities and memories as they support their children	CCL, BR. & TLE: "The stories that parents shared with their daughters illustrate the cultural and familial resources of their homes and communities, their 'funds of knowledge' (Moll et al., 1992) and 'pedagogies of home' (Bernal, 2001) that are embedded in the narratives they shared with their daughters" (p. 341).
		TLE: "Through reflection, writers 'bear witness' to the deep emotions contained within these memories and the learning attached to these experiences of strength, survival, and resistance" (p. 339).
Future	These findings are future-focused – encouraging children to "pursue their dreams and choose they life they want," which is often contrasted with the experiences of parents.	BR: "Valente, Samuel, Alma, and Rose support their daughter's happiness by encouraging them to pursue their dreams and choose the life they want for themselves" (p. 343). Flores provides a quote from each of them to illustrate this finding.
		CCL: "Together, parents and their daughters are co-constructing a new narrative, a counternarrative, in which they (de)construct their lived realities to (re)construct their futures." (p. 344)

A Metasynthesis of Scholarship **161**

Flores (2018) Findings (Across three analyses)
A Sampling of Code Definitions and Illustrative Examples

Finding Code	Definition	Illustrative Examples
Own Words	This finding is often unstated/understated, it is a representational finding. This finding highlights the significance of attending to the actual words (and stories) of participants.	BR: "Together, CRT and LatCrit worked to center the experiential knowledge of these parents through the sharing of their stories in their own words, allowing us to hear and see the voices and knowledges that are many times excluding, thus breaking silences" (p. 344). The use of both Spanish quotes and English translations speaks to the need to honor participants' words and stories.

Writing in the same year, both Delgado-Gaitan (1992) and Gadsden (1995) described the significant impact that the past has on families and how parents support their children. Delgado-Gaitan (1992) emphasized how families are connected across generations through culture, history, and language. She illustrated intergenerational connections – many of which were presented in the form of stories – that connected family members across time and space through networks of mutuality and sharing. Highlighting family educational values and morals, she notes, "An important aspect of socialization is the transmission of values, which vary from culture to culture and from family to family" (p. 497). Much of this work is done through "Family stories about their life in Mexico... [that] guided the children's moral and emotional learning" (p. 507). This ancestral practice – carried out through family literacy practices – taught children values including consideration, cooperation, and respect for elders. Delgado-Gaitan (1992) wrote,

> Parents believed that education meant being considerate of others, kindness, respect for elders and authority, and cooperation. In Spanish, children are said to be "buen educado" (well educated) when they are well mannered, speak to others kindly and respectfully, and are helpful to those in need. A person who is "buen educado" may not have been formally schooled. (p. 506)

Delgado-Gaitan (1992) also raised an issue that was later taken up by Li (2003). She suggested that "Parents shared with their children their own educational limitations as well as their desire that the children remain in school, complete their education, and go beyond the parents' accomplishments" (Delgado-Gaitan, 1992, p. 507); thus, parents were depicted as valuing education in order to provide their children with advantages that were not available to them.

TABLE 6.6 A Sampling of the Sorted Code Definitions for List #1

Clusters/Categories	1 – Moll et al. (1992)	2 – Gadsden (1995)	3 – Delgado-Gaitan (1992)	4 – Li (2003)	5 – Gonzalez (1993)
This cluster of findings examines relationships between homes and schools. Mismatch and discontinuity are highlighted as well as the transformative potential of reciprocity and collaboration.	**Symmetrical Relationships (Home/School)** This set of findings emphasizes the mutuality that is created between home and school when families' are seen as partners in education. That is, their household resources become material for learning in the classroom.			**Counternarratives, discontinuities, and mismatch** This set of findings focuses on mismatches between the Chinese home culture and the school. These mismatches are sometimes presented in the data as counternarratives. Li also refers to them as discontinuities.	**Transformative power of reciprocity and collaborative visits** This set of findings relates to the reciprocal power of the home community visits and the impact they have of teachers' understandings of families and communities.

This cluster of findings examines the past and the future as informing the opportunities that children encounter.	**Intergenerational and Ancestral Linkages (Time, History, Transitions, Futures)** This set of findings focus on how families' literacy practices are connected across time and context, linking generations and also part of imagining futurities.	**Intergenerational and Ancestral Linkages** **Time, History, Futurities** This set of findings speaks to the intergenerational connections and threads – many of which are discursive – that connect family members across time and context.	**Parental opportunities missed, unfulfilled expectations for children** These findings highlight lost opportunities for parents alongside unfulfilled expectations/hopes for the children.	**Anthropological Imagination** This set of findings is about possibilities for the future. It is about shifts in thinking and action that can lead to new possibilities for children and families.

(Continued)

TABLE 6.6 Continued

Clusters/Categories	1 – Moll et al. (1992)	2 – Gadsden (1995)	3 – Delgado-Gaitan (1992)	4 – Li (2003)	5 – Gonzalez (1993)
This cluster of findings highlights the exclusionary effects of race, systemic inequities, and the failure of schools.		**Families as Sites where Race is Critically Read and Navigated** This set of findings focus on how families engage in critically reading and navigating race and racism. Their literacy practices engage with and respond to their lived experiences with racism.	**Families as Sites to Read and Navigate Systemic Inequities** The findings in this set focus on examples of how members of the family read, respond, and resist systemic inequities.	**Schools as exclusionary, unresponsive, and not doing their job.** These findings point to the failure of school alongside exclusionary practices. Schools do not provide the Liu children with the skills and abilities that they need for success.	**Survival at School and in life** These findings highlight overcoming challenges through the use of the word "survival." The need for survival extends to both school and life.

This cluster
of findings
highlights value
and respect for
children as well
as how teachers
might rethink
their ideas
about children,
particularly
children from
underserved
communities

**Care and Value
Placed on
Children's
Education**
Woven through
this set of find-
ings are the
care, value, and
respect placed
on children's
education. These
findings included
emotionalities
(e.g., frustration,
emotional sup-
port, confidence)
throughout the
excerpts.

**Representational
Finding:
Unlearning
Previous
Assumptions**
This set of findings
highlights the need
for teachers to revisit,
rethink, and unlearn
previous beliefs and
assumptions about the
families.

166 A Metasynthesis of Scholarship

Gadsden (1995) reiterated the idea that family practices were connected across time and context, through linking generations and imagining futures. Unlike Delgado-Gaitan (1992), she focused on literacy practices across time. As she noted in her abstract, "literacy should be seen as a continuous, ever-changing activity, transformed by critical life events, translated as a result of life-span transitions, and defined and shaped by cultural and community beliefs about the price of education and the expected rewards of learning" (Gadsden, 1995, p. 352). She used the word "survival" – which recurred several times in our cross article analysis – to highlight the significance of literacy in African American communities. As she wrote, "In the words of Ms. Lennie 'if you want to know how I would define literacy as a Black person, let's say it's reading; let's say it's writing or knowing how to survive in this world – and most of all knowing how to combine all of these things so that you appreciate who you are as a Black person and so you never forget your history'" (p. 367). Literacy practices crossed generations to create a shared historical consciousness that was rooted in identity, family, and community. Remembering history and lessons learned by past generations was considered to be crucial for survival.

While Gadsden (1995) referenced how "the acquisition of literacy and uses of knowledge are tied to the transitions that people make and to understanding life and work in communities" (p. 367), Li (2003) explicitly highlighted parents' lost opportunities for schooling alongside their dashed hope and unfulfilled expectations for their children. While Delgado-Gaitan (1992) and Gadsden (1995) named the possibilities of education and literacy for changing the futures of children, Li (2003) was less convinced. She noted that although the parents in her study had "missed the opportunity to learn English, they hoped that their children would grow up literate in English. However, after their children went to school, they brought home only disappointment and unfulfilled expectations" (p. 189). Li explicitly attended to the exclusive nature of schools, noting "as Daniel entered school, Kathy and Peter's dream for their only son was broken" (p. 192). Thus, while schools, education, and literacy were described by participants as spaces of opportunity, these beliefs were then questioned by Li who explicitly named the failure of schools to help the children in her sample become literate in English when misalignments existed between home and schools.

Gonzalez and her colleagues (1995) offered a possible solution grounded in what she referred to as the "anthropological imagination" (p. 465) of teachers. Her study foregrounded teachers' inquiries into families' household networks, survival strategies, and resources. She noted that "[a]n anthropological imagination paved the way for teachers" (p. 465) to see students and families in new ways. Specifically, "teachers were not given predigested methods to use unreflexively. Emerging from the teachers' own theoretical understanding of ethnography, home visits because participant-observation, and insights from the households were tied into broader regional, social, economic, and gender related patterns" (p. 465). In this way, ethnography was identified as a "tool for social action that

A Metasynthesis of Scholarship **167**

can enable persons to transform the confines of their circumstances" (p. 467). Notably, in this account, the onus was on teachers to revisit, retheorize, and reimagine their work with children, families, and communities. As parents were recognized as experts with family funds of knowledge, the relationships between parents and teachers grew through mutuality, respect, and reciprocity. Gonzalez and colleagues (1995) wrote:

> Parents have come to view themselves as agents capable of changing their child's educational experiences. As parents responded with personal narratives concerning their own unique and singular life course, a heightened historical consciousness began to emerge (p. 467).

This historical consciousness – grounded in ancestral wisdom – that offered a pathway for imagining new futures. Claims about transformation were evident in Gonzalez's ongoing work with Moll and his colleagues (Moll et al., 1992); however, this focus on future imaginings and possibilities were explicitly articulated by Gonzalez through the future-oriented nature of her findings.

Across the five papers included in List #1, we see a confluence of attention to temporality and how what happens in families is tied to ancestral wisdom and practices (Delgado-Gaitan, 1992; Gadsden, 1995) as well as possibilities for the future (Gonzalez et al., 1995). In some accounts, the past and imagined futures operate are simultaneous influences as parents compare their lost experiences with the advantages of their children (Li, 2000) or when teachers revisit and relearn leading to new possibilities for children (Gonzalez et al., 1995).

Aside from sharing an initial cluster of findings from our metasynthesis, we want to make explicit our process for arriving at these findings. Figure 6.2 illustrates our pathway from reading primary studies, through the ART process to coding of the findings, defining our codes, and identifying clusters of findings to represent.

An important point to consider when representing a metasynthesis is the recontextualization of synthesized clusters of findings culled from primary studies. Thus, we intentionally highlight significant features from each study in a descriptive table for readers to reference as they consider our methodology and synthesized findings. This final step provides readers with essential background information to consider as they reflect on our metasynthetic findings. See Appendix M for this descriptive table for our List #1.

Going Public and Publication of Our Metasynthesis

Our metasynthesis project continues as we analyze the findings from List #2, and may be adding additional articles to that data set. Our goal is to publish our metasynthesis in a highly ranked and highly cited literacy journal. In short, because we are addressing what we believe is a problematic silence in our field, we aspire for

168 A Metasynthesis of Scholarship

a large audience. We believe that not only will this article synthesize important insights from a group of scholars who are under-represented in our field, but it will also provide a model for scholarship that not only synthesizes findings from across qualitative studies, but also creates spaces for attending to the voices of scholars who work must inform what we do as literacy scholars with an interest in families and communities.

Disseminating this synthesis to educators who work with families is another important step. Indeed, the studies included in this metasynthesis may not rise to the top of Google searches and yet, taken collectively, we have identified impressive set studies written by BIPOC scholars that center how diverse families use,

Step 1: Reading the Primary Study	BILINGUAL RESEARCH JOURNAL 2018, VOL. 41, NO. 3, 329–348 https://doi.org/10.1080/15235882.2018.1496955 **R** Routledge Taylor & Francis Group RESEARCH ARTICLE ✱ Check for updates ***Chicas fuertes:* Counterstories of Latinx parents raising strong girls** Tracey T. Flores The University of Texas at Austin **ABSTRACT** In this article, I explore the narratives and experiences of four Latinx mothers and fathers, Alma, Rose, Valente and Samuel, who participated with their adolescent daughters (grades nine-10), Blanca, Elizabeth, Rocky and Reyna in Somos Escritores/We are Writers writing workshops. Somos Escritores was a family engagement space, created with and for Latinx mothers and fathers and their adolescent daughters, that invited families to draw, write and share stories from their lived experiences. Workshops were designed with and for Latinx parents and their adolescent daughters to open space for the intergenerational exchange of stories and experiences within a political context that continuously and increasingly works to silence and control their voices and experience. Drawing upon written narratives, interview transcripts and ethnographic field notes, I provide insights into the ways that these parents are raising their daughters to be "chicas fuertes/strong girls." Through the sharing of consejos, stories, and experiences – their "pedagogies of the home," (Delgado Bernal, 2001), these parents provide their daughters with strategies and tools to navigate their daily lives, including their personal, social and academic worlds, while ensuring that they stay connected to their familial, cultural and linguistic roots. **KEYWORDS** family engagement; intergenerational storytelling; Latina girls; Latinx parents; writing
Step 2: Completing the Analytic Review Template (ART)	**Organization (Categories, Use of Participants' Voices, Questions, Chronological?)** • Stories of resistance: "I write to let my daughter know that I am here" (p. 339). • Stories of family: "Family is the most important thing." • Stories for the future: "I want her to be happy."
	Findings (note from which section of the article the findings are extracted) • Three categories emerged: stories of resistance, stories of family, and stories. Stories of resistance: "I write to let my daughter know that I am here" • "Through reflection, writers "bear witness" to the deep emotions contained within these memories and the learning attached to these experiences of strength, survival, and resistance" (p. 339). • Alma's scar story is not only a story in which she recounts a painful time in her life but also a story of growth, learning, and healing (Anzaldúa, 1999). In her words, she resists the temptation to let this pain and grief hold her back from what lies ahead in her future and her daughter's future. Through sharing this experience with her daughter, she teaches and models for her daughter how challenges and struggles prepare us to be más fuerte ("stronger") and más valiante ("more valiant") in life.

(a)

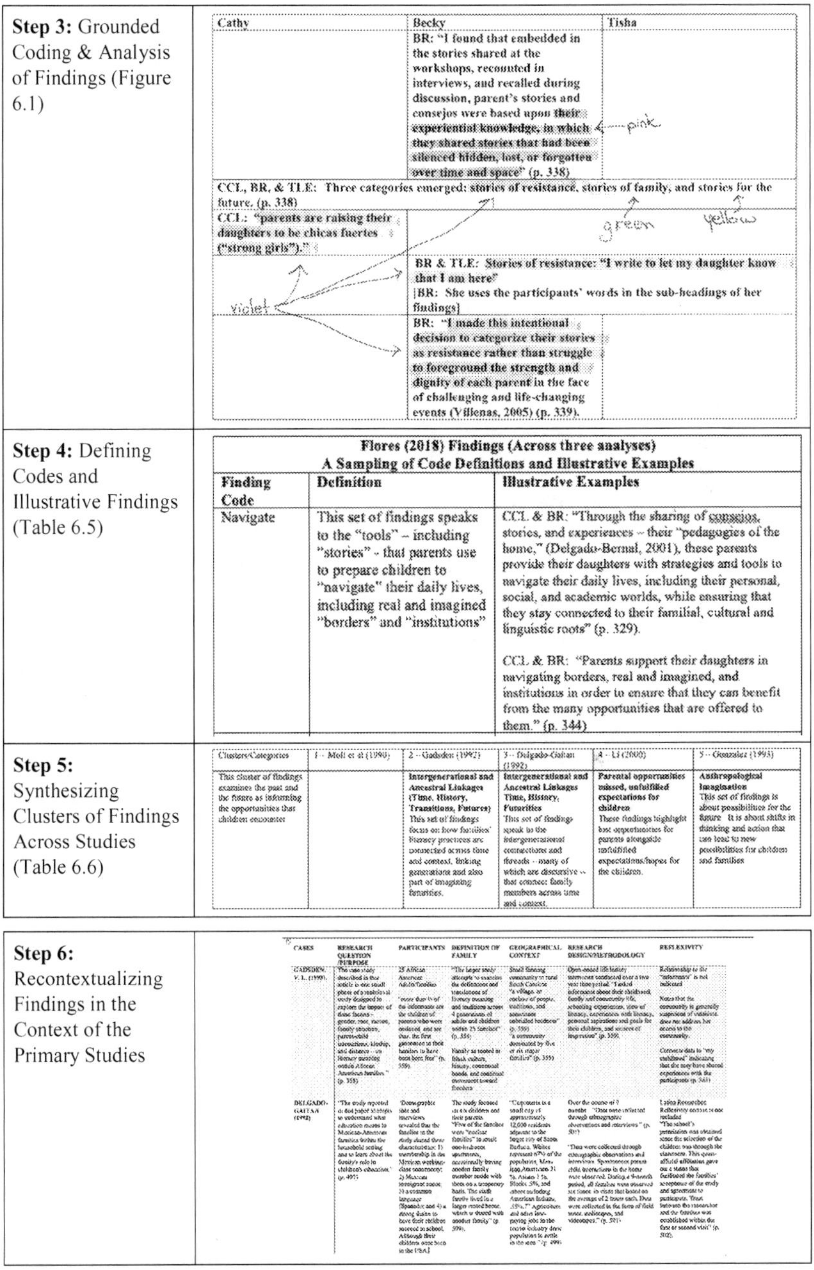

Step 3: Grounded Coding & Analysis of Findings (Figure 6.1)

Cathy	Becky	Tisha
	BR: "I found that embedded in the stories shared at the workshops, recounted in interviews, and recalled during discussion, parent's stories and consejos were based upon their experiential knowledge, in which they shared stories that had been silenced hidden, lost, or forgotten over time and space" (p. 338) ← pink	
CCL, BR, & TLE: Three categories emerged: stories of resistance, stories of family, and stories for the future. (p. 338) (green) (yellow)		
CCL: "parents are raising their daughters to be chicas fuertes ("strong girls")."		
violet	BR & TLE: Stories of resistance: "I write to let my daughter know that I am here" [BR: She uses the participants' words in the sub-headings of her findings]	
	BR: "I made this intentional decision to categorize their stories as resistance rather than struggle to foreground the strength and dignity of each parent in the face of challenging and life-changing events (Villenas, 2005) (p. 339).	

Step 4: Defining Codes and Illustrative Findings (Table 6.5)

Flores (2018) Findings (Across three analyses)
A Sampling of Code Definitions and Illustrative Examples

Finding Code	Definition	Illustrative Examples
Navigate	This set of findings speaks to the "tools" – including "stories" - that parents use to prepare children to "navigate" their daily lives, including real and imagined "borders" and "institutions"	CCL & BR: "Through the sharing of consejos, stories, and experiences – their "pedagogies of the home," (Delgado-Bernal, 2001), these parents provide their daughters with strategies and tools to navigate their daily lives, including their personal, social, and academic worlds, while ensuring that they stay connected to their familial, cultural and linguistic roots" (p. 329). CCL & BR: "Parents support their daughters in navigating borders, real and imagined, and institutions in order to ensure that they can benefit from the many opportunities that are offered to them." (p. 344)

Step 5: Synthesizing Clusters of Findings Across Studies (Table 6.6)

Clusters/Categories	1 – Moll et al (1990)	2 – Gadsden (1992)	3 – Delgado-Gaitan (1992)	4 – Li (2000)	5 – Gonzalez (1993)
This cluster of findings examines the past and the future as informing the opportunities that children encounter		**Intergenerational and Ancestral Linkages (Time, History, Transitions, Futures)** This set of findings focus on how families' literacy practices are connected across time and context, linking generations and also part of imagining futurities.	**Intergenerational and Ancestral Linkages Time, History, Futurities** This set of findings speak to the intergenerational connections and threads – many of which are discursive – that connect family members across time and context.	**Parental opportunities missed, unfulfilled expectations for children** These findings highlight lost opportunities for parents alongside unfulfilled expectations/hopes for the children.	**Anthropological Imagination** This set of findings is about possibilities for the future. It is about shifts in thinking and action that can lead to new possibilities for children and families

Step 6: Recontextualizing Findings in the Context of the Primary Studies

CASES	RESEARCH QUESTION /PURPOSE	PARTICIPANTS	DEFINITION OF FAMILY	GEOGRAPHICAL CONTEXT	RESEARCH DESIGN/METHODOLOGY	REFLEXIVITY
GADSDEN, V. L. (1990).	The case study described in this article is one small phase of a multi-level study designed to explore the impact of these factors – gender, race, racism, family structure, parent-child interactions, kinship, and distance – on literacy meaning within African American families." (p. 353)	25 African American Adults/Families "more than ⅔ of the informants are the children of parents who were enslaved, and are thus, the first generation in their families to have been born free" (p. 359).	"The larger study attempts to examine the definitions and transference of literacy meaning and traditions across 4 generations of adults and children within 25 families" (p. 354) Family as rooted in Black culture, history, communal bonds, and continual movement toward freedom	Small farming community in rural South Carolina "a village, an enclave of people, traditions, and sometimes unbridled hardness" (p. 359) "a community dominated by five or six major families" (p. 355)	Open-ended life history interviews conducted over a five year time period. "I asked informants about their childhood, family and community life, schooling experiences, view of literacy, experiences with literacy, personal aspirations and goals for their children, and sources of inspiration" (p. 359).	Relationship to the "informants" is not indicated Notes that the community is generally suspicious of outsiders; does not address her access to the community. Connects data to "my childhood" indicating that she may have shared experiences with the participants (p. 361)
DELGADO-GAITAN (1992)	"The study reported in this paper attempts to understand what education means to Mexican-American families within the household setting and to learn about the family's role in children's education." (p. 497)	"Demographic data and interviews revealed that the families in the study shared these characteristics: 1) membership in the Mexican working-class community; 2) Mexican immigrant status; 3) a common language (Spanish); and 4) a strong desire to have their children succeed in school. Although their children were born in the USA]	The study focused on six children and their parents. "Five of the families were "nuclear families" in small one-bedroom apartments, occasionally having another family member reside with them on a temporary basis. The sixth family lived in a larger rented home, which is shared with another family" (p. 500).	"Carpinteria is a small city of approximately 12,000 residents adjacent to the larger city of Santa Barbara. Whites represent 67% of the population, Mexican Americans 21%, Asians 1%, Blacks 5%, and others including American Indians, .55%." Agriculture and other low-paying jobs in the tourist industry drew population to settle in the area" (p. 499).	Over the course of ? months. "Data were collected through ethnographic observations and interviews." (p. 501) "Data were collected through ethnographic observations and interviews. Spontaneous parent-child interactions in the home were observed. During a 9-month period, all families were observed six times, in visits that lasted on the average of 2 hours each. Data were collected in the form of field notes, audiotapes, and videotapes." (p. 501)	Latina Researcher. Reflexivity section is not included "The school's permission was obtained since the selection of the children was through the classroom. This quasi-official affiliation gave me a status that facilitated the families' acceptance of the study and agreement to participate. Trust between the researcher and the families was established within the first or second visit" (p. 502).

(b)

FIGURE 6.2 Illustrative Metasynthesis Pathway for Gadsden (1995)

170 A Metasynthesis of Scholarship

mediate, critique, and transform literacy practices in their homes, communities, workplaces, and schools. Indeed, one of the powerful aspects of metasynthesis is the representation of findings across a body of scholarship. As we have shown, there are many primary qualitative studies conducted by BIPOC scholars that document how diverse families engage with literacy. Each of these studies makes a unique contribution to our understandings about literacy in families and communities. Yet, taken together, there are important findings that resonate across the studies and have the potential to inform educational practices in schools and communities.

If educators truly want to center family knowledge and practices in schools, the voices, insights, and perspectives of BIPOC scholars must be recognized. In order to reach educators, we might, for example, write a short piece for a practitioner-oriented journal such as *Journal of Adolescent and Adult Literacy*, *The Reading Teacher*, *Language Arts*, or *Educational Leadership*. We could share the paper with organizations that reach practitioners including the *National Parent Teacher Association*, *National School Boards Association*, and *American Association of School Administrators*. These organizations include people who make policy and practice decisions that concern families and communities.

We have been intentionally transparent about our process in the hope that subsequent metasynthesists might find our process helpful as they design and implement their own metasynthesis. We highlight the importance of not only research collaborations that include both BIPOC and non-BIPOC scholars. While reading each other's work, listening to each other's voices, and becoming responsive to the challenges faced by historically underserved communities is important, we must also find ways to work together to examine, analyze, and interrogate assumptions and practices. These collaborations are essential and will inform transformative research that can move us toward equity.

Going Critical: Decolonizing Metasynthesis

As we have worked our way through this metasynthesis project, we have continuously reminded ourselves of our goal to respond to a silence involving the voices of BIPOC scholars in family literacy scholarship. These concerns arose as we completed our integrative literature review (Compton-Lilly et al., 2012) and lamented the relatively low citation rates for BIPOC scholars. It continued as we conducted our meta-ethnography and attended to resounding silences around racism and the challenges faced by Families and Communities of Color. We asked ourselves, "How do we challenge ourselves to see beyond what we know?" Each step in creating and conducting this metasynthesis was subject to careful scrutiny about our assumptions and about ourselves. Our longitudinal research partnership has provided opportunities to understand and challenge the lenses, contexts, assumptions, and silences in our individual and collective work.

Indeed, as we designed our metasynthesis, we found ourselves reflecting on and revisiting previous methodological decisions. Importantly, we managed to switch gears and tried different approaches even when they did not align with our earlier work. For example, counting citations is a highly positivist act that implies that scholarly impact can be measured. However, List #2 is not based on citation counts precisely because we have come to recognize inequities in the field and the need to recognize the contribution of bilingual, indigenous, and raced BIPOC scholars who continue to be excluded from scholarly conversations due to segregated flows of knowledge (e.g., Solórzano & Yosso, 2002).

As noted across this volume, researchers bring their own subjectivities to research syntheses, which include internalized hierarchies related to knowledge, mentor/mentee relationships, language practices, evidentiary sources, and claims to credibility. These hierarchies have impacted our careers and every step of our research syntheses process: from developing our samples, to reviewing primary studies, and analyzing and synthesizing across studies.

As we documented the decision-making processes and reflections that informed our metasynthesis, we continually wondered while whether we were capturing what we know about family literacy or merely ventriloquizing dominant voices and positions. Reflection has been an ongoing part of the process. For example, as Becky conducted the ART for the Moll, Amanti, Neff, and Gonzalez (1992) study, she wrote,

> Even though I have read and used this article so many times – early in my doctoral career, in my courses, with teacher-research groups, my reading path through this article for the metasynthesis was quite different. I picked up on the layers of interpretation – the authors of the article, the teachers in the study, the families (the Lopez'). There were different layers of interpretation, different angles of insight across the article, different types of claims made. My awareness of these layers was heightened because I realized that I was treating the findings as if they were primary data in order to create new insights across the "sites" or studies.

As noted above, the process of selecting the primary scholarship for this synthesis was not unproblematic. Indeed, the selection and synthesis of these studies was subject to the gaze of two white researchers (Becky and Cathy) and a Black researcher (Tisha). How do we reconcile our "gaze" – our entitlement – as we peered into the inner workings of empirical research written by people who do not share our racial, linguistic, and/or cultural backgrounds? What does it mean to identify synthetic findings, especially when representational findings, for example, are not explicitly stated? Rather than being invited into the homes or lives of participants to observe and/or participate in family literacy practices, we have invited ourselves to sit down and study the findings of BIPOC scholars. If we were to have asked consent to study their findings, would they have granted it?

172 A Metasynthesis of Scholarship

As it should be clear from our illustration of our emerging process, the terminology of "extracting" findings suggests a technical and mechanistic process. However, we have found our discussions to entail interpretation and dialogue as we collaboratively synthesized findings from the primary studies. We continually reminded each other to treat study findings as primary data. Our process seemed and felt conceptual and artful, as we considered and synthesized primary study findings. However, we extracted those findings from the homes and lives of the participants. We even pulled them out of carefully written, revised, and published papers. We inserted them into a new context – our ART and then looked across these ARTS to envision a new context where the findings were synthesized across context, time, and participants to identify similarities, differences, nuances, and anomalies. In this way, we created and sustained a space for a cacophony of voices engaged in dialogue. Yet, what does it mean for us to do this? What dynamics of coloniality and racism are still at play? Throughout this process of reading and re-reading the findings from the original studies, we challenged ourselves by asking: "How do we hear and see beyond what we know? How do we preserve the meaning of original texts as when we are expected to extract findings, a process of decontextualization?"

Hoon and Baluch (2019) propose "dialectical interrogation" (p. 18) as a means for heightening reflexivity and trustworthiness in metasyntheses. For them, dialectical interrogation "entails scrutinizing the underlying theoretical, ontological or methodological assumptions that are reinforced and clung to in a research field" (p. 18). They tell us that for fields that are well established – like family literacy – "disruptive interrogation may aid in prompting a different ontological emphasis from those used in initial research on the phenomenon of interest. Especially mature areas of research can benefit from adopting an alternative philosophical approach regarding the nature of the phenomenon as well as the knowledge about this phenomenon" (p. 18).

To paraphrase their argument, our disruptive interrogation – as articulated in our metasynthesis – "unpacks the individual paradigmatic premises" thereby leading us to reframe family literacy scholarship "via a shift in ontological and epistemological emphasis" (p. 18). This shift constitutes "a richly generative step" and "an impetus for adopting a new or broader perspective "based on previously undervalued theoretical foundations" (p. 18) that honors the voices of BIPOC scholars. This is particularly important since – like much educational scholarship – family literacy initiatives and programs are designed to serve Families and Communities of Color. In the same way that we need more Teachers of Color in North American Classrooms, we also need to hear and value the voices of BIPOC scholars.

Discussion: Limits, Possibilities, and Reflections

Hoon (2013) reminded us that "the metasynthesis is understood as a complete study itself that aims at extracting, analyzing, and synthesizing qualitative evidence to build theory" (p. 573). Our metasynthesis focused on scholarship of

BIPOC scholars led us to expand in our conceptualization of the field of family literacy studies. As we designed the study, we revised our understandings of "families" and "literacies" and "research/representation." As we extracted, analyzed, and interpreted findings from individual studies, we realized the complexity of this interpretive work and the types of findings that operate in and across scholarship, including explicit, implicit, and representational claims. We leveraged this understanding as we synthesized findings across the studies. Our representation of what we have learned from BIPOC scholars invites educators to expand their understandings of how twenty-first century families – in different geographic contexts, in the United States and in Peru, United Kingdom, Canada, and Mexico – navigate, critique, and design literacy practices to accomplish social, personal, and community goals. Metasynthesis holds promise for looking across research studies to arrive at refined, extended, and new understandings. In essence, the studies included in our metasynthesis operate as a new multisite study of family literacy practices that honors the insights and perspectives of BIPOC scholars who bring deep and vested interest to the communities that they serve.

Related Appendices

Appendix L: Analytic Review Template (ART) for our Meta-Synthesis of Family Literacy Scholarship conducted by Scholars of Color

Appendix M: Descriptive Table – List #1

References

Beck, C. T. (2009). Metasynthesis: A goldmine for evidence-based practice. *Aorn Journal*, 90(5), 701–710.

Bernal, D. D. (2001). Learning and living pedagogies of the home: The mestiza consciousness of Chicana students. *International Journal of Qualitative Studies in Education*, 14(5), 623–639.

Campano, G., Ghiso, M., Yee, M., & Pantoja, A. (2013). Toward community research and coalitional literacy practices for educational justice. *Language Arts*, 90(5), 314–326.

Compton-Lilly, C., Rogers, R., & Lewis Ellison, T. (2020). A meta-ethnography of family literacy scholarship: Ways with metaphors. *Reading Research Quarterly*, 55(2), 271–289.

Compton-Lilly, C., Lewis Ellison, T., & Rogers, R. (2019). The promise of family literacy: Possibilities and practices for educators. *Language Arts*, 97(1), 25–35.

Compton-Lilly, C., Rogers, R., & Lewis, T. (2012) Analyzing epistemological considerations related to diversity: An integrative critical literature review of family literacy scholarship. *Reading Research Quarterly*, 47(1), 33–60.

Cooper, H. (2010). *Research synthesis and meta-analysis: Step-by-step approach* (4th ed.). Sage.

Delgado-Gaitan, C. (1992). School matters in the Mexican American home. *American Educational Research Journal*, 29(3), 495–513.

Evans-Winters, V. E., & Esposito, J. (2010). Other people's daughters: Critical race feminism and Black girls' education. *Educational Foundations*, 24, 11–24.

174 A Metasynthesis of Scholarship

Flores, T. T. (2018). Chicas fuertes: Counterstories of Latinx parents raising strong girls. *Bilingual Research Journal*, 41(3), 329–348.

Gadsden, V. L. (1995). Literacy, education, and identity among African-Americans: The communal nature of learning. *Urban Education*, 27(4), 352–369.

González, N. (2006). *I am my language: Discourses of women and children in the borderlands.* University of Arizona Press.

Gonzalez, N., Moll, L. C., Tenery, M. F., Rivera, A., Rendon, P., Gonzales, R., & Amanti, C. (1995). Funds of knowledge for teaching in Latino households. *Urban Education*, 29(4), 443–470.

Hagerman, M. A. (2014). White families and race: Colour-blind and colour-conscious approaches to white racial socialization. *Ethnic and Racial Studies*, 37(14), 2598–2614.

Hare, J. (2012). 'They tell a story and there's meaning behind that story': Indigenous knowledge and young indigenous children's literacy learning. *Journal of Early Childhood Literacy*, 12(4), 389–414.

Heath, S. B. (1983). *Ways with words: Language, life and work in communities and classrooms.* Cambridge University Press.

Hoon, C. (2013). Metasynthesis of qualitative case studies: An approach to theory building. *Organizational Research Methods*, 16(4), 522–556.

Hoon, C., & Baluch, A. (2019). The role of dialectical interrogation in review studies: Theorizing from what we see rather than what we have already seen. *Journal of Management Studies*, 57(6), 1–26.

Kabuto, B. (2010). Code-switching during parent—child reading interactions: Taking multiple theoretical perspectives. *Journal of Early Childhood Literacy*, 10(2), 131–157.

Kalman, J. (2001). Everyday paperwork: Literacy practices in the daily life of unschooled and underschooled women in a semiurban community of Mexico City. *Linguistics & Education*, 54, 523–538.

Kwon, J. (2019). Parent–Child translanguaging among transnational immigrant families in museums. *International Journal of Bilingual Education and Bilingualism*, 1–16.

Lewis, T. Y. (2013). "We txt 2 sty cnnectd": An African American Mother and Son Communicate: Digital Literacies, Meaning-Making, and Activity Theory Systems. *Journal of Education*, 193(2), 1–13.

Li, G. (2003). Literacy, culture, and politics of schooling: Counternarratives of a Chinese Canadian family. *Anthropology & Education Quarterly*, 34(2), 182–204.

Luke, C. (2003). Glocal mobilities: Crafting identities in interracial families. *International Journal of Cultural Studies*, 6(4), 379–401.

Marin, A., & Bang, M. (2018). "Look it, this is how you know:" Family forest walks as a context for knowledge-building about the natural world. *Cognition and Instruction*, 36(2), 89–118.

McCormick, J., Rodney, P., & Varcoe, C. (2003). Reinterpretations across studies: An approach to meta-analysis. *Qualitative Health Research*, 13(7), 933–944.

Moll, L., Amanti, C. Neff, D., & Gonzalez, N. (1992). Funds of knowledge for teaching: Using a qualitative approach to connect homes and classrooms, *Theory into Practice*, 31(2), 132–141.

Orellana, M. F. (2009). *Translating childhoods: Immigrant youth, language, and culture.* Rutgers University Press.

Pahl, K., & Pollard, A. (2010). The Case of the disappearing object: Narratives and artefacts in homes and a museum exhibition from Pakistani heritage families in South Yorkshire. *Museum and Society*, 8(1), 1–17.

de la Piedra, T. (2009). Hybrid literacies: The case of a Quechua community in the Andes. *Anthropology & Education Quarterly*, 40(2), 100–128.

Prendergast, C. (2003). *Literacy and racial justice: The politics of learning after Brown v. Board of Education*. Southern Illinois: University Press.

Pritchard, E. D. (2014). 'Like signposts on the road': The function of literacy in constructing Black Queer Ancestors. *Literacy in Composition Studies*, 2(1), 29–56.

Rowe, S. M., Wertsch, J. V., & Kosyaeva, T. Y. (2002). Linking little narratives to big ones: Narrative and public memory in history museums. *Culture & Psychology*, 8(1), 96–112.

Sandelowski, M., & Barroso, J. (2003). Classifying the findings in qualitative studies. *Qualitative Health Research*, 13(7), 905–923.

Sandelowski, M., Docherty, S., & Emden, C. (1997). Qualitative metasynthesis: Issues and techniques. *Research in Nursing & Health*, 20(4), 365–371.

Sarroub, L. K. (2002). In-betweenness: Religion and conflicting visions of literacy. *Reading Research Quarterly*, 37(2), 130–148.

Solórzano, D. G., & Yosso, T. J. (2002). Critical race methodology: Counter-storytelling as an analytical framework for education research. *Qualitative Inquiry*, 8(1), 23–44.

Song, K. (2016). "Okay, I will say in Korean and then in American": Translanguaging practices in bilingual homes. *Journal of Early Childhood Literacy*, 16(1), 84–106.

Souto-Manning, M. (2018). Disrupting Eurocentric epistemologies: Re-mediating transitions to centre intersectionally-minoritised immigrant children, families and communities. *European Journal of Education*, 53(4), 456–468.

Suri, H. (2014). *Towards methodologically inclusive research syntheses: Expanding possibilities*. Routledge.

Taylor, D. (1983). *Family literacy: Young children learning to read and write*. Heinemann.

Taylor, D., & Dorsey-Gaines, C. (1988). *Growing up literate: Learning from inner-city families*. Heinemann.

Thorne, S., Jensen, L., Kearney, M. H., Noblit, G., & Sandelowski, M. (2004). Qualitative metasynthesis: Reflections on methodological orientation and ideological agenda. *Qualitative Health Research*, 14(10), 1342–1365.

Trigos-Carrillo, L. (2019). Community cultural wealth and literacy capital in Latin American communities. *English Teaching: Practice & Critique*, 19(1), 3–19.

Trigos-Carrillo, L. M. (2016). *A critical approach to academic, community, and family literacies of first-generation college students in Latin America* (Doctoral dissertation, University of Missouri Columbia).

Valdés, G. (1996). *Con respeto: Bridging the distances between culturally diverse families and schools: An ethnographic portrait*. Teachers College Press.

Winddance Twine, F. W. (1996). Brown skinned white girls: class, culture and the construction of white identity in suburban communities. *Gender, Place and Culture: A Journal of Feminist Geography*, 3(2), 205–224.

Yosso, T. J. (2005). Whose culture has capital? A critical race theory discussion of community cultural wealth. *Race Ethnicity and Education*, 8(1), 69–91.

7

CONCLUSIONS

Since before literacy education was recognized as an academic field, scholars have been intrigued by review-centric approaches. This was particularly apparent in the case of reading scholarship, which extended across 70 years with the annual publication of *Summary of Reading Investigations*, as described in Chapter 1. Over time, these summaries of research related to reading were housed at Universities and published in various journals. In 1966, the Education Resources Information Center (ERIC) – an early online digital library of education research and information – was created in by the Institute of Education Sciences at the U.S. Department of Education. Today, we witness the creation of CITE-ITEL – an ongoing public knowledge project that operates as an interactive repository for research related to literacy teacher education. As scholars, we have witnessed this lineage of research synthesis approaches change over time based on the development of the field, advancements in methodological and theoretical procedures, and technological advances. What has stayed consistent is a scholarly imagination that seeks to understand the depth and scope of our fields in order to contribute new knowledge.

This book presents a lineage of approaches to research syntheses from **dissertation literature reviews,** to **traditional reviews, critical integrative syntheses, meta-ethnographies,** and **metasyntheses.** Across our trajectory, we have problematized taken-for-granted assumptions and advocated for the attention to reflexivity, transparency in representational decisions, and dissemination choices. Explicit attention to these aspects of reviewing are relatively new developments in the genre of the research syntheses. In this chapter, we address a range of issues relate to research syntheses and present a set of considerations for contemporary and future research synthesists. Specifically, we revisit the process for curating and reviewing primary studies, explore forms of research syntheses not explicitly addressed in this volume, raise international considerations, reflect on the sometimes problematic impact of research syntheses, and examine a set of emerging approaches to research synthesis.

Curating a Bodies of Scholarship

When designing a research study or writing a grant proposal, reading relevant research syntheses is often a first step. Research syntheses tend to be highly cited guides to large bodies of scholarship. For research synthesists, analytic curation involves organizing and publicly presenting a body of scholarship. For social scientists, approaches to curation have changed and matured over time. Approaches may be chronological, thematic, or comparative and may explore controversies, gaps, and/or the cumulation of knowledge in a field. Yet, the procedural decisions involved in designing and conducting research syntheses have remained mysterious to many scholars. In this book, we have highlighted processes and practices for carrying out five different kinds of research syntheses – dissertation literature reviews, traditional and follow up reviews, integrative critical reviews, meta-ethnographies, and metasyntheses. Each research syntheses involves its own set of methodological and theoretical considerations.

While we have showcased different approaches, we have simultaneously highlighted a shared pathway that involves designing a research synthesis, searching and sampling relevant scholarship, analyzing and synthesizing scholarship, representing the synthesis, going public with the results, and decolonizing the synthesis through intentional reflexivity. In this section, we revisit a few of these threads and pose additional questions that synthesists might find useful as they synthesize primary studies.

One thread – *designing a research synthesis* – depends on the purpose, goal, and research questions posed by the synthesist. As the preceding chapters illustrate, the purpose of a research synthesis can range from completing a dissertation to exploring a problematic silence in a field. With purpose in mind, scholars must always interrogate the assumptions, biases, beliefs, and hopes they bring to a synthesis project. These questions will lead the scholar to consider the type of research synthesis (e.g., literature review, meta-ethnography, metasynthesis) that will best serve their purpose. This design process may involve learning more about available synthetic methodologies and corresponding analytic procedures. As noted in Chapters 2 through 6, our design process for each review required us to learn new vocabulary, analytical practices, and new ways of approaching published research. Our process was always iterative as we proposed next steps, and then revisited and revised those steps as we moved forward.

In Chapter 2, we shared goals and questions that might accompany the writing of a dissertation literature review. Because the dissertation literature reviewer is often a novice to field, the sampling and discernment process looks different

178 Conclusions

from that of an experienced scholar. The goal of a dissertation literature review is often to present a reading of a given body of scholarship to justify the design and implementation of an empirical study. The goal of the dissertation literature review is to place a study in dialogue with other scholarship in the field and provide a framework for making sense of empirical findings. The questions that guide a dissertation literature review generally reflect the dissertator's research questions. Of course, dissertation literature reviews could also assume the forms of historical reviews or a full-blown metasyntheses. However, most dissertators – and their respective committee members – find value in requiring novice researchers to curate a conventional review of scholarship related to the questions they raise, the participants they address, and the practices they examine.

The goal of a metasynthesis is quite different. Metasynthesists focus specifically on the findings from a set of empirical studies that explore a shared or similar issue. Close analysis of reported findings allows the metasynthesist to make claims about what we know, identify patterns across primary studies, and examine nuances of understanding that might reflect cultural differences, available resources, or historic inequities. While conducting a metasynthesis might on the surface appear to be a simple process of compiling findings from across empirical studies, as illustrated in Chapter 6 of the current volume, conducting a metasynthesis requires rich knowledge of a given field, which is needed to inform the sampling of primary studies, the analysis of those studies, and adapting a sufficiently reflexive approach for looking across findings. Thus, metasyntheses are generally conducted by scholars who have extensive experience with a given body of scholarship.

As we wrote each chapter, we emphasized the importance of being transparent in regard to the design and methodology used for research syntheses. We are hopeful that the research syntheses highlighted this book act as touchstone examples for various types of reviews. However, we do not view our efforts as perfect. In fact, we recognize that each attempt was flawed, imperfect, and probably will not directly transfer to other research contexts. Thus, we have worked to illustrate our methodological and theoretical decision-making, highlight the challenges we encountered, and recognize the limits of our synthetic efforts.

Along the way, we have emphasized that writing research reviews is theoretical and methodological work. We have provided windows into our methodological procedures because we know that scholars often struggle with the technical details of synthesizing bodies of qualitative research. Yet, we have also surrounded these procedural details – which are always interpretive – with information about our research reflexivities and theoretical inclinations.

Before moving on, it is important to address issues that scholars and editors are often not quick to discuss. First, there are self-promotional reasons for conducting research syntheses. All of us recall senior scholars advising us to design and publish a synthetic study early in our careers. In part, this is because research syntheses are frequently cited enhancing one's visibility in the field, research

Conclusions **179**

portfolio and citation rates. Similarly, conducting a research syntheses can establish a scholar as a recognized expert on a particular topic, which is important as scholars strive to claim a place in an academic field.

While generally recognized for his theories related to forms of capital that advantage people within particular social fields, Bourdieu (1993, 2003) also wrote extensively about reflexivity and the need for scholars to be fully cognizant of the professional advantages of asking particular questions, implementing particular methodologies, and referencing particular theories. Drawing on Bourdieu, Swartz noted that "Reflexivity means viewing intellectual practices as being interest–oriented rather than being motivated exclusively by objective ideas or values" (Swartz, 1997, p. 279). In short, writing and publishing a research synthesis is one way to obtain professional recognition. Bourdieu warned scholars of the need to break up the "small circles of mutual admiration" (Wacquant, 1992, p. 57) that characterize academic fields. Thus, we recognize the context within which we publish our research syntheses and the advantages of exploring emerging and novel research synthesis approaches that are at the cutting edge of literacy educational scholarship. As we write these words, we are distinctly aware of the academic capital associated with publishing a book that addresses multiple forms of research syntheses. Not only is this an intellectually riveting experience, but it is also a good career move.

For example, in Chapter 3, Rebecca reflected on two literature reviews related to critical discourse analysis (Rogers, Malancharuvil-Berkes, Mosley, Hui, & Joseph, 2005; Rogers & Schaenen, 2014), which have been among her most cited publications. Why is this? What is the appeal of these syntheses? As scholars, we know that research syntheses provide accessible and helpful curated accounts of scholarship that assist with writing tasks (e.g., an IRB application, research proposal, grant proposal, book). Reviews assist us in locating relevant research, getting a handle on the types of arguments that are being made, and pinpointing how emergent research ideas might speak to a field.

Similarly, journal editors are often pleased to receive research syntheses as submissions because they know they are often well cited and can enhance the impact factor of the journal. Admittedly, writing research syntheses individually and collectively has shaped how we review research syntheses and advise doctoral students and colleagues. Based on this work, we are more likely to expect a clear methodological description describing the synthesist's searching, sampling, and analytic processes. We expect authors to be clear about the type of research synthesis they are writing and to articulate the purpose of their review. As reviewers, synthesists, and journal editors, we have watched the field change over the past 20 years. Synthesists are more likely to be held accountable for reporting on their research design, methodological procedures, and their reflexivity as synthesists. This, in turn, creates new standards for what count as trustworthy syntheses.

Next, we pivot to the thread of *searching and sampling scholarship.* Across the chapters, we emphasize the interpretive and power-laden nature of locating and

180 Conclusions

accessing primary scholarship. Given the technological tools that are now available, it may seem that processes for searching and sampling vast bodies of scholarship are relatively simple and straightforward. However, as described in each chapter, our initial attempts soon became complicated. We recognized that finding workable search terms often required multiple attempts and the use of various terms to refer to similar ideas. Based on the primary studies that we located, we began to notice patterns in how search engines worked – specifically, the dramatic over-representation of scholarship written in English by scholars located in the United States. We began to wonder what else was out there and how those primary studies might have informed our analyses. These complexities relate to the geo-politics of databases and vendors, the economics of publishing companies, and the status of particular journals, which are discussed later in this chapter. We also faced difficult decisions related to articles that we felt were significant and important contributions, but did not always meet the criteria we had established.

As we moved through the searching and selection process, we found that we constantly revisited our inclusion criteria to ensure that our sample addressed the purposes we posed and was systematic. This entailed clarifying criteria based on patterns encountered as we searched. This does not mean that criteria was tweaked to include particular studies, but that certain patterns across studies caused us to revise and revisit our criteria. For example, when attending to citation rates for highly cited scholars, we noticed that family literacy studies that reported on particular family literacy programs relied heavily on the work of the scholars who created those programs. We decided to omit those studies from our sample as they over-represented particular scholars who were not extensively represented in the larger data set. Thus, inclusion criteria evolved through a process of considering what we found as we searched, which also required us to revisit our sample multiple times to ensure that all studies included in the sample continued to meet our evolving criteria.

As we look back on the research syntheses that we have conducted, we inevitably identify shortcoming in our selection and sampling processes. For example, for our meta-ethnography, our focus on citation counting resulted in our failure to include the voices of many BIPOC scholars, which led to an additional challenge of figuring out how to systematically respond to this gap as we conducted our metasynthesis. Finally, we must recognize the important contributions made by reviewers and editors as our research syntheses were submitted, revised, and resubmitted to academic journals. These comments often required us to revisit our samples and re-examine our stated inclusion criteria.

Analyzing and synthesizing primary studies can be a particularly daunting thread in the research synthesis process. As Hart (2018) noted research synthesis entails "reading to review" (p. 53) rather than reading for information. As Hart explained, this meant approaching primary studies with a particular set of questions. Analyzing primary studies often involved our use of code books and matrices, which were familiar qualitative analytic strategies that we had used in

Conclusions **181**

our own empirical research projects. For each research synthesis, we designed an analytic review template (ART) that helped us to identify and organize significant information about each primary study.

Our attempts to analyze were often troubling as we grappled with tensions that accompanied efforts to standardize our readings of primary students. In particular, we worried about simplifying complex issues, decontextualizing findings from participants' lived experiences, and losing sight of salient factors. We handled these tensions by creating detailed matrices that helped us to document, and thus continually revisit, the complexities of primary studies (Appendix M).

Our analysis was also complicated by the particular analytical tools – including discourse analysis – that we brought to the primary studies. For example, in our meta-ethnography, we attended to the metaphors used by highly cited family literacy scholars. We also attended to their explicit use of the words "race" and "racism." In our metasynthesis, we attended to findings identified by BIPOC scholars. Once again, these processes were not as simple as we expected. For example, what counts as a metaphor? What counts as a finding? In order to achieve clarity, we engaged in reliability tests with each other – individually analyzing particular studies, comparing our analyses, and arriving at shared definitions to drive our collective analysis.

As we conducted our analyses, we experienced many false starts and procedural revisions. We sometimes rejected approaches that were too time intensive and sought alternative yet viable means. We continuously asked ourselves, which approaches were most useful and which were taking us down pathways that distracted from our synthetic purposes. Our tendency was to try to do too much and on multiple occasions future publications emerged out of our frustration in not being able to address all the questions and issues raised by our analyses.

Another thread through each of the chapters has been the choices involved in *representing and distributing research syntheses.* Indeed, across time and across synthesis approaches there are differences. We have found that the publication venue has a significant influence on the writing and presentation of research syntheses. Because the published reviews described in this volume appeared in highly ranked peer-reviewed journals, they assumed the form of formal academic papers, complete with extensive theoretical and methodological sections. Across time and publication venues, we note that reviewers have been mixed in their expectations for the amount of procedural detail to be included in research syntheses. We see academic venues moving toward increasingly high expectations for detail. This reflects our belief that disclosing details about each methodological step is important for enhancing trustworthiness. In addition, detail provides a road map of decisions for readers to consider and reveals the emergent, subjective, and inherently partial nature of all syntheses. Paradoxically, an adequate description of procedures should raise questions and considerations for readers.

In the opening of each chapter, we referenced related reports that were generated by each synthesis. Not all of these products were published in major research

182 Conclusions

journals. For example, we wrote an invited column for *Language Arts*, a practitioner-oriented journal (Compton-Lilly, Lewis Ellison, & Rogers, 2019), to share the results of our research synthesis with practitioners. Research syntheses can be put to work in different ways. In an era of calls for evidence for educational decisions, it is important to find ways to synthesize research findings for various audiences. However, as with all research syntheses, all evidence is partial and even the best conducted research syntheses are never neutral; they inevitably bring ideological and political aims as discussed later in this chapter.

Thus, we are also left with lingering questions:

- What other types of research syntheses might be possible?
- What new directions do we imagine for publishing and disseminating research syntheses?
- In what ways have journals shaped the genre of research syntheses?
- What flexibility and advances might be necessary to accommodate a variety of approaches?
- How might research syntheses reach a broader audience?
- What representational choices are possible given the constraints of print-based publishing?
- How might synthetic methodologies be used to attend to and represent multimodal research findings?

For example, research synthesists have reviewed performance-based methodologies, including dance, art, and theatre. Yet to truly attend to this body of scholarship, synthesists must be sensitive to not only explicitly stated findings but also to representational choices (e.g. modalities, dissemination venues, attention to participants' words). We are starting to see examples of podcasts and videos linked to articles and journals. The *Journal of Literacy Research* and *Teachers College Record* provide short video podcast summaries of published articles. These methods disseminate key findings more quickly and to a broader audience. Similarly, executive summaries, abstracts, and briefs often appeal to policy makers at local, state, and national levels. For example, CITE-ITEL – a public knowledge project related to literacy teacher education – may soon include a webpage devoted to review-centric studies and provide easily accessible abstracts to a larger audience. As it becomes common practice for tables, figures, and appendices to be published as online companion materials to articles, research synthesists might consider publishing descriptive summaries of key synthesis findings online to increase dissemination and access to decision-making audiences.

As we revisit the chapters in the book, we again turn to the thread of *decolonizing research syntheses*. In making transparent our decisions and positionalities, we make the case for humanizing research syntheses. Often, research synthesists are treated as if they are neutral or absent from analytic processes. This is an artifact of post-positivism and reflects the assumption that researchers can be objective in how they select research sites and participants, generate data, and report findings. These ideas have long been debunked by qualitative researchers, yet continue to operate in regard to research syntheses. In each chapter, we have provided examples of how we turned a reflexive lens on ourselves as research synthesists as we made decisions about how to synthesize primary studies and/or in our retrospective analysis of the process.

What might it mean to decolonize research syntheses? We are cautious to not overstate our claims about decolonization of academic spaces. We are aware of critiques of decolonization as a metaphor that detracts attention from scholars who have historically been marginalized by dominant ideas and traditions (Tuck & Yang, 2012). Whether engaging in discussions about reclaiming land or academic spaces, questions are raised about intellectual property, knowledge, voice, and representation. We cannot deny an academic legacy that has privileged white male thought, narrow definitions of logic, and the manifest destiny of certain ideas and truths.

We move closest to a decolonizing stance in Chapter 6, where we intentionally designed our metasynthesis to focus on the family literacy scholarship of BIPOC scholars. At the same time, we recognize very real dangers related to the presumption of scholarly discovery, re-presenting ideas, and ultimately claiming authorship. A process of decolonizing and/or colonizing our research syntheses occurred with each choice we made – from the composition of the authorship team, to the identification of guiding questions, our choices of databases, exclusion criteria for scholarship, representation of the findings, and the language choices made and used along the way. We recognize that our attempts at decolonization are partial and limited, despite our best and critical intentions.

To assist research syntheses in negotiating the challenges inherent in producing a research synthesis that is useful, systematic, and decolonizing, we offer questions to be considered at each stage in a research synthesis process (see Table 7.1).

The Vast Range of Research Syntheses

As discussed in the introduction to this book, there are many types of research syntheses (see Appendix A). We have focused on five different types of syntheses, but these examples only begin to capture the full landscape of research synthesis scholarship. Furthermore, research syntheses have influenced not only our scholarly work, but also various aspects of our lives. For example, Stephen Hawking's *A Brief History of Time: From the Big Bang to Black Holes* (1988) is a popular science text that explores the structure, origin, development, and future of our universe. This text reviews a vast range of issues related to the universe and has inspired both a film and an opera. Hawking's text is one of a historical lineage of popular scientific syntheses that can be traced back to Darwin's *On the Origin of Species by Means of Natural Selection* (1859) which claimed the attention of non-specialist readers and attracted widespread interest, and eventually scientific agreement regarding theories of evolution. These books reviewed large bodies of

184 Conclusions

scholarship and have transformed how people locate themselves within time, on earth, and within the universe.

A close analysis of academic fields reveals a vast range of research syntheses that are not explicitly addressed in our book. These include historical reviews, conceptual mapping reviews, methodological syntheses, theoretical reviews,

TABLE 7.1 Questions to Consider Each Stage of the Research Synthesis Process

Designing a Research Synthesis	What is your purpose for looking across research in a given field?
	What conversations, tensions, and/or issues do you plan to explore?
	Do you seek to describe and interpret the landscape of a field?
	Are you interested in methodological, theoretical, or practical aspects presented in/across a body of scholarship?
	Are you updating a previously published literature review?
	Are you making a case for instructional practice based on a metasynthesis of findings?
	Are you seeking to reveal and/or explore gaps and silences in/across primary studies?
	What "mentor" articles might inform the design of your research synthesis?
	How was your inquiry team formed? What other voices might be needed?
	Who is not at the synthesis planning table that should be?
Searching and Sampling Relevant Literature	What databases and search terms might you start with and why?
	What types of research (e.g., published, peer-reviewed, cross-disciplinary) will you include?
	What databases will you not search and why?
	What body of scholarship will you explore?
	What timeframe will be examined?
Analyzing and Synthesizing the Studies	How will you organize the primary studies (e.g., thematically, chronologically, methodologically)?
	What aspects of the primary studies are of more or less interest?
	How will you maintain attention to significant contextual information (e.g., participants, setting, and structural challenges) as you analyze primary studies?
	How will you ensure that your analysis process is both thorough and manageable?

Representing and Distributing Research Syntheses	What is the best balance between authors' interpretations and participants' voices in the synthesis of studies?
	How might syntheses attend to and represent the multimodal nature of the primary studies?
	Who is your audience and what do they need to know?
	What details are necessary for your audience?
	What will make your research synthesis useful and compelling to your audience?
	How might we use social media and Internet-based platforms to support dissemination of and access to the synthesis?
Decolonizing Research Syntheses	What role have the researchers, dominant ideas in the field, and academic conventions played in your research synthesis process? Have these considerations silenced or dismissed other ways of making sense of a body of scholarship?
	Whose voices have you included or ignored?
	What dominant ways of thinking have been sustained, challenged, questioned, or extended?
	What are the histories of these ideas which may extend much further than articles published in academic journals?
	What does the syntheses help scholars or practitioners to understand that was formerly invisible, ignored, or unexamined?

international reviews, and reviews that are explicitly designed to inform practice. While most of the research syntheses discussed in this book have focused on education, and specifically literacy education, in this section, we intentionally broaden our scope to include a few illustrative reviews that extend beyond the field of education. While we have presented each of these review types as separate categories, in several cases, there is clear overlap across the typology presented.

Historical Reviews

Historical reviews draw on primary research and historical documents to track the development of practices, policies, and ideas over time. These reviews are often presented chronologically starting with early research and moving toward more current examinations of practice and thought. Many of these reviews propose possibilities for future research, theorizing, practice, and/or policy. For example, in their introduction to a special issue of the *Journal of Educational Media, Memory, and Society*, Fuchs, Bruch, and Annegarn-Gläß (2016) present a chronological review of the history of educational films and identify five main themes

186 Conclusions

that have defined the course of their development. They maintained that the "detailed study of the history of educational films within the fields of historical educational research and historical film research ... [is] one aspect of the sustained 'media revolution' that is now affecting schools and education" (p. 10).

In some cases, historical reviews have been credited with creating a foundational knowledge base that has defined an emerging body of scholarship. For example, Smagorinsky (personal communication) recently noted that when Braddock (1963) published a review of studies related to writing composition, "It was the first time in which composition research had ever been brought together under one heading, under one roof. Before that it had been scattered widely." This synthetic volume identified several factors that affected writing (e.g., environmental factors, instructional factors, rhetorical considerations, assessment measures) and summarized five studies that were identified – using an extensive list of selection criteria – as "the most soundly based studies" (p. 55). Smagorinsky noted that this review had a powerful effect on writing scholars and helped to establish composition as an academic field.

Conceptual Mapping Reviews

Some scholars have used particular analysis and presentation tools to synthesize bodies of scholarship. Concept maps, originating in the field of science education, have been used in nursing education scholarship for over 25 years. These visual representations can take the form of charts, graphic organizers, tables, flow-charts, Venn Diagrams, timelines, or T-charts. The goal is to represent conceptual ideas within a field. Daley, Morgan, and Beman (2016) reviewed 221 articles, books, and book chapters to examine emergence of concept mapping practices in nursing research. Through their synthesis, they track the emergence and use of concept mapping and propose future research ventures to better understand how these tools might be used to support the learning of nursing candidates. This kind of conceptual mapping might also prove useful to educational researchers to understand the history and trajectory of knowledge flows.

Methodological Syntheses

Methodological syntheses attend to the methodological tools that have been used within a particular area of study. They may trace the lineage of methodological changes that have occurred within an area of study, propose the use of previously underutilized methodologies, and/or critique of an over-reliance on particular methodological approaches. For example, Liu and Brown (2015) presented a methodological synthesis of research that explored the effectiveness of corrective feedback for L2 writers. Based on an analysis of 32 published studies and 12 dissertations, they identified methodological limitations and inconsistencies including inadequate reporting of research contexts, methodologies, and statistical analyses; research designs with questionable ecological validity; and the wide array of quality indicators used to evaluate both writing and feedback. They offered recommendations for improving the methodological approached used for future research.

Theoretical Reviews

Theoretical reviews attend to the theoretical frameworks that have been used within bodies of scholarship. Specifically, they can consider not only which frameworks have been used, but also how they have been applied and described. Hodges, Feng, Kuo, and McTigue (2016) identify various bodies of theory (e.g., schema theory, transactional theory, sociocultural theory) that have been used to frame reading and writing research. They focused on the theories used to frame studies published in the *Journal of Adolescent and Adult Literacy* and suggest that future research should clarify differences between commonly used theories and extend the range of theories that are applied to the teaching of reading and writing. Theoretical reviews can suggest possibilities for moving areas of research forward by proposing potentially useful lenses, frames, and theoretical constructs. While Hodges et al. (2016) identify and define theoretical frameworks that have been used in literacy research, other scholars (Hoon & Baluch, 2020) have identified how research syntheses can operate as spaces of "dialectical interrogation" (p. 1246) as scholars analyze primary studies as sites of theoretical consolidation and/or disruption. In these research syntheses, "theory is conceptualized as a continuum where single theorizing outcomes represent interim struggles that are part of an emerging story and/or are a stimulus to further theorizing" (Hoon & Baluch, 2020, p. 1251).

International Reviews

International reviews examine bodies of research across international borders. These reviews might aspire to international comparison, attend to research within a section of the globe or synthesize research from around the globe. Omolewa (2007) examined that how indigenous modes of education in Africa might inform educational practice beyond Africa. Specifically, this review identified characteristics, goals, modes of transmission, and teaching and learning strategies used across indigenous African educational spaces and suggested how adopting these elements might improve international educational practices.

Drawing on a set of studies conducted mostly in English-speaking nations, Kyriacou (1987) identified teacher stress and burnout as an international problem. Specifically, she reviewed a range of studies that collectively "have led to a much clearer understanding of teacher stress and burnout" (p. 146). She suggested that seeking ways to reduce stress in schools should be an international priority.

188 Conclusions

Reviews Designed to Inform Practice

Some reviews of scholarship are designed to synthesize large bodies of information to directly inform practice. These reviews generally include clearly articulated practice or policy implications. For example, Hattie (2003) drew on an extensive synthesis of research related to the role teachers play in student learning. After identifying the respective contributions of home, schools, principals, and peers, he identified teachers as playing an essential and significant role and reviewed scholarly claims made about expert teachers. Finally, he drew on primary studies to inform the design of an empirical study that explicitly compared the practices and thinking of "expert teachers" to teachers that he described as "experienced" but not expert (p. 10).

Drawing on scholarship grounded in cognitive and educational psychology, Dunlosky, Rawson, Marsh, Nathan, and Willingham (2013) reviewed scholarship related to effective learning techniques. They identified "10 learning techniques in detail and offer recommendations about their relative utility" (p. 5). They selected techniques that were relatively easy to use, could be adapted to various learning contexts, and that students identified as helpful (e.g., summarizing, highlighting/underlining, keyword mnemonics, imagery, rereading). They argued that these techniques were widely useful to students and could contribute to increased learning.

The Contribution of Technology to Research Synthesis

As we have reiterated across this volume, it is a productive and promising time for research syntheses. Since the 1980s – when qualitative research began to emerge as a respected and viable scholarly venture – thousands of qualitative studies across a vast range of disciplines have been published. Virtually all of these studies suffer the same enduring criticism, they are not generalizable. However, given this vast amount of work alongside the systematic and grounded nature of the studies, collectively they must tell us something. Thankfully, we are working in an era when technology has become a powerful tool for storing, accessing, and analyzing large bodies of scholarship.

The Emergence of Academic Databases

In 1968, Summers noted that "regardless of whether one would call the ever expanding volume of published materials a flood or an explosion, the issue is … one of system control, organization and dissemination" (p. 8). In short, the number of studies in literacy, and other fields, was increasing exponentially, raising significant questions about the ability of scholars to organize, synthesize, and disseminate that research. Technology provided possible solutions. Drawing on the annual *Summary of Reading Investigations* by Gray and others, Summers made

Conclusions **189**

"the first attempt to work with the total corpus of research material, assess the utility of using the summaries as a part of the data base for information retrieval, and define some of the salient characteristics of the document collection" (pp. 10–11). In short, Summer accessed the complete bibliographic information for each annual summary and had that data transcribed onto paper tapes and punch cards, which were then converted to magnetic tapes. Summers (1968) noted that this repository was one of 18 clearinghouses that were combined, with support from the International Reading Association and Indiana University, to become ERIC (the *Educational Resources Information Center*, later the *Educational Research Information Center*). ERIC was originally a microfiche database and is now an online repository of abstracts and full-text publications that continue to be sponsored by the U.S. Department of Education. ERIC database coverage extends to conferences, meetings, government documents, theses, dissertations, reports, audiovisual media, bibliographies, directories, books, and monographs. This early online database was an essential resource for scholars long before modern search engines and databases became readily available.

Online resources continue to provide access to educational research. For example, *Research in the Teaching of English* (RTE), a literacy education journal sponsored by the National Council for the Teaching of English (NCTE) has published the annual *Annotated Bibliography of Research in the Teaching of English* since 2003 (Frederick et al., 2019; available at https://ncte.org/resources/journals/research-in-the-teaching-of-english/). This annotated list of scholarship presents research published in the area of English language arts that has been identified as being of interest to RTE readers. Other curated lists and archives include the previously mentioned CITE-ITEL archive, an interactive repository for research related to literacy teacher education. These resources supplement established academic search engines (e.g., *Academic Search*, *Education Full Text*, *ProQuest*, and *JSTOR: The Scholarly Journal Archive*) and public Web search engines, including *Google Scholar*.

As noted in Appendix C, which provides a partial list of available research-oriented databases, some databases focus on national bodies of scholarship. For example, the Australian Education Index is produced by Cunningham Library at the Australian Council for Educational Research. It provides access to nearly 220,000 entries relating to educational research, policy, and practice, from 1979 to the present.

Other databases target areas of the world or particular language communities. For example, African Journals Online (AJOL), an independent database of journals published in Africa across disciplines, is the world's largest online library of peer-reviewed, African-published scholarly journals. It hosts 524 Journals, including 262 open access journals. Serving scholars who are speakers of Spanish and Portuguese, Fuente Académica is a collection of academic journals from Latin America, Portugal, and Spain, with particular emphasis on agriculture, biological sciences, economics, history, law, literature, philosophy, psychology, public administration, religion, and sociology. This database can be purchased through

190 Conclusions

EBSCO and includes full-text articles from scholarly journals. There are also open access databases such as Redalyc and SciELO.

While some databases aspire to be truly international, closer analysis reveals that this is rarely the case. For example, Dissertation Abstracts International, currently ProQuest Dissertations and Theses database is a bibliography of international dissertations and theses published since 1938. However, most of the texts included are from American and British Universities with a limited number of dissertations from the rest of the world.

Bibliometrics as a Tool for Research Synthesis

As we write in the year 2020, it is essential to recognize the development of bibliometric mapping and science mapping processes that offer tools for identifying and organizing large bodies of scholarship, identifying influential publications within a field, reporting citation patterns rates, and analyzing historical developments within fields of study. In recent years, several options have become available, including VOSViewer and CitNetExplorer. For example, VOS stands for *Visualization of Similarities* and draws on the logic of social network analyses. This tool allows for quicker and comprehensive analyses of citation patterns and networks operating within a data set. Using these bibliometric tools, researchers can map networks and connections between and among documents, authors, keywords, and geographical areas. These quantitative analyses rely on metrics and the primary studies available in major databases, including SCOPUS and Web of Science.

Bibliometric analyses use descriptive statistics to document topographical trends in an area of study. Questions that might be asked of bibliometric reviews include:

- What is the volume, growth, and geographic distribution of research within a field over a period of time?
- What journals, authors, and articles have the highest citation rates?
- What thematic foci have garnered the most attention during a particular time period?
- What topics have particular journals addressed or not addressed during a particular time period?
- What relationship(s) exist between any of the above patterns?

Bibliographic tools can also be used to create visual representations – network maps – to depict relationships among multiple features of a literature search. In these maps, distances between items reflect similarities or relatedness (Van Eck & Waltman, 2009). Below, we present a worked example of "critical literacy research" to illustrate the potential of these tools. We close this section by reflecting on some of the limits that accompany the use of bibliometric tools.

A Worked Example of Bibliometric Mapping

We present this analysis to illustrate the potential of bibliometric analyses, specifically VOSViewer. Because VOSViewer is designed to search scholarship included in the SCOPUS database, only peer-reviewed journals included in that database are referenced in this illustrative example. Specifically, we searched peer-reviewed journals in SCOPUS using the search term "critical literacy research" between 2017 and 2019. We then scrubbed the records to exclude non-relevant scholarship that was inadvertently included in our search (e.g., biomedical, engineering, psychological research unrelated to literacy research). The remaining articles ($n =$ 374) were exported into a .CSV file which we then imported into VOSViewer. The following maps were generated:

- Citation analysis by journal sources
- Citation analysis by country
- Bibliographic coupling
- Co-authorship by country
- Co-occurrence of author keyword(s)

While there is no space here to present our full analysis, we offer two network maps focused on *co-authorship by country* and *co-occurrence of author keyword*. These maps provide a sense of the utility of Bibliometric tools for exploring critical literacy research. Note that across both these examples, our search was limited by the primary studies available in the Scopus database and by authors who used "critical literacy" as a keyword.

Our analysis of co-authorship by country identified 58 countries of origin for studies related to critical literacy research. Of these, we focused on 16 counties, based on researcher home institution, that meet our criteria of producing more than five publications. This allowed us to focus only on countries that had produced substantial amounts of critical literacy scholarship. Our map (Figure 7.1) illustrates the frequency of authorship by geographic location (home institution). This map not only reveals which counties have produced the most critical literacy scholarship, but also reveals international collaborations, represented by the lines and colors that connect geographic locations. For example, scholars from the USA frequently collaborate with scholars in Canada and the Netherlands, as indicated by the green-threaded network. Readers should be reminded that our search only represents the years of 2017–2019 and, as discussed below, geopolitical biases are built into the database.

Our second search examined the co-occurrence-author keywords across a different subsample of studies from across the same original SCOPUS search. VOSViewer identified 1167 author keywords (see Figure 7.2). Again, we limited our search to occurrences of five or more in order to focus on substantial patterns. Sixty-two author keywords meet our criteria. On the resulting map, clustering of

192 Conclusions

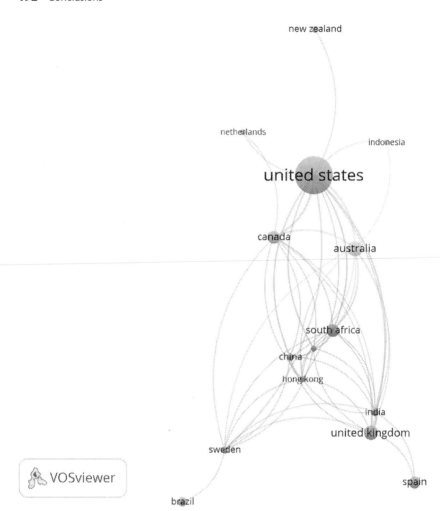

FIGURE 7.1 Frequency of Authorship by Geographic Location of Home Institution

keywords provides insight into the foci of critical literacy scholarship. The size of the nodes represents the frequency/prevalence of each keyword. For example, there are two main clusters of co-occurring keywords in this particular data set: critical literacy and teacher education. Scholarship related to teacher education tends to fall into two clusters, related to adolescence and digital media literacies. Around the critical literacy node, we see orbiting areas of focus – as represented through keywords – that include information literacy, media literacy, and urban education. Based on its size, the keyword *teacher education* appeared frequently. Based on its relative proximity to adolescence and digital media literacies, teacher education is more connected with these bodies of scholarship than critical literacy scholarship.

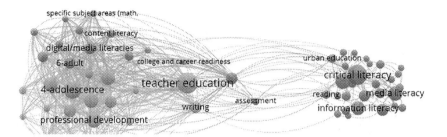

FIGURE 7.2 Co-occurrence of Author Keywords across Subsample of Studies

In VOSViewer, multiple representational modes are used to present information, including color, proximity, size, frequency, and linkages. With VOSViewer, scholars can zoom in to highlight each node and examine subnetworks of scholarship. It is also possible to overlay *time as a factor* in order to identify shifts in keywords across time.

Limits of Bibliometrics

As the examples presented above attest, bibliometrics have the potential to make significant contributions to how scholars make sense of large bodies of scholarship. However, these tools are still evolving and their potential is always limited by which databases, and thus which primary studies, are searched and sampled. In addition, the imprecision of search terms, complexities related to geographic location/home institution, and the researchers' flawed interactions with search engines (Zimmer, 2009) can complicate and diminish the validity of resulting findings. In our own use of VOSViewer, we found that appropriately using this tool required multiple attempts, including several abandoned efforts, before we were able to conduct a viable search. In short, we needed to carefully review results each time we conducted a search, adjust analytic settings, and explore various features of the online tool.

In addition, it is important to recognize that all search engines systematically exclude certain sites and certain types of texts. While some search engines include only peer-reviewed research, other search engines include unpublished and non-peer-reviewed products that some scholars might prefer not to include. As noted above, even a careful search will sometimes include texts that are far-removed from the target body of scholarship; thus, it is essential for scholars to review and scrub the data elicited through a computerized search.

As Wallin (2005) reported, too often scholars use bibliometric tools without being aware of the shortcomings of these tools. For example, qualitative work is often published in a larger range of journals than is represented in the data set associated with a particular tool. For example, some scholars have found that SCOPUS, the database used by VOSViewer, provides relatively extensive coverage

194 Conclusions

of social sciences texts (Hernández-Torrano, 2019). In contrast, Hammarfelt (2016) found both the *Web of Science* and *SCOPUS* "insufficient" (p. 126) for research in the humanities. These mechanical limitations are further confounded by conceptual ones including whether or not citation rates truly represent the impact a publication has on a field, privileging of particular journals based on visibility, overattention to first-authors over authorial teams, and international publication and citation patterns (Wallin, 2005). In addition, the detailed citation mining that could systematically track the impact of particular publications over a long time periods of time is rare. This mining might entail comparing the citation rates for particular articles to citations rates within a particular journal and/ or the statistical normalization of citation rates for a defined cluster of articles.

Finally, some scholars have argued that search engines can be constructed to deliberately contribute to the construction of particular political and ideological discourses. These efforts can be intentionally expansive if they generate exposure to diverse and opposing views. However, they can also be used to restrict the range of ideas and perspectives available to scholars. For example, drawing on her analysis of mainstream media, (Noble, 2013) highlighted the forms of cultural privileging that operate through Google searches that "prioritize the interests of its commercial partners and advertisers, rather than rendering the social, political and economic interests of Black women and girls visible" (p. 2). Zimmer (2009) noted that "Web search engines indirectly contribute to political organization and deliberative discourse by generating unintentional exposures to diverse and opposing views" (p. 513). The results of these types of actions are apparent not only in the continuing depiction of racial, linguistic, and gendered stereotypes, but also in the dissemination of conspiracy theories, fake news, and anti-scientific rhetoric.

We would hope that academic search engines are immune to these tendencies, but it is clear that search engines do serve as gatekeepers, particularly in regard to international publications. As we access and use these tools, we must remain cognizant of the potential for these tools to present particular values, ethical stances, and claims. As presented below, these ideological considerations are relevant not only to the curation of digital resources, but can also accompany traditional research syntheses and affect their use.

Politics and Research Syntheses

Education has always been a political enterprise. From the use of the bible as a central text for teaching children to read, through the McGuffey readers with their messages about God and nature, the value of work, and focus on social conduct (Bohning, 1986), through Sunday School texts that highlighted social consciousness, interdependence, and the benefits of cooperative economic and industrial relations (Teitelbaum, 1990), political ideologies have always influenced education. This has been true of the creation and use of research syntheses related

Conclusions **195**

to literacy education. Below, we offer a brief review of two significant research syntheses that reviewed literacy scholarship with the explicit intent to impact literacy educational practices and policies at state and local levels.

In 1985, the National Academy of Education produced *Becoming a Nation of Readers* (BNR; Anderson et al., 1985) which drew on three broad areas of research related to human cognition – linguistics, child development, and behavioral science "to synthesize a diverse, rich body of scientific information into a systematic account of beginning reading and the comprehension of language" (p. 6). The report was explicitly focused on educational practice and ended with a four-page list of implications for parents, teachers, schools, and teacher educators. However, this publication was met with concern and critique from literacy organizations and their members (Davidson, 1988) leading to the publication of an edited "counterpoint" volume, which was described as providing a forum for the "responses of a number of reading authorities" to … issues in BNR that are considered to be controversial, incomplete, or in consistent" (Davidson, 1988, p. 1).

Becoming a Nation of Readers (Anderson et al., 1985) while clearly controversial at the time of its publication, may seem less contentious to contemporary literacy scholars in regard to its stated implications for educating children and in comparison to more recent documents including the *National Reading Panel: Teaching Children to Read* report (2000). For example, *Becoming a Nation of Readers* recommended that "teachers of beginning reading should present well-designed phonics instruction," "reading primers should be interesting, comprehensible, and give children opportunities to apply phonics," and "teachers should devote more time to comprehension instruction" (p. 118). While the report was a clear call for more systematic phonics instruction, it pales in comparison to the supposedly scientific findings of the *National Reading Panel Report*. Problematic claims about the importance of systematic phonic approaches, phonemic awareness, and fluency were particularly evident in the widely read summary of the report, which Allington (2005) described as "misrepresenting the evidence" (p. 464) presented in the full report. He noted:

> Errors of fact in the Summary are not simply the result of a difficulty in dumbing down complicated stuff for public consumption. The errors in reporting the findings reflect, to my mind, a simple ideological bias in favor of a particular sort of reading instruction for beginning readers and for struggling readers—the sort of reading instruction that the full NRP report doggedly avoided recommending. (p. 464)

In addition to the *errors* represented in the widely read summary, there were also significant concerns about the corpus of primary studies included. As Garan (2001) noted, the analysis included only studies with "experimental or quasi-experimental control groups." In addition, each study had to "measure reading as an outcome" (p. 501). Critics of the report lamented the significant amounts

196 Conclusions

of literacy research were ignored including research related to writing, student interests and motivation as well as research that recognizes the significance of children's cultural, linguistic, and socioeconomic backgrounds. Perhaps most unsettling were Garan's concluding comments, which are particularly relevant to our discussion of research syntheses presented in this book. Garan wrote:

> If *Teaching Children to Read* [the NRP report] were a typical research study, published in an education journal and destined to be read only by other researchers, then I could simply end my analysis by saying that the panel's own words have established that the research base in its report on phonics is so flawed that the results do not even matter. However, as we have seen, this study has clout. It has a public relations machine behind it that has already promulgated the results throughout a very wide, very public arena as representing unbiased scientific "truth." Both Congress and the National Institute of Child Health and Human Development are committed to ensuring that the findings of the NRP report affect classroom instruction.
>
> (Garan, 2001, p. 506)

In the years that followed the release of the National Reading Panel Report, educators in the United States witnessed a barrage of initiatives that both drew on the findings of the report and further truncated the abilities of teachers to make decisions about what and how they taught. Specifically, the NRP Report opened a door to more federal oversight of schools and the subsequent implementation of *No Child Left Behind*, *Reading First*, *Race to the Top*, and the *Common Core State Standards*. As Garan reported, the NRP report played a significant role in literacy initiatives that followed and continues to impact educational experiences for children across the United States, despite significant critiques of the original report (Allington, 2005; Garan, 2001, 2005; Garan, Shanahan, & Henkin, 2001; Krashen, 2001; Shanahan, 2003) and the limited empirical evidence for related initiatives (e.g., Reading First, see Gamse, Bloom, Kemple, & Jacob, 2008).

We present *Becoming a Nation of Readers* (Anderson et al., 1985) and the *National Reading Panel Report* (2000) as cautionary examples of how research syntheses have been used to endorse and support particular ideological positions. Problematic uses of research syntheses have been used to impact literacy educational practice and policies in many parts of the world. Sometimes this results when U.S.-based reports are taken up and applied to international contexts. In other cases, other countries have supported the creation and dissemination of ideologically based research syntheses. For example, the *Rose Report* in the United Kingdom (Rose, 2006) despite being titled an "independent review," has been heavily critiqued as an ideologically informed analysis that argued for the use of synthetic phonics as a major dimension of early reading instruction.

This report has been heavily critiqued for misrepresenting available scholarship (Wyse, & Goswami, 2008; Wyse, & Styles, 2007).

In some fields, high-quality and methodologically explicit systematic reviews that present comprehensive or exhaustive searches of the field are considered essential resources for framing research within particular fields. These systematic reviews often include detailed protocols for reviewing experimental and/or quasi-experimental work. However, as noted above, educational research is an applied field. What works in particular experimental conditions may not transfer to the real complexities of teaching and learning contexts. Thus, it is always questionable whether any single research synthesis can provide a definitive truth. Regardless, the public's research imagination can be shaped by systematic reviews of quantitative/experimental and experimental.

In this book, we have argued for the expansion of our collective research imagination to explore how synthesizing qualitative research can be useful, trustworthy, and transferable. Given the breadth and scope of qualitative research in so many areas of social sciences, it is important in order to advance our methodological tool kit in order to synthesize what has been learned across primary studies. Educators often hear about the importance of "evidence-based" practices. Yet, what counts as evidence? Who decides? As educators, we have witnessed the broadening of these conversations to include classroom-based studies that examine the complexities of literacy practices within local contexts. As a field, we need to be able to point to the collective evidence from this research to inform practice and policy decisions.

Conclusions

While research syntheses are sometimes treated as applying reductionist processes to primary studies and then looking across their subcomponents, we have attempted to illustrate diversity in research synthesis techniques and have raised important issues related to methodological and theoretical integrity across this genre of scholarship. As a research team, we have engaged in collaborative synthetic scholarship for over a decade. This volume chronicles our journey in conducting review-centric work in literacy studies. Our focus has been on synthesizing qualitative research to advance theoretical and methodological transparency. As we reflect on our process, we recognize the significance of our team approach. All of our syntheses – even our doctoral dissertation literature reviews – benefited from collaboration. These collaborations have influenced and improved the questions we asked, the resources we consulted and the methodological moves we made.

As the field of education moves forward, we recommend assembling international teams of scholars from across the world, scholars from different cultural, religious, and linguistic backgrounds, and racially diverse scholars. Diversity is an asset that must be channeled as we consider the potential and power of collective

198 Conclusions

knowledge. Not only will these collaborations improve our syntheses, but they will also help to ensure that scholarship is produced and distributed across diverse geographical contexts.

As we approached the close of this book, we asked ourselves "How do we imagine this book building on and advancing the landscape of research syntheses?" One potential consequence of focusing on research synthesis is elevating the status of high-quality syntheses of qualitative research into public sphere decisions that require evidence-based practices. Often, "evidence-based" practices are equated quantitative rather than qualitative evidence. Yet, this is short-sighted due to the collective wealth of findings that have been presented by qualitative researchers.

In the case of family literacy, it is common for educational leaders in schools to recognize that traditional approaches to collaborating with families do not work; particularly for children and youth whose cultural and linguistic backgrounds differ from white, middle class norms and values. At the same time, there is an avalanche of research conducted by BIPOC scholars that describes, interprets, and explains literacy practices in families and communities. This research could be the basis for building connections with teachers and schools. By synthesizing qualitative research that includes lengthy observations, in-depth interviews and the generation of artifacts, the perspectives, voices, and practices of families are honored. Looking across these studies to identify patterns and promising practices has the potential to inform new respectful and responsive approaches to working with families. These syntheses could also provide important information that highlights gaps in the field and identifies new directions for research.

Our hope is that this book contributes to strengthening review designs and reporting practices. This might, in turn, expand the vista of the types of research syntheses that can be carried out not only in literacy studies, but also across the educational spectrum and beyond.

Related Appendices

Common Qualitative Research Synthesis Designs

Appendix C: Databases Used by University Scholars for Educational Research

Appendix M: Descriptive Table – List #1

References

Allington, R. L. (2005). Ideology is still trumping evidence. *Phi Delta Kappan, 86*(6), 462–468.

Anderson, R. C., Hiebert, E. H., Scott, J. A., Wilkinson, I. A., Becker, W., & Becker, W. C. (1985). *Becoming a nation of readers: The report of the commission on reading*. National Academy of Education, National Institute of Education, and the Center for the Study of Reading.

Bohning, G. (1986). The McGuffey Eclectic Readers: 1836–1986. *The Reading Teacher, 40*(3), 263–269.

Bourdieu, P. (1993). *Sociology in question*. Sage.

Bourdieu, P. (2003). Participant objectivation. *The Journal of the Royal Anthropological Institute*, 9(2), 281–294.

Braddock, R. (1963). *Research in written composition*. National Council of Teachers of English.

Compton-Lilly, C., Lewis Ellison, T. & Rogers, R. (2019). The promise of family literacy: Possibilities and practices for educators. *Language Arts*, 97 (1), 25–35.

Daley, B. J., Morgan, S., & Beman, S. B. (2016). Concept maps in nursing education: A historical literature review and research directions. *Journal of Nursing Education*, 55(11), 631–639.

Darwin, C. (1859). *On the origin of species by means of natural selection*. Murray.

Davidson, J. L. (1988). *Counterpoint and beyond: A response to "Becoming a Nation of Readers"*. National Council of Teachers of English.

Dunlosky, J., Rawson, K. A., Marsh, E. J., Nathan, M. J., & Willingham, D. T. (2013). Improving students' learning with effective learning techniques: Promising directions from cognitive and educational psychology. *Psychological Science in the Public Interest*, 14(1), 4–58.

Frederick, A., Crampton, A., David, S., Baker, J., Beach, R., Fogarty, E., … Thein, A. (2019). Annotated bibliography of research in the teaching of English. *Research in the Teaching of English*, 53(3), AB1–AB43.

Fuchs, E., Bruch, A., & Annegarn-Gläß, M. (2016). Educational films: A historical review of media innovation in schools. *Journal of Educational Media, Memory, and Society*, 8(1), 1–13.

Gamse, B. C., Bloom, H. S., Kemple, J. J., & Jacob, R. T. (2008). *Reading First Impact Study: Interim Report. NCEE 2008–4016*. National Center for Education Evaluation and Regional Assistance.

Garan, E. M. (2001). Beyond the smoke and mirrors: A critique of the National Reading Panel report on phonics. *Phi Delta Kappan*, 82(7), 500–506.

Garan, E. M. (2005). Murder your darlings: A scientific response to the voice of evidence in reading research. *Phi Delta Kappan*, 86(6), 438–443.

Garan, E. M., Shanahan, T., & Henkin, R. (2001). What does the report of the National Reading Panel really tell us about teaching phonics? *Language Arts*, 79(1), 61.

Hammarfelt, B. (2016). Beyond coverage: Toward a bibliometrics for the humanities. In M. Ochsner, S. E. Hug, & H. D. Daniel (Eds.), *Research assessment in the humanities* (pp. 115–131). Springer.

Hart, C. (2018). *Doing a literature review: Releasing the social science research imagination*. Sage.

Hattie, J. A. C. (2003). *Teachers make a difference: What is the research evidence? Paper presented at the ACER Research Conference*, Melbourne, Australia. Retrieved from http://research. acer.edu.au/research_conference_2003/4/

Hawking, S. (1988). *A brief history of time: From Big Bang to Black Holes*. Random House.

Hernández-Torrano, D. (2019). Mapping global research on child well-being in school contexts: A bibliometric and network analysis (1978–2018). *Child Indicators Research*, 42, 1–22.

Hodges, T. S., Feng, L., Kuo, L. J., & McTigue, E. (2016). Discovering the literacy gap: A systematic review of reading and writing theories in research. *Cogent Education*, 3(1), 1–13.

Hoon, C., & Baluch, A. M. (2020). The role of dialectical interrogation in review studies: Theorizing from what we see rather than what we have already seen. *Journal of Management Studies*, 57(6), 1246–1271.

200 Conclusions

Krashen, S. (2001). More smoke and mirrors: A critique of the National Reading Panel report on fluency. *Phi Delta Kappan*, 83(2), 119–123.

Kyriacou, C. (1987). Teacher stress and burnout: An international review. *Educational Research*, 29(2), 146–152.

Liu, Q., & Brown, D. (2015). Methodological synthesis of research on the effectiveness of corrective feedback in L2 writing. *Journal of Second Language Writing*, 30, 66–81.

National Reading Panel. (2000). *National reading panel: Teaching children to read: An evidence-based assessment of the scientific research literature on reading and its implications for reading instruction: Reports of the subgroups.* Washington, DC: U.S. Department of Health and Human Services, Public Health Service, National Institutes of Health, National Institute of Child Health and Human Development.

Noble, S. U. (2013). Google search: Hyper-visibility as a means of rendering Black women and girls invisible. *In Visible Culture*, (19), 1–31.

Omolewa, M. (2007). Traditional African modes of education: Their relevance in the modern world. *International Review of Education*, 53(5–6), 593–612.

Rogers, R., & Schaenen, I. (2014). Critical discourse analysis in literacy education: A review of the literature. *Reading Research Quarterly*, 49(1), 121–143.

Rogers, R., Malancharuvil-Berkes, E., Mosley, M., Hui, D., & Joseph, G. O. G. (2005). Critical discourse analysis in education: A review of the literature. *Review of Educational Research*, 75(3), 365–416.

Rose, J. (2006). *Independent review of the teaching of early reading.* Department for Education and Skills Publications.

Shanahan, T. (2003). based reading instruction: Myths about the National Reading Panel report. *The Reading Teacher*, 56(7), 646–655.

Summers, E. G. (1968). Reading research literature: Identification and retrieval. *Reading Research Quarterly*, 4(1), 5–48.

Swartz, D. (1997). *Culture and power: The sociology of Pierre Bourdieu.* Chicago University Press.

Teitelbaum, K. (1990). "Critical Lessons" from Our Past: Curricula of Socialist Sunday Schools in the United States. *Curriculum Inquiry*, 20(4), 407–436.

Tuck, E., & Yang, K. W. (2012). Decolonization is not a metaphor. *Decolonization: Indigeneity, Education & Society*, 1(1), 1–40.

Van Eck, N., & Waltman, J. (2009). Software survey: VOSViewer, a computer program for bibliometric mapping. *Scientometrics*, 84, 523–538.

Wacquant, J. D. (1992). Toward a social praxeology: The structure and logic of Bourdieu's sociology. In P. Bourdieu & J. D. Wacquant (Eds.), *An invitation to reflexive sociology* (pp. 1–6). University of Chicago Press.

Wallin, J. A. (2005). Bibliometric methods: Pitfalls and possibilities. *Basic & Clinical Pharmacology & Toxicology*, 97(5), 261–275.

Wyse, D., & Goswami, U. (2008). Synthetic phonics and the teaching of reading. *British Educational Research Journal*, 34(6), 691–710.

Wyse, D., & Styles, M. (2007). Synthetic phonics and the teaching of reading: The debate surrounding England's "Rose Report". *Literacy*, 41(1), 35–42.

Zimmer, M. (2009). Web search studies: Multidisciplinary perspectives on web search engines. In J. Hunsinger, L. Klastrup, & M. Allen (Eds.). *International handbook of internet research* (pp. 507–521). Springer.

APPENDIX A

Common Qualitative Research Synthesis Designs

Conceptual Literature Reviews

Conceptual reviews are intended to provide new insights and describe the theoretical landscape of a research area (e.g., Kennedy, 2007; Kucan & Palincsar, 2010). Hadley and Dicinkson (2020), for example, described their purpose in writing a conceptual review was to "work towards a more robust theoretical framework for vocabulary knowledge, focusing especially on the understudied dimensions of vocabulary depth, which can be used to evaluate and design measures for early childhood learners" (p. 1).

[1]Dissertation Literature Review

Dissertation literature reviews are generally forms of traditional literature reviews. The goal of these reviews is to analyze a body of scholarship to reveal themes, trends, gaps, controversies, and areas of confluence. This review will also raise awareness of various patterns and/or to argue for or against positions within the field.

Grounded Formal Theory

The goal of *grounded formal theory* is to "create a model explaining variations arising from differences in time and context that the contributing researchers could not have captured in their more circumscribed venues" (Thorne et al., 2004, p. 1355). Thus, grounded formal theory involves reflexively looking

---

[1] Indicates the types of research syntheses we highlight in this book.

202 Appendix A

across research studies to identify conditions under which generalizations might be warranted.

[1]Integrative Literature Reviews

Integrative literature reviews view primary research studies and the phenomenon explored in those studies through a particular lens or perspective. These reviews are "critical" if they appraise and analyze the scholarship being reviewed in relation to issues related to equity, representation, and bias.

Meta-analysis

Statistical analysis of research findings with a focus on cumulative and quantifiable sense of primary studies. Emphasis is generally placed on effect sizes. The goal is to produce generalizable findings.

[1]Meta-ethnography

Noblit and Hare's (1988) book is perhaps the best-known methodological sourcebook on this synthesis approach. Rather than focusing explicitly on findings from ethnographic studies, meta-ethnography involves analyzing the metaphors used in ethnographic studies to compare, synthesize, and create new understandings. Meta-ethnography aims to "account for all important similarities and differences in language, concepts, images, and other ideas around a target experience" (Sandelowski, Docherty, & Emden, 1997, p. 369). Specifically, meta-ethnographers identify and translate key metaphors in existent research studies to trace the development, refinement, and expansion of conceptual frameworks that continue to frame family literacy scholarship.

Metastudy

Metastudy involves a three-pronged process that includes "metatheory, meta-method and meta-data analysis" (Thorne et al., 2004, p. 1355). It involves a "set of detailed guidelines for search and retrieval, for creating an analytic dialogue, and for interpreting the findings deriving from a diverse set of studies into one another and into the possibilities of a coherent new whole" (p. 1356).

[1]Metasynthesis

These forms of systematic review integrate the findings from various research studies – quantitative and/or qualitative – that focus on a particular issue or body of scholarship. These primary studies involve the analysis of data collected through a wide range of quantitative and/or qualitative methodologies.

Narrative Review

The goal of a narrative review is to sample the field, tell a story about the research landscape, and situate one's work in a dialogue with existing research in a given field.

Qualitative Metasummary

This form of systematic review integrates qualitative findings that focus on a particular issue or body of scholarship. In the case of qualitative metasummary, the findings from primary studies are summarized, rather than integrated to create novel interpretations and insights into a body of scholarship. Sandelowski's and Barroso's (2003) description of qualitative metasummary involves the extraction of relevant findings statements from primary studies, the identification of themes across those findings and the calculation of effect sizes, which involves quantifying quantitative results. This process might entail calculating the frequency of particular types of findings across studies.

Qualitative Metasynthesis

Thorne and her colleagues (2004) explain that qualitative metasynthesis is an umbrella term that references various qualitative approaches that aspires toward the development of new knowledge through rigorous analysis of the findings from existent qualitative research. Metasynthesis can take a variety of forms including meta-ethnography, grounded formal theory, metastudy, and qualitative research integration. These forms of systematic review integrate the findings from various qualitative research studies that focus on a particular issue or body of scholarship. They involve the analysis of data collected through various analytic methods that include ethnography, grounded theory, and phenomenological analyses.

Qualitative Research Integration

Qualitative research integration references empirical studies that are directed "toward the combination of research findings in reports of qualitative studies" (p. 1357). Unlike metasummaries, which are simply an aggregation of qualitative findings, qualitative research integration references the "interpretive integration of qualitative findings… that offer novel interpretations" (p. 1358).

Research Synthesis

This is a broad umbrella term to reference any form of review that looks across primary studies. Research syntheses analyze and interpret research reports rather than collecting raw data. A synthesis is connective in that it tells a story of what

204 Appendix A

is known across the findings of a study. We side with Suri (2014) who argues that the purpose of syntheses is to create new knowledge by making connections or integration across studies visible. As evidenced by the chart/glossary, there are several subtypes of integrative research syntheses including: critical research syntheses, interpretive syntheses, and participatory syntheses.

Scoping Review

A scoping review is a tool for determining the scope or amount of coverage for a particular body of literature. It attends to the volume of research available as well as the general focus of that research. Its aim is to provide an "overview or map of the evidence" (Munn et al., 2018, p. 3) and is often used to identify the types of available evidence, methodologies used, relevant factors/characteristics, and/ or to identify gaps in a given field. A scoping review is sometimes a precursor to a systematic review.

Systematic Review

This kind of review is often described as "comprehensive" or "exhaustive" searches. There is an emphasis placed on protocols, explicit inclusion-exclusion criteria, evaluation of the quality of the methodology, and comprehensive searches. Suri (2014) critiques the systematic/unsystematic distinction which claims false objectivity and transparency, and has the "political impact of favoring post-positivism" (p. 22).

[1]Traditional Literature Review

Through collecting, analyzing, and representing findings across a corpus of studies, traditional literature reviews provide perspective on a field of study. They do so both in the breadth and depth of the primary studies reviewed.

APPENDIX B

Final Analytic Review Template for the Meta-Ethnography (ART)

Article #_____   Reviewer Initials _____

Analytical Review Template (ART)
for Family Literacy Meta-Ethnography
Coding of Handbook Chapters, Review Chapters, and
Literature Reviews Sections

Comments to reviewers:

Use direct quotes whenever possible

Attempt to capture the terminology/language used

APA reference for the article

Authors' name(s):

Author's institutional affiliation/location(s):

Author's department(s)/division(s), college(s) (if known):

Ethnicity of the author(s) (if known):

Summary of the chapter/article:

Term(s) used (circle one or more):

family literacy or

literacy in families

home literacy

funds of knowledge

Other: _____

206 Appendix B

Definition of literacy if provided (please quote):

What type of paper/chapter/handbook? (circle one or more)
Review
Empirical study
Theoretical paper
Position paper
Practitioner Information
Other: _____

What methodologies are used? (circle one or more)
Qualitative
Case study
Ethnography
Quantitative
Discourse Analysis
Other: _____
NA

What theoretical frameworks are privileged in this review?

This article addresses… (circle one or more)
Race
Cultural diversity
Linguistic diversity
Gender differences
SES differences
Other: _____

To what extent are these dimensions of difference addressed?

1. Racial, cultural, social class, and language differences were not discussed.
2. Differences were alluded to but only in general terms.
3. Differences are treated as methodological variables that correlated with specific literacy practices and/or eventual school success.
4. Race, social class, language, gender, or other difference are treated as central to the analysis.

Additional comments on diversity:
How, when, and to what extent are larger, macro contextual issues/factors addressed?

1. Not at all
2. In general terms
3. Discussed in depth

How does this review article relate to other review articles?

What is the role/position of the researcher?

What do/does the author/s cite as future directions?

What researchers are central to this author's arguments? (List all references coded as P or C)

Additional comments:

APPENDIX C

Databases Used by University Scholars for Educational Research

Database	Description of Data Bases	Audience	Index/Full Text	Country & Language
Academic OneFile	Gale's premier periodical resource, Gale Academic OneFile, provides millions of articles from over 17,000 scholarly journals and other authoritative sources – including thousands of podcasts and transcripts from NPR and CNN as well as videos from BBC Worldwide Learning (more info from the link).	Academic institutions	Mixed	Farmington Hills, Michigan Operates in 165 countries
Academic Search Complete	Academic Search Complete was first published in 2007 as Academic Premier. Academic Search Complete is a scholarly, multidisciplinary full-text database, with several thousand full-text periodicals, most of which are peer-reviewed journals. In addition to full text, this database offers indexing and abstracts for many more journals, monographs, reports, conference proceedings, etc. The database features PDF content going back as far as 1887, with the majority of full-text titles in native (searchable) PDF format. A selection of AP News videos is also available in this database. Note: Videos are only available if you are on campus or if you are using a VPN connection to campus. This resource is partially funded by MOREnet, the Missouri Research and Education Network.	Academic institutions	Index and abstract	Ipswich, Massachusetts
Academic Search Premier	(Also see Academic search premier) Academic Search Premier (EBSCO): More than 3,100 active full-text journals and magazines Nearly 2,800 active full-text peer-reviewed journals More than 1,200 active full-text peer-reviewed journals with no embargo More than 2,200 active full-text journals indexed in Web of Science or Scopus.	Academic libraries, government		Ipswich, Massachusetts

(*Continued*)

210 Appendix C

Database	Description of Data Bases	Audience	Index/Full Text	Country & Language
Academic Search	Academic search is a monthly indexing service. It was first published in 1997 by EBSCO Publishing in Ipswich, Massachusetts. Its academic focus is international universities, covering social science, education, psychology, and other subjects. Publishing formats covered are academic journals, magazines, newspapers, and CD-ROM.			Ipswich, Massachusetts
African Journals Online	This is an independent database of journals published in Africa across disciplines. African Journals Online (AJOL) is the world's largest online library of peer-reviewed, African-published scholarly journals. AJOL hosts 524 Journals, including 262 open access journals.	Researchers in numerous disciplines	Index, abstract, & full-text	Grahamstown, South Africa
Al Manhal	Al Manhal is the leading Arabic electronic information provider. They are the world's only provider of full-text searchable databases of scholarly and scientific publications from the Middle East, Africa, and Asia.	University, government, corporate, schools, public libraries	Full text	Dubai – United Arab Emirates Arabic
Art Index	Art Index is an art research database providing high-quality indexing for hundreds of national and international art journals, plus thousands of art dissertations. The index covers fine, decorative, and commercial art, as well as photography, film, and architecture.	Academic, libraries, public libraries, government	Index	Ipswich, Massachusetts English
ArticleFirst	ArticleFirst (also see FirstSearch) offers citations for nearly 12,500 journals in science, technology, medicine, social science, business, the humanities, and popular culture, 1990 to the present, updated daily.		Index	Dublin, Ohio

Australian Education Index	Australian Education Index (AEI) is produced by Cunningham Library at the Australian Council for Educational Research as one of its specialist databases. The Australian Education Index provides a complex and sophisticated subscription database consisting of nearly 220,000 entries relating to educational research, policy, and practice. Relevant to a wide range of people interested in education from schools and universities as well as the researcher, it covers the period 1979 to the present.	School and university-based educators and researchers	Index	Australia English
AUSTROM	A compilation of Australian databases that cover a wide range of subjects. Subjects include public affairs, the Australian economy, politics, legal studies, policing and criminology, architecture, education and English language teaching, consumer and information sciences, family studies, multicultural affairs, and sports and tourism.	Education, government and corporate sectors	Index, abstract, & full-text	Melbourne, Australia English
British Education Index	Bibliographic database covering journal literature on education and training. Also includes British Education Theses Index. Coverage from 1976 onwards.	Education, government	Index	United Kingdom English

(*Continued*)

Database	Description of Data Bases	Audience	Index/Full Text	Country & Language
Best Evidence Encyclopedia	The Best Evidence Encyclopedia is a free website created by the Johns Hopkins University School of Education's Center for Data-Driven Reform in Education under funding from the Institute of Education Sciences, U.S. Department of Education. It is intended to give educators and researchers fair and useful information about the strength of the evidence supporting a variety of programs available for students in grades K-12. The Best Evidence Encyclopedia provides summaries of scientific reviews as well as links to the full texts of each review.	Educator, researcher	Full text	English
Biological Abstracts	*Biological Abstracts* is a collection of bibliographic references for life science and biomedical research literature, covering peer-reviewed article abstracts from U.S. and international journals. Abstracts from more than 4,300 peer-reviewed journals. Coverage dating back to 1969.	Academic libraries, corporations, government, healthcare	Index	Philadelphia, Pennsylvania English
C2-SPECTR	The Campbell Collaboration is an international research network that produces high-quality, transparent, and policy-relevant evidence syntheses, plain language summaries and policy briefs in the social sectors. The first issue of the new journal, *Campbell Systematic Reviews* – a double issue – is now available on Wiley Online Library.	Systematic researcher		Oslo, Norway
CITE-ITEL	An Introduction to the CITE-ITEL Database: https://www.citejournal.org/volume-19/issue-2-19/english-language-arts/an-introduction-to-the-cite-itel-database-access-dialogue-and-possibility/			United States English

Appendix C **213**

Name	Description	Type	Format	Location
ComDisDome	Deep coverage on communication disorders, Over 300,000 A&I records, Latest research, trends, and findings in the field. ComDisDome is an indexing and abstracting tool covering the communications disorders literature, with focus on speech-language pathology and audiology.	Academic, government	Index and abstract	Ann Arbor, Michigan
Comprehensive Dissertation Index	Part of the ProQuest collection of dissertations.	Academic		
Current Contents on Disc	Current Contents is a rapid alerting service database from Clarivate Analytics. Current Contents Connect is a multidisciplinary current awareness resource with this unique feature set: Browse journals by discipline Browse an issue's complete table of contents Set up alerts to be notified when new issues of a journal have been released. It is now included in Web of Science family of products.	Academic, government	Alert service	Philadelphia, Pennsylvania English
Dissertation Abstracts	Alternative Name(s) & Keywords: Dissertation & Thesis A&I (ProQuest). This database is a comprehensive collection of dissertations and theses from around the world, spanning from 1743 to the present day. Most entries are abstracts & citations only, but full text is provided for open access dissertations & theses.	Academic		Ann Arbor, Michigan

(Continued)

Database	Description of Data Bases	Audience	Index/Full Text	Country & Language
Dissertation Abstracts International	All content previously contained in Dissertation Abstracts International is now available online in ProQuest Dissertations & Theses Global.	Academic		Ann Arbor, Michigan
e-Marefa	e-Marefa is an integrated database of full text and comprehensive metadata of over 700,000 journals, research papers, theses and dissertations, conference papers, statistical reports, and e-books, which has produced 22 specialized databases covering all disciplines.			Amman, Jordan
EconLit	EconLit covers economics publications as far back as 1886, including peer-reviewed journal articles, working papers from leading universities, PhD dissertations, books, collective volume articles, conference proceedings, and book reviews. All these are indexed, classified, and linkable to full-text library holdings.		Full text	Ipswich, Massachusetts English
Education Research Complete	*Education Research Complete* is a robust database for education students, professionals and policymakers. Providing hundreds of full-text education journals, it covers all levels of education, from early childhood to higher education, plus multilingual education, health education, and testing.		Full text	Ipswich, Massachusetts
Educational Abstracts	*Education Abstracts* is an education research database providing high-quality indexing and abstracts for hundreds of journals. Coverage spans all levels of education and includes adult education, multicultural education, and teaching methods.		Index & abstract	Ipswich, Massachusetts

ERIC	The ERIC (Educational Resources Information Center) database, sponsored by the U.S. Department of Education, provides access to over one million bibliographic records of journal articles and other education-related materials. In addition to ERIC's indexing of educational journal content, ERIC's Document coverage includes conferences, meetings, government documents, theses, dissertations, reports, audiovisual media, bibliographies, directories, books, and monographs.	Academic libraries, public libraries, government	Index, abstract, & full-text	Ipswich, Massachusetts English
ESRC (ESRC Data Service, ESRD Data Store)	Launched in 2008, ESRC Data Store was a self-archiving system for the storage and sharing of primary research data from the social and behavioral sciences. The initial phase was aimed at ESRC award holders, who are required to offer data outputs for sharing their award contract. In 2012, ESRC Data Store was incorporated into the UK Data Service, and in 2014 it was extended and improved under the name ReShare. Today ReShare accepts digital data from researchers beyond the social sciences, and offers access to open and safeguarded data collections for anyone involved in social science research and learning. Data can be found via Discover, the discovery portal of the UK Data Service.	Anyone involved in social science research and learning		Colchester, United Kingdom (University of Essex) English
Expanded Academic ASAP	Expanded Academic ASAP contains more than 3,800 peer-reviewed journals, including Social science journals, Humanities journals, General interest magazines, Science and technology journals, and National and global news sources.	Academic libraries, public libraries, government	Search service	Dublin, Ohio Multiple

(*Continued*)

Database	Description of Data Bases	Audience	Index/Full Text	Country & Language
Fuente Académica	Fuente Académica is a collection of academic journals from Latin America, Portugal and Spain. Many subject areas are covered with particular emphasis on agriculture, biological sciences, economics, history, law, literature, philosophy, psychology, public administration, religion and sociology. This is a database that can be purchased through EBSCO which includes full-text Spanish- and Portuguese-language scholarly journals.		Full text	Ipswich, Massachusetts Spanish, Portuguese
GoogleScholar	Search all scholarly literature from one convenient place. Locate the complete document through your library or on the web. Check who's citing your publications, create a public author profile. Rank documents the way researchers do, weighing the full text of each document, where it was published, who it was written by, as well as how often and how recently it has been cited in other scholarly literature.	All	Search engine, Index, & linked full text if open sourced	Mountain View, California Can Translate
InfoTrac	InfoTrac is a family of full-text databases of content from academic journals and general magazines, of which the majority are targeted to the English-speaking North American market. As is typical of online proprietary databases, various forms of authentication are used to verify affiliation with subscribing academic, public, and school libraries.	Schools, academics	Indexed, full text and abstract	Farmington Hills, Michigan Mostly English

Ingenta	Ingenta was formed in 1998 and floated on the London Stock Exchange in April 2000. Jointly operating from Europe (Oxford) and North America (Boston and New Jersey), they have local teams in Brazil, India, China and Australia. Ingenta serves over 400 trade and scholarly publishers. Ingenta produces and sells a range of publishing products and platform solutions to help manage and deliver content. With over 40 years of experience producing publishing platforms, Ingenta today provides a wide range of management products, tools and services, which are not exclusive for trade, scholarly and academic sectors, book publishers, journal publishers, newspaper and magazine industries, retail, and music industry. Unlock your tomorrow and discover more about their different solutions.	Best known for offering solutions to publishers	Oxford, United Kingdom; Boston, Massachusetts
International Political Science Abstracts	*International Political Science Abstracts* is published bimonthly by the International Political Science Association. It provides non-evaluative abstracts of articles in the field of political science published in journals and yearbooks all over the world.	Academic libraries, public, libraries, government	Abstract	Newbury Park, California
ISI Web of Science (previous name: *ISI Web of Knowledge*; current name: *Web of Science*)	Web of Science (previously known as Web of Knowledge) is a website which provides subscription-based access to multiple databases that provide comprehensive citation data for many different academic disciplines. It was originally produced by the Institute for Scientific Information (ISI) and is currently maintained by Clarivate Analytics.		

(*Continued*)

Database	Description of Data Bases	Audience	Index/Full Text	Country & Language
JSTOR	JSTOR contains articles, usually at least 3–5 years old, from scholarly journals in the humanities, social sciences, and sciences. Some journal issues are available from as far back as the 1800s. For more recent material, try using Summon or one of the individual databases. UMSL has access to selected JSTOR Collections: Arts & Sciences I, II, III & IV, Ecology and Botany I, Health & General Sciences, Early Journal Content (journals published in the United States before 1923 and published in other countries before 1870).	Academic libraries, public libraries, government		New York
Linguistics and Language Behavior Abstracts	Linguistics and Language Behavior Abstracts (LLBA) abstracts and indexes the international literature in linguistics and related disciplines in the language sciences. The database covers all aspects of the study of language including phonetics, phonology, morphology, syntax, and semantics. Complete coverage is given to various fields of linguistics including descriptive, historical, comparative, theoretical, and geographical linguistics. The database provides abstracts of journal articles and citations to book reviews drawn from over 1,500 serials publications, and also provides abstracts of books, book chapters, and dissertations.	Academic institutions	Index & abstract	Ann Arbor, Michigan

| MEDline | Created by the U.S. National Library of Medicine, MEDLINE contains citations and abstracts for biomedical and health journals used by healthcare professionals, nurses, clinicians, and researchers engaged in clinical care, public health and health policy development. Many find the EBSCO version easier to use, but an OVID version is also available. Content Includes: Over 19 million references to journal articles in life sciences with a concentration on biomedicine Records are indexed with NLM Medical Subject Headings (MeSH) Citations from approximately 5,600 worldwide journals in 39 languages, and older journals in 60 languages Citations created by the NLM Coverage from 1946 to the present, with some older material Majority of publications are scholarly journals Includes a small number of newspapers, magazines, and newsletters Majority of journals selected based on the recommendation of the Literature Selection Technical Review Committee (LSTRC). | Biomedical & healthcare | Index & abstract | Bethesda, Maryland Multiple |
| **MLA International Bibliography** | Indexes critical materials on modern language, literature, linguistics, and folklore. Covers over 3,000 journals and series, books, working papers and proceedings, and bibliographies. Produced by the Modern Language Association (MLA), the electronic version of the bibliography dates back to the 1920s and contains millions of citations. | Academic, teacher, student | Index & abstract | New York Multiple |

(*Continued*)

Database	Description of Data Bases	Audience	Index/Full Text	Country & Language
Professional Development Collection	Designed for professional educators, this database provides a highly specialized collection of high-quality education journals, including peer-reviewed titles and educational reports.	Academic libraries, public libraries, government, schools	Full text	Ipswich, Massachusetts English
Project Muse	Project MUSE's Standard Collection provides full-text access to scholarly journal titles, primarily in the Humanities and Social Sciences.	Academic libraries, public libraries	Index, abstract, & full text	Baltimore, Maryland English
ProQuest Research Library	A list of DB procured by ProQuest.			
PsycARTICLES	PsycARTICLES offers full-text, peer-reviewed scholarly and scientific articles in psychology published by the American Psychological Association. Access over 70 top, full-text psychology journals covering the disciplines of Human Physiology, Personality Psychology, Social Psychology, Educational Psychology, and more. For a more extensive and in-depth search use PsycINFO.	Academic libraries, public libraries	Full text	Washington, DC English
PsycCRITIQUES	PsycCRITIQUES was discontinued as of December 31, 2017. Full PsycCRITIQUES archived database is now available to the public through the Center for the History of Psychology at the University of Akron.			Washington, DC

PsychLIT	PsycLIT was a CD-ROM version of Psychological Abstracts. It was merged into the PsycINFO online database in 2000. PsycLIT contained citations and abstracts to journal articles, and summaries of English-language chapters and books in psychology, as well as behavioral information from sociology, linguistics, medicine, law, psychiatry, and anthropology.			Washington, DC
Psychological Abstracts	Psychological Abstracts was an abstract and index periodical and the print counterpart of the PsycINFO database. It was published by the American Psychological Association and was produced for 80 years, ceasing publication at the end of 2006.			Washington, DC
Psychology & Behavioral Sciences Collection	Psychology & Behavioral Sciences Collection provides access to hundreds of full-text journals and offers particularly strong coverage in child and adolescent psychology and various areas of counseling. Subject area: Anthropology, emotional and behavioral characteristics, mental processes, observational and experimental methods, psychiatry, and psychology.	Academic, government, healthcare sectors	Full text	Ipswich, Massachusetts English
PsycINFO	PsycINFO® is the American Psychological Association's renowned resource for abstracts of scholarly journal articles, book chapters, books, and dissertations, containing over 3 million citations and summaries dating as far back as the 1600s.	Academic, government, healthcare sectors	Abstract	Washington, DC

(Continued)

Database	Description of Data Bases	Audience	Index/Full Text	Country & Language
PubMed	PubMed has been available since 1996. Its more than 27 million references include the MEDLINE database. PubMed citations often include links to the full-text article on the publishers' Web sites and/or in PMC and the Bookshelf. MEDLINE is the largest subset of PubMed.	Audience in bioscience field	Index & Full text	USA English
Redalyc	The Redalyc project is a bibliographic database and a digital library of open access journals, supported by the Universidad Autónoma del Estado de México with the help of numerous other higher education institutions and information systems. The project started in 2002 with aim of building a scientific information system made up by the leading journals of all the knowledge areas edited in and about Latin America.	Science field, academic	abstract, full-text, & citation	Mexico Spanish & Portugal
SAGE	SAGE Publishing, formerly SAGE Publications, is an independent publishing company founded in 1965 in New York by Sara Miller McCune and now based in Newbury Park, California. It publishes more than 1,000 journals, more than 800 books a year,[1] reference works and electronic products covering business, humanities, social sciences, science, technology and medicine. SAGE also owns and publishes under the imprints of Corwin Press[2] (since 1990), CQ Press[3] (since 2008), Learning Matters[4] (since 2011), and Adam Matthew Digital (since 2012).[5] It has more than 1,500 employees in its principal offices in Los Angeles, London, New Delhi, Singapore, Washington, DC, and Melbourne.	Academic Libraries, Public libraries, government		Newbury Park, California

Science Direct	The ScienceDirect platform provides full text access to over 1,600 Elsevier journal titles. The journals are grouped into four main sections: Physical Sciences and Engineering, Life Sciences, Health Sciences, and Social Sciences and Humanities.	Academic Libraries, Public libraries, government	Index, abstract, & full-text	Amsterdam, Netherlands
SIGLE	The "System for Information on Grey Literature in Europe" (SIGLE) was established in 1980, Operated by a network of national information or document supply centers active in collecting and promoting gray literature, SIGLE was an on line, pan-European electronic bibliographic database and document delivery system. Integrated into OpenSIGLE in 2007.	Any interested party	Index & Full text of gray literature	French/EU
Sociological Abstracts	Sociological Abstracts indexes the international literature in sociology and related disciplines in the social and behavioral sciences. The database provides abstracts of journal articles and citations to book reviews drawn from over 1,809 serials publications, and also provides abstracts of books, book chapters, dissertations, and conference papers.	Academic libraries, public libraries, government	Index & abstract	Ann Arbor, Michigan
The Social Sciences Citation Index	The Social Sciences Citation Index (SSCI) is a commercial citation index product of Clarivate Analytics. The SSCI citation database covers some 3,000 of the world's leading academic journals in social sciences across more than 50 disciplines. It is made available online through the Web of Science service for a fee. The database records which articles are cited by other articles.	Academic libraries, public libraries, government	index	Philadelphia, Pennsylvania English

Database	Description of Data Bases	Audience	Index/Full Text	Country & Language
The Cochrane Library	The Cochrane Library is a collection of databases in medicine and other healthcare specialties provided by Cochrane and other organizations. At its core is the collection of Cochrane Reviews, a database of systematic reviews and meta-analyses, which summarizes and interprets the results of medical research. The Cochrane Library aims to make the results of well-conducted controlled trials readily available and is a key resource in evidence-based medicine.	Healthcare sector	Reviews	London, England English
Theses A&I	See above under "Dissertation & Thesis A&I"			
Theses Full Text	See above under "Dissertation & Thesis A&I"			
Theses Global	See above under "Dissertation & Thesis A&I"			
Web of Science	Web of Science is the world's most trusted publisher-independent global citation database. Guided by Dr. Eugene Garfield, inventor of the world's first citation index, Web of Science is the most powerful research engine. Their multidisciplinary platform connects regional, specialty, data, and patent indexes to the Web of Science Core Collection, the world's only true citation index. The comprehensive platform allows you to track ideas across disciplines and time from over 1.7 billion cited references from over 159 million records. Science, social science, arts, and humanities (supports 256 disciplines).	Academic Libraries, Public libraries, government	Index	Philadelphia, Pennsylvania Eng-lish

Wiley InterScience (replaced by Wiley Online Library)	Wiley InterScience is part of the Wiley Publishing. Wiley made a major foray into scientific, technical, and medical (STM) publishing in 1961 when it acquired InterScience Publishers (weblink is Wiley Online Library). Wiley Online Library is a subscription-based library that launched on August 7, 2010, replacing Wiley InterScience.	Researcher, librarians, author		Hoboken, New Jersey
Wilson Select Plus	Part of H. W. Wilson Publishing database, the periodical titles are selected by subscriber vote with assistance from subject specialists and ALA's Reference and User Services Association. Wilson Select Plus comprises the core, peer-reviewed journals in each field, providing authoritative information for the user. Users continue to request more full-text information online, and Wilson Select Plus significantly increases the amount of full text that can be provided through the new FirstSearch service.		Full text	Hackensack, New Jersey
Wilson's Omni File (OmniFile Full Text Mega, or OmniFile Full Text Select)	OmniFile: Full Text Select Edition is a multidisciplinary database providing only the full-text articles, with their accompanying indexing and abstracts, from the following Wilson databases: Applied Science & Technology Full Text, Art Full Text, Biological & Agricultural Index Plus, Education Full Text, General Science Full Text, Humanities Full Text, Index to Legal Periodicals Full Text, Library Literature & Information Science Full Text, Readers' Guide Full Text, Social Sciences Full Text, and Wilson Business Full Text.	Academic libraries	Full text	Hackensack, New Jersey

Database	Description of Data Bases	Audience	Index/Full Text	Country & Language
WorldCat	(Also see FirstSearch) WorldCat is an OCLC catalog of books, web resources, and other materials. It contains millions of bibliographic records cataloged by OCLC member libraries worldwide. This database contains all material cataloged by OCLC member libraries including books, computer data files, computer programs, films and slides, journals, magazines, manuscripts, maps, musical scores, newspapers, sound recordings, and videotapes.	General audience	Searches multiple libraries; locate text in nearby library	Dublin, Ohio Multiple

APPENDIX D

Code Book from 2005 Literature Review

1. Publication date for study:
   Authors' institutional affiliation and location:
   What type of article is this? (e.g., empirical study, theoretical paper, review of literature, and position paper)
2. How is Critical Discourse Analysis (CDA) defined? Use the author's words to define CDA.
3. What theorists/researchers are cited in reference to CDA?
   What mode of language is studied? (spoken, written, interactional)
   What theoretical frameworks does the researcher use in the paper? List the theoretical frameworks and cite all theorists referenced.
   What theories of language are used? Use the author's words to describe the theory of language and cite the linguists and discourse analysts the author references.
4. Who are the research population/participants?
5. What is the ethnicity of the research participants if applicable?
6. What is the grade level of the participants if applicable?
7. What is the geographic location of the study?
   What is the context of the study? (community agency, newspaper, school)
8. What is the research question?
9. How is learning addressed (intertextuality references)?
   How is the analysis conducted? (e.g., what aspects of CDA are used) [Specifically describe the method of conducting CDA]
10. What are the data sources?

228 Appendix D

11. What is the role of the researcher (e.g., text analysts and participant observer)?
12. Is there a theory of learning in the research?
13. What are the noted limitations of the work? [the author's words]
    What are critiques of the work?
    How does this article relate to other articles?

APPENDIX E

Code Book from 2016 Literature Review

Analytic Review Template (ART) from 2016 Follow-Up Literature Review

Reviewer Initials:

Date the Review was Complete:

Comments to Reviewers: Use direct quotes and add page numbers. Attempt to capture the terminology/language used. As we synthesize the scholarship, we will be taking direct quotes from each of these categories, across articles in a disciplinary area. Err on the side of more rather than less information in each category. Some of this information will be plugged directly into a spreadsheet for quantitative analysis. Other portions of this ART will be qualitatively analyzed. With four of the questions on this ART, you will consult a schemata (context, social action, reconstruction–deconstruction, and reflexivity) and plug your score and justification into the ART.

APA Reference

1. What type of article is this? (e.g., empirical study, theoretical paper, review of literature, and position paper)
2. Summary of the article (can be taken from the abstract or lines from key sections of the study).
3. How is CDA defined? Use the author's words to define CDA (defined as a goal, a purpose, a stance, a theory, etc. They may define CDA more than once in the article)
4. Does the author describe any critiques or limitations of CDA? What do they state as limitations or critiques of CDA (e.g., Trainor (2005) critiques CDA's shortcomings around affect and emotions).

230 Appendix E

5. What theorists/researchers are cited in reference to CDA? [*We will use this information for counting the most frequently cited scholars in CDA. Include complete reference from the bibliography.*]

6. What theoretical frameworks does the researcher use in the paper? List the theoretical frameworks and cite all theorists referenced.

7. What theories of language are used? Does the author specifically address a theory of language? Use the author's words to describe the theory of language and cite linguists and discourse analysts/theorists the author references.

    For example, Martínez-Roldan unites Chicana feminist theory and CDA; Rogers & Mosley merge critical race theory with CDA.

8. Who are the research participants?

    We want to know: Who is doing research with whom? Do CDA researchers tend to look at the discourses of historically marginalized groups? Do they tend to work with small or large numbers of participants or texts? Include the NUMBER of participants and other descriptive information that the author provides. For example, 10 white boys

9. What is the ethnicity of the research participants if applicable?

10. What educational level does the article focus on?

    In what learning contexts is CDA being conducted? We coded each study at one of nine educational contexts: early childhood, elementary, middle, secondary, PK-12, adult, higher education, community contexts, teacher education, and professional development. Please include other descriptors as you see fit and we will discuss.

11. What is the geographic location of the study?

12. Where does the article fall on the context scale and why?

13. What is the research design (case study, teacher-research study, part of larger, ethnographic study)?

14. What is the sociopolitical focus of the research? Choose one primary area (and a secondary emphasis area, if necessary)

    (1) Assessment, Standards, Commercialization of Education; (2) Cultural & Linguistic Diversity, Teachers' Identities, Discourses & Learning; (3) Cultural & Linguistic Diversity, Students' Identities, Discourses and Learning; (4) Social Class, (5) Racism, Anti-Racism, Ethnicity & Diversity, (6) Sexualities & Gender. There will undoubtedly be others in the larger dataset (e.g., neoliberalism). Please identify what you see as the sociopolitical focus and then as we look across the studies, we will group these areas.

15. What is the research question?

    Quote specifically from the article and include page numbers. It is possible the question may be posed as a statement of purpose. (Imagine putting the research questions into a table so readers can see the range of questions asked in each area).

16. How is the analysis conducted? (e.g., what aspects of CDA are used)

    [Could you "replicate" the study based on the description of their methodology? Specifically describe the method of conducting critical discourse analysis, use the authors description from the analysis section. We want to be able to discuss the range

of analytic approaches used within each disciplinary area and across the dataset. Do the authors take more of a deductive or inductive approach to CDA? Likewise, if the analytic procedures are not described, note that as well.]

17. What is the analytic focus/unit of analysis (e.g., on-task/off-task conversations, moments of tension, episodes, and idealized lines)?
18. What is the level of detail in describing the analytic procedures?
    1. 1–2 paragraphs or less would be considered minimal description of procedures;
    2. 3–4 paragraphs of DA procedures might be considered adequate;
    3. 5–10 paragraphs and beyond would be considered detailed description of procedures.
19. Did the authors carry out a multimodal analysis? Y/N – If Yes, explain.
20. Did they include a multimodal transcript? If yes, describe and reference the page number.
21. What data sources are generated for the study?
22. Are global technologies included? Y/N – If Yes, explain.
23. Where does this article fall on the **reflexivity scale**? Provide a number and a justification. Cite page numbers.
24. Related to reflexivity, does the researcher describe herself (himself) specifically with respect to identity or other social or cultural or demographic qualities? Circle NO or YES. If yes, how (include direct quotes and page numbers)?
25. Is there a theory of learning in the research? How is learning addressed (e.g., intertextuality developmental theories, and sociocultural theories)?
26. Where does this article fall on the **reconstructive–deconstructive scale** and why? Provide a number and a justification. Cite page numbers.
27. What are the key findings? Use the author's words and include page numbers.
    Imagine putting this information into a table so readers could see a summary of key findings within a discipline.
28. How are the findings represented (e.g., three sections with tables; chronological arrangement of findings, through narratives and illustrations)
29. What do the authors cite as implications of this research?
    [Include specific quotes and page numbers]
30. Where does the article fall on the **action scale** and why?
31. What are the noted limitations of the work? [the author's words]
32. What do/does the author/s cite as future directions?

Additional Comments/Insights/Connections across the Articles in this Area:

APPENDIX F

Coding Chart for Spreadsheet

General Feature	Range	Code for Data Entry	Notes
Publication Date (PD)	Year of Publication	PY-####	Enter the year (Ex. PY = 2008)
Authorship (A)	Number of Authors	A-###	Enter the number of authors (ex, A = 3; A = 1, etc)
Article Type (AT)	Empirical	AT-EMP	
	Theoretical	AT-THEO	
	Review of literature	AT-REV	
	Position paper	AT-POS	
Data Source (DS)	Written docs	DS-WRT	
	Interactions	DS-INTERAC	
	Interviews	DS-INTERV	
Disciplinary Field (DF)	Teacher Education	DF-TCHED	
	Literacy Ed	DF-LED	
	Education Policy	DF-EDPOL	
	Higher Education	DF-HIGHED	
	Art & Music	DF-AM	
	CDA	DF-CDA	
	Character & Citizenship	DF-CC	
	Curriculum & Instruction	DF-CURR	
	S.T.E.M.	DF-STEM	
	Vocational WorkForce	DF-VOC	
Study Design (SD)	Case Study	SD-CASE	

General Feature	Range	Code for Data Entry	Notes
	Teacher-Research	SD-TAR	
	Part of Larger Ethnographic Study	SD-PART	
	Survey	SD-SURVEY	
	Historical/Archival	SD-HIST	
	Quasi-experimental	SD-QUASI	
Research Question (RQ)		RQ-XXXXX	Enter specific text of question and page number.
CDA Definition (DEF)		DEF-YES	If yes, enter the specific definition and page number.
		DEF-NO	
Research Participants (RP)	Number	RP = 1 RP = 2–9 RP = 10–20 RP = 21–40 RP = 40+	Enter the number if authors say it. If authors do not specifically state, estimate – more than 10 or less than 10.
Educational Setting (ES)	Early Childhood	ES-EC	
	Elementary	ES-ELEM	
	Middle School	ES-MID	
	Secondary	ES-SECOND	
	PK-12	ES-PK12	
	Adult	ES-ADLT	
	Higher Education	ES-HIGHED	
	Community	ES-COMM	
	Teacher Education	ES-TCHED	
	Professional Development	ES-PD	
Socio-Political Focus (SP)	Assessments, Standards, Curriculum, Evaluations, Outcomes, Commercialization of Education	SP-STAND	
	Cultural/Linguistic Diversity & Teacher Identities	SP-CLTID	
	Cultural/Linguistic Diversity & Student Identities	SP-CLSID	

(*Continued*)

234 Appendix F

General Feature	Range	Code for Data Entry	Notes
	Cultural/Linguistic Diversity – International, National, State or Local Ideologies and Identities	SP-CLGID	
	Racism/Anti-Racism	SP-RAC	
	Sexualities & Gender	SP-SEX	
	Disability, Construction of Disability/Ability or Tracking	SP-DIS	
	Democracy, Citizenship, Civil Rights & Human Rights (includes violence, peace, or criminalization)	SP-DEM	
Multimodal Analysis (MMA)		MMA-YES	
		MMA-NO	
Multimodal Transcript (MMT)		MMT-YES	
		MMT-NO	
Global Technologies (GT)		GT-YES	
		GT-NO	
Geographic Location (GL)	United States	GL-US	
	United Kingdom	GL-UK	
	Australia	GL-AUS	
	Canada	GL-CAN	
	Europe	GL-EUR	
	Asia	GL-ASIA	
	Latin America	GL-LA	
	Africa	GL-AFR	
Analytic Procedures (AP)	None	AP-0	
	Minimal (1–2 paragraphs or less)	AP-1	

General Feature	Range	Code for Data Entry	Notes
	Adequate (3–4 paragraphs)	AP-2	
	Detailed (5–10 paragraphs or more)	AP-3	
Reflexivity (R)		R-1	
		R-2	
		R-3	
Reconstructive/ Deconstructive (RD)		RD-1	
		RD-2	
		RD-3	
Social Action (SA)		SA-1	
		SA-2	
		SA-3	
Journal Name			

APPENDIX G

Sample Response Letter to Editors and Reviewers

December 10, 200X

Dear Editors and Reviewers:

Enclosed you will find a revised and resubmitted version of the paper, "Critical Discourse Analysis in Education: A Review of the Literature," for consideration in *Review of Educational Research.* Thank you for your careful review and suggestions for revision. We have attended to all of the suggestions from the reviewers and the editors and believe the manuscript is much stronger as a result. What follows is a summary of the revisions that have been made on the paper.

First, as all of the reviewers suggested, we rewrote the introduction to provide a clearer and more motivating beginning. Next, to address another issue that each of the reviewers raised, we included a new section called "Critical Discourse Analysis: Key Concepts" (pp. 4–9). This section is organized by the constructs of "critical," "discourse," and "analysis." This section allowed us to respond to many of the questions and concerns of the reviewers such as clarifying terms, expanding on frameworks, and people, reducing jargon for non-experts in the field, and linking CDA to the larger field of discourse analysis.

Second, in the "Methodology" section, we noted that we integrated books into our review, as was suggested of two of the reviewers. We agree that this is an important move because research and theory development in emerging fields is often published first in books. We took out the descriptions of who we are as researchers in the "Delimitations" section. We agree this was not an authentic reflexive move and, instead, have included our institutional information in the "Author's biography" section. We aligned the content of the section "Organization of the Review" with the outline of the "Findings" section that can be found on the same page (p. 13).

Third, in the "Findings" section of the review, we made many substantive revisions to address the reviewers' concerns. We introduced each of the sections in the review to give the reader a sense of why each of the sections is important and how each section relates to the next. We also took out the long sections of citations and instead referred readers to Appendix B where each of the studies is summarized. Given this, we request that Appendix B is either published as part of the paper in the journal or put online so readers can refer to it. One of the reviewers also felt this was important. Further, from our experience and knowledge of RER, including a chart of the studies reviewed is fairly common practice and we think it helps to ground the reader in the studies reviewed and reduce overlap in the paper. Further, we cut the majority of the lengthy quotes and instead summarized the important points throughout each of the sections. We also eliminated the repetition that was found in the last version of the manuscript.

In addition to clarifying the manuscript, we have significantly reduced the page length which resulted in a much more succinct paper, a suggestion made by several of the reviewers and the editor.

Finally, we added a section in the "Discussion" section about what we have learned from studies that use CDA in educational contexts. One of the reviewers noted that a synthesis of the findings of the studies reviewed was an aspect of the manuscript that was missing. We thought this worked nicely in the "Discussion" and "Conclusion" sections.

We are enthusiastic about the revisions we have made to this manuscript. We believe it is a greatly improved version and could be a real contribution to *Review of Educational Research*. We look forward to hearing from the reviewers and the editors. We are, of course, willing to make further revisions.

APPENDIX H

Final Analytic Review Template for the Integrative Critical Review (ART)

Family Literacy Integrative Critical Literature
Article number: _____   Reviewer initials: _____

APA Citation:

Institutional affiliation(s)/location(s) of author(s):
Department(s)/division(s) and college(s) (if known) of author(s):

1. Summary of the chapter/article/book:
2. Term(s) used (circle one or more):
   family literacy, literacy in families, home literacy, funds of knowledge
   Other:
3. Family literacy definition (please quote):
4. What type of paper/chapter/book is it? (circle one or more)
   Review, Empirical study, Theoretical/position paper, Practitioner
   Other:
5. What methodologies are used? (circle one or more)
   Qualitative/quantitative, Case study, Ethnography, Discourse analysis, Not applicable
   Other:
6. What theoretical frameworks are privileged in this review?
7. This article addresses... (circle one or more):
   Race, Cultural diversity, Linguistic diversity, Gender differences, Socioeconomic status differences
   Other:
   Additional comments:

Appendix H **239**

8. To what extent are these dimensions of difference addressed?

___ Racial, cultural, social class, and language differences are not discussed.

___ Differences are alluded to but only in general terms.

___ Differences are treated as methodological variables that correlate with specific literacy practices and/or eventual school success.

___ Race, social class, language, gender, or other differences are treated as central to the analysis.

Additional comments:

9. How, when, and to what extent are larger, macrocontextual issues/factors addressed? (circle one)

Not at all, In general terms, Discussed in depth

Additional comments:

10. How does this review article relate to other review articles?

11. What is the role/position of the researcher(s)?

12. What does the author(s) cite as future directions?

13. Additional comments:

APPENDIX I
Inter-Rater Reliability Check

ART Inter-Rater Reliability Check

These are the questions that we will use to determine inter-rater reliability among the three of us. As I am sure you appreciate, it is critical that we give each of these questions careful consideration as poor cores related to reliability could complicate making a case for the validity of the ART analysis.

APA Bibliographic Data (copy from the list I sent):

1. Term(s) used (underline one or more):
   Family literacy

   Literacy in families

   Home literacy

   Funds of knowledge

   Other: _____

2. What type of paper/chapter/handbook? (underline one or more)
   Review

   Empirical study

   Theoretical paper

   Position paper

   Practitioner Information

   Other: _____

Appendix I **241**

3. What methodologies are used? (underline one or more)
Qualitative

Case study

Ethnography

Quantitative

Discourse Analysis

Other: _____

NA

4. What theoretical frameworks are privileged in this review?
5. This article addresses ... (underline one or more)
Race

Cultural diversity

Linguistic diversity

Gender differences

SES differences

Other: _____

6. To what extent are these dimensions of difference addressed? (CHOOSE ONLY ONE)
   1. Racial, cultural, social class, and language differences were either not mentioned or not discussed as relevant to the research.
   2. Differences were eluded to but only in general terms. These studies used terms such as "non-mainstream," "multiple perspectives," and "language differences" to reference diversity, but did not discuss specific literate practices in diverse communities nor did they examine what these practices meant in terms of schooling, access to resources, or school trajectories.
   3. These quantitative studies treated difference as a methodological variable that correlated with specific literacy practices and eventual school success. These predictive and causal research studies focused on family literacy in diverse populations of students including children from low-income families or children from particular racial, ethnic, or linguistic groups.
   4. These studies identified culture, social class, race, gender, ethnicity, and/ or language as central to their analyses. Many researchers noted the inextricable connections between various dimensions of diversity. For example, Wasik and Hendrickson (2004) noted "any serious study of literacy development must include an examination of family culture and beliefs" (p. 158). These studies discuss specific literate practices in diverse communities and/or they examine what these practices meant in terms of schooling, access to resources, and/or school trajectories.

242 Appendix I

7. To what extent are larger, macro contextual issues/factors addressed (i.e., social histories, institutions, political pressures, and general economic conditions)?
   1. Not at all
   2. In general terms
   3. Discussed in depth

APPENDIX J

Response Letter to Editors for Our Critical Integrative Literature Review

---

Dear RRQ Editors,

Thank you so much for your support in helping me revise this paper for publication in RRQ. I have tried to address all of the issues identified by the editors. I am happy to make any additional changes and truly appreciate all of the excellent feedback from reviewers and editors.

Much appreciated!
Cathy Compton-Lilly

Purpose and Contribution

1. We have revised the introduction of the paper to further clarify the goals of the paper and have restated the goals of the review in the paragraph before the "Methodology" section (pp. 16–17)

2. A clearer statement of conclusions has been crafted on pages 50–54. The final paragraph on page 54 clarifies the new and substantive contribution of this review.

Distinction of Modernist and Postmodernist Epistemologies

3. We have clarified our language to avoid categorizing studies as either "modernist" or "postmodernist." Instead, we have adopted language that identifies "modernist" or "postmodernist" dimensions of the various studies. In addition to rereading and editing the paper to support this distinction, we have edited the following introductory sections (page 36, para 1; page 40, para 2; page 44, para 2). In these sections, care was taken to identify various

244 Appendix J

"modernist" or "postmodernist" dimensions that were discernible in the various studies.

4. The authors of the studies we analyzed did not explicitly characterize their studies in terms of modernist and postmodernist epistemologies. In line with our response to item 3, we have worked to craft a more nuanced discussion of the underlying epistemologies by rewording claims across the study and by specifically identifying the dimensions of studies rather than identifying studies as either modernist or postmodernist.

5. We have omitted references to modernist epistemologies as serving school purposes with the exception of a quote from Carrington and Luke (2003) – "schooling remains modernist in its assumptions about both the family and the traditional print medium" (p. 222).

6. We have provided more clarity about the conclusions being made in relation to the epistemological foundations of studies of family literacy on pages 50–54.

Framing and Defining "Diversity Scholarship"

7. We have clarified the relationship between our analyses of diversity scholarship and family literacy scholarship on the bottom of page 2 – "We then explore various epistemological stances that operate in scholarship related to diversity. Insights from this analysis will be applied to family literacy scholarship later in the paper."

8. We present a definition of "diversity scholarship" on page 7.

Miscellaneous Issues

9. We have revised the paper to clarify the argument that is being built relative to diversity scholarship. This has been addressed on page 6 ("In this section, we analyze epistemological dimensions of work that theorizes and operationalizes diversity. In line with our contention that family literacy scholars have not yet grappled sufficiently with the significance of diversity, we turn to the work of diversity scholars who have placed diversity at the center of their analyses of schools and communities") and on page 16 (para 2).

10. We did not add the description of the detailed CDA techniques to Appendix A as this CDA analysis was NOT conducted on all 213 studies that were analyzed using the ART (analytic review template). CDA was only conducted on the 88 studies that identified diversity as central to their discussion of family literacy.

    While some changes have been made on the description of CDA used with the "comprehensive edited volumes" (pp. 21–22), a much more detailed account has been added to the description of analyses conducted on the 88 "diversity central" studies. This is presented on page 22.

11. References to the work of Orellana et al. (2003) have been added on pages 15, 37, 39, 46, and 48.

12. Figure 4 has been deleted.

Additional Issues/Changes:

- In line with reviewer #2 comments, we have deleted the paragraph about "fairly synonymous terms" for family literacy (previously on page 2) as it did not contribute to the arguments presented in the paper.
- The significance of the race/nationality of highly cited diversity scholars has been noted on page 26 – "This under-representation of Scholars of Color is potentially problematic, as articulated by Scheurich and Young (1994) in that white scholars are susceptible to "epistemological racism" (p. 4) that could define the assumptions they bring to their work."
- We appreciate the editors' request that we consider including references to a recent meta-analysis of family literacy programs to the current paper (e.g., van Steensel et al., 2011). We have examined that meta-analysis and have decided not to include the paper or references to it, as the current review did not analyze reviews of family literacy programs.

APPENDIX K

Response Letter to Editors for Our Meta-Ethnography

Dear Editors,

Thank you for your very kind and thoughtful review of our article, previously titled *Ways with Metaphors and Silence: A Meta-Ethnography of Family Literacy Scholarship*. It is now titled *A Meta-Ethnography of Family Literacy Scholarship: Ways with Metaphors and Silence*.

Again, we very much appreciate the time and attention granted by the reviewers and believe that this feedback contributes to a much stronger article. We have identified areas of revision on the chart below as well as a description of how we have responded to those comments.

1. Reviewers asked that you specify and limit your claims concerning the family literacy research. Please consider reviewer 2's request to "qualify your generalizations." This reviewer noted that your conclusions apply "to the sources that were analyzed and the indeterminate scope of those influenced by these sources, not necessarily the field as a whole." We think that by addressing this issue, you will also resolve some of the problems noted by reviewer 1.	The specific points mentioned by the editors and reviewer 1 have been revised. We have taken care to qualify generalizations across the paper.

2. Reviewer 2 also asked that you note that some movement in the field exists "to establish a critical perspective that attends to issues of power and privilege, race and gender." We ask that you consider this point and respond to it.	On pages 28 and 29, we have noted efforts in the field of literacy to attend to more closely to race, power, and privilege. We have qualified our analysis to the highly cited articles
3. In general, more information on the methods is needed. On page 8, you wrote, "we conducted an integrated critical review of family literacy scholarship (Authors, 2012) that focused on how researchers addressed and treated diversity (e.g., race, class, and culture) as well as the nature of literacy, its purposes and its development. We found that 59% of [the X] analyzed studies [limited to reviews, etc] failed to treat diversity as central." Can you say more about this? The information in Figure 1 is helpful, but a quick summary (number of studies analyzed and main criteria) would be helpful. As part of that, what was considered "academic reviews of family literacy"?	These details have been added on pages 7 and 8. We have extended some of the ideas from the chart in our narrative. We have removed the phrase," "academic reviews of family literacy" and replaced it with clearer language.

248 Appendix K

4. On pages 8 and 9, you indicate that the rationale for including studies that might be 10+ years old is that these are the metaphors that are guiding the current conversation (via the many citations). Wouldn't this argument also be valid for the older, highly cited arguments? (Later, we see it in your findings, but this was not clear from the methods.) A stronger rationale for looking at these less highly cited (yet still often cited) scholars would be helpful. Additionally, was there any look at whether there were differences in the metaphors between these older, highly cited scholars and the ones used? Also, you said that a seminal piece per scholar was identified. How was that identified? As mentioned, you were "not studying the evolution of metaphors across each scholar's body of scholarship," so it makes sense, then, that the piece chosen was important because a scholar's metaphors may not be consistent across their scholarship.	We have clarified the rationale for the inclusion of more recent articles on page 8. While we believe that more recent articles contribute to lines of argument, and we did consider trying to identify how the more recent articles differed from earlier articles, no clear trends in metaphor use were apparent. We are not confident that we can make claims at this point. We describe the selection of each seminal article on the bottom of page 8.

5.	On pages 9 and 10, can you list the articles analyzed? On page 10, why are there seven articles? We thought that three articles were first analyzed (and these three are older, so are these practice/training articles?). We are confused here. What was the overlap in the three training articles? What was unique? Why did just two authors code the remaining four articles?	This has been clarified on page 9. Analysis of the first three has been clarified as a process of arriving at a shared definition for metaphor.
6.	On page 7, you wrote, "We used these phases to design our meta-analysis and to guide our analysis of family literacy research." Did you mean "meta-ethnography" here? Or, are you reinvesting the word "meta-analysis" with a more comprehensive meaning?	Yes, we meant "meta-ethnography." This has been corrected.
7.	On page 11, move the word "the" in this sentence from after to before the word "current": "These memories were contrasted with current the home literacy practices that parents created for their children, which were described as 'more low key' (p. 98)."	Thank you. This has been corrected.

250 Appendix K

8.	Ensure that references include complete author initials with no space between initials, ampersand for multiauthored works, year, full titles of books including edition/volume, page numbers for book chapters, month for presentations, and volume and issue number for journal articles. Ensure that authors for a single source are listed in correct order.	Two co-authors have again carefully checked references for adherence to APA guidelines.

Thank you so much for your careful attention to our work. We believe that the review process has made this a much stronger paper and we look forward to seeing it in press in RRQ. We are of course, very happy to make any additional changes that might be needed.

Thank you!
Catherine Compton-Lilly
comptonlilly@sc.edu

APPENDIX L

Analytic Review Template (ART) for our
Metasynthesis of Family Literacy Scholarship
Conducted by BIPOC Scholars

Article Number 1	*List Number 1*
Citation	Flores, T. (2018). Chicas Fuertes: Counter-stories of Latinx parents raising strong girls. *Bilingual Research Journal, 41*(3), 329–348.
Purpose Goal/Research Question	"explore the narratives and experiences of four Latinx mothers and fathers…who participated with their adolescent daughters (grades nine-10), Blanca, Elizabeth, Rocky and Reyna in Somos Escritores/We are Writers writing workshops" (p. 329).
	"What can we learn from the written and oral words, stories, and experiences of Latinx mothers and fathers about who they are, what matters to them, and what they envision for their daughter's futures" (p. 330).
Methodology	• Qualitative Case study – based on dissertation research
	• Somos Escritores/We are Writers 90 min. creative writing workshops
	• "Workshops were designed with and for Latinx parents and their adolescent daughters to open space for the intergenerational exchange of stories and experiences. At workshops, parents and their daughters drew, wrote, and orally shared stories from their lives that addressed the stereotypes, tensions, and contradictions they navigate on a daily basis at the intersections of age, gender, race, language, and immigrant status" (p. 330).
	• Writing samples, interview transcripts (45 min. semistructured interviews), and ethnographic field notes
	• June and July 2016; met weekly
	• Guiding questions, conversations, writing, and mentor texts
Participants	4 Latinx mother and fathers – Alma, Rose, Valente, and Samuel, with
	4 adolescent daughters – Blanca, Elizabeth, Rocky, and Reyna (9–10th graders)
Geography/ Context	Arizona/local university campus
Theoretical Frameworks	• Chicana Feminist Epistemology (CFE, Delgado Bernal, 1998)
	• Critical Race Theory (CRT, Ladson-Billings & Tate, 1995)
	• Latino Critical Race Theory (LatCrit, Solórzano, 1998; Solórzano & Yosso, 2001)
	"These frameworks provide tools to help us to imagine and (re)imagine more inclusive and socially just educational spaces that recognize and privilege the knowledge that resides within Latinx parents' experiences and realities to transform classrooms, schools, and communities" (p. 332).

Sampling Process	"To recruit Latinx parents and their daughters to participate in workshops, I contacted the director of a university-sponsored outreach program for Latina middle and high school girls aimed at increasing the enrollment of first-generation Latinas by directly involving families in the education of their children. She invited me to present a short writing workshop at their monthly session for eighth-grade girls and their parents. My presentation provided a glimpse into Somos Escritores, as I invited girls and parents to participate in a drawing, writing, and sharing activity similar to what was planned for the summer" (p. 336).
After the presentation, I handed out information about the summer workshops. Initially 22 families (44 girls, mothers, and fathers) signed up to participate. After following up with all parents and girls via email, personal phone calls, and letters, five families enrolled in the program and the study. Of the initial five families that enrolled, four families participated in all workshops and the study. Two families were father and daughter writing pairs and two families were mother and daughter writing pairs" (p. 336).
Types of Data	• Writing samples, interview transcripts (45 min. semistructured interviews), and ethnographic field notes • Pens, pencils, crayons, markers, paper, and a writer's notebook • Used mentor texts per workshop • Drawing, oral storytelling, reflections • Print-based and digital poetry, picture books, short stories, and autobiographies
Length of the Study	6 weeks
Analysis Process	• Data collection and analysis were recursive throughout the study • Grounded theory coding techniques and narrative inquiry methods • "As I coded, I created categories, collapsing and expanding throughout analysis…Looking across the data, I continued to analyze, confirm, and revise existing codes and categories to ensure alignment with the theoretical and epistemological lens that I brought to the study" (p. 339).
Organization (Categories, Use of Participants' Voices, Questions, Chronological?)	• Stories of resistance: "I write to let my daughter know that I am here" (p. 339) • Stories of family: "Family is the most important thing." • Stories for the future: "I want her to be happy."

(Continued)

Article Number 1	*List Number 1*
Findings (Note from Which Section of the Article the Findings are Extracted)	• Three categories emerged: stories of resistance, stories of family, and stories.

Stories of resistance: "I write to let my daughter know that I am here"
- "Through reflection, writers 'bear witness' to the deep emotions contained within these memories and the learning attached to these experiences of strength, survival, and resistance" (p. 339).
- Alma's scar story is not only a story in which she recounts a painful time in her life but also a story of growth, learning, and healing (Anzaldúa, 1999). In her words, she resists the temptation to let this pain and grief hold her back from what lies ahead in her future and her daughter's future. Through sharing this experience with her daughter, she teaches and models for her daughter how challenges and struggles prepare us to be más fuerte ("stronger") and más valiante ("more valiant") in life.
- "Valente's story is one example of the ways that Somos Escritores opened up space for the sharing of a story of resistance in which Valente illustrates the challenges of immigrating to a new country while continuing to resist and let his daughter know he exists for her and their family. Through their stories, parents are enacting control of the conditions of their lived realities while modeling courage and resistance for their daughters" (p. 340).

Stories of family: "Family is the most important thing."
- "The stories that parents shared with their daughters illustrate the cultural and familial resources of their homes and communities, their 'funds of knowledge' (Moll et al., 1992) and 'pedagogies of the home' (Delgado Bernal, 2001) that are embedded in the narratives they shared with their daughters" (p. 341).
- "In sharing this family story with his daughter and the group, Samuel not only honored his parents but also opened dialogue with his daughter to help her to understand how he was raising her and the sacrifices he is making so that she may have more opportunities in her life than he was afforded"
- "These family stories that parents shared with their daughters illustrate the cultural strength (Delgado-Gaitan, 1994; Valdés, 1996), love, and support of the generations that came before them. Most importantly, these stories highlight the deep love of family and provide their daughters with the lesson that 'family is the most important thing'" (p. 342).

Stories for the future: "I want her to be happy."

- "Alma explained that from these experiences she learned that this "wasn't suffering" but "tests," and from these tests she learned and grew. She wanted to be happy and model for her own daughters what a healthy relationship is and that the most important thing in life is to be happy. She continued: Yo estoy muy contenta porque yo veo a … Lo que mi inspira son mis hijas a salir adelante; las dos. ("I am very happy because I see … what inspires me to keep going are my daughters, both of them.")
- "Valente, Samuel, Alma, and Rose support their daughter's happiness by encouraging them to pursue their dreams and choose the life that they want for themselves. They shared the following: Valente: … queremos que ella sea una profesional de bien y esperando la carrera que ella escoja… esperamos que llegue a la universidad y que se gradúe y que la carrera que escoja. ('… we want her to become a professional who does good by choosing the career she likes … We hope she'd get to the university and graduate in the area she chooses.') Samuel: I encourage her to explore all her options and not put all her eggs in one basket. She needs choices. Alma: Y su meta siempre es … Siempre ella tiene bien claro que ella quiere ir a la universidad. Y la apoyo. [And, her goal always … She always has been clear that she wants to go to the university. And I support her.] Rose: Stay in school. Study, study, study … because books are food for your brain. Follow your heart and find a job that will make you happy. In their encouragement, they also provide tough love and honesty to ensure that their daughters follow their hearts while staying focused on the future" (p. 343).

(Continued)

Article Number 1	List Number 1
	Second-generation, Latinx/Chicana woman, biliterate, former K–8 Title 1 teacher for culturally and linguistically diverse students and families.
	Through Flores' experiences as a teacher working with her students' families, it was "foundational in the creation of Somos Escritores" (p. 330). "Invited my students and their families, majority Latinx and Spanish speaking, to participate in after-school family writing workshops because of my belief in the power of writing to break silence, amplify voices, and build community. These workshops became a space to learn and grow together through the collective and reciprocal sharing of our stories while building strong relationships" …
Researcher background: race, Culture, Language, Nationality, Positionality	"Based upon the stories of my childhood and my work alongside my students and families in family writing projects, I imagined and (re)imagined Somos Escritores as a space that would value and honor the experiential knowledge of Latinx parents and their adolescent daughters by placing their stories at the center of workshops. Therefore, I intentionally organized and designed workshops to welcome and invite Latinx parents and their daughters into Somos Escritores as experts of their lived realities, thus positioning them as 'holders and creators of knowledge' (Delgado Bernal, 2002) while working to disrupt traditional notions of family engagement spaces" (p. 331).
	Facilitator/participant observer: "I share stories from my work alongside these Latinx parents and their adolescent daughters in Somos Escritores" (p. 330).
	Flores was very vulnerable with her participants, sharing personal stories about her pregnancy, etc., which humanized her and allowed her participants to be humanized and expressive to share their personal stories within this safe space throughout the workshops.
Limitations of the Research as Described by Authors	NA
Implications for Educators, Researchers, Policymakers, & Literacy Education	• "safe and humanizing spaces for the students, families, and communities that we serve" • "there is a heightened sense of urgency for counterspaces like Somos Escritores, in which educators and families can come together to learn alongside one another, share resources, advocate, and mobilize to support our daughters, children, and one another" • "we need to not only open spaces but hold space for our Latinx families and communities in which we enter as learners to understand the material conditions of their lived realities, moving from bearing witness to action for change" (p. 345).

APPENDIX M

Descriptive Table for BIPOC – List #1

Cases	Research Question/ Purpose	Participants	Definition of Family	Geographical Context	Research Design/Methodology	Reflexivity
1. **Moll et al. (1992)**	"The primary purpose of this work is to develop innovations in teaching that draw upon the knowledge and skills found in local households." (p. 132) "The goal of the study was to explore teacher-researcher collaborations in conducting household research and in using this information to develop classroom practices." (p. 135)	Researchers, teachers, family members, and children	"Household/family literacy: This view of households, we should mention, contrasts sharply with prevailing and accepted perceptions of working-class families as somehow disorganized socially and deficient intellectually; perceptions that are well accepted and rarely challenged in the field of education and elsewhere (however, see McDermott, 1987; Moll & Diaz, 1987; Taylor & Dorsey-Gaines, 1988; see also Velez-Ibanez, in press)." (p. 134)	"working-class, Mexican communities in Tucson" (p. 132)	"We have developed a research approach that is based on understanding households (and classrooms) qualitatively. We utilize a combination of ethnographic observations, open-ended interviewing strategies, life histories, and case studies that, when combined analytically, can portray accurately the complex functions of households within their socio-historical contexts. Qualitative research offers a range of methodological alternatives that can fathom the array of cultural and intellectual resources available to students and teachers within these households. This approach is particularly important in dealing with students whose households are usually viewed as being 'poor,' not only economically but in terms of the quality of experiences for the child." (p. 132) We utilize a combination of ethnographic observations, open-ended interviewing strategies, life histories, and case studies. Timeline is not specified although we infer it was a significant amount of time.	Reflexivity not specifically addressed. Multiracial and bi/multilingual research team, Puerto Rican, Mexican-American, White American

2. **Gadsden (1993)**	"The case study described in this article is one small phase of a multilevel study designed to explore the impact of these factors – gender, race, racism, family structure, parent–child interactions, kinship, and distance – on literacy meaning within African American families." (p. 358)	25 African American adults/families "more than ½ of the informants are the children of parents who were enslaved, and are, thus, the first generation in their families to have been born free" (p. 359)	"The larger study attempts to examine the definitions and translations of literacy meaning and traditions across 4 generations of adults and children within 25 families" (p. 358) Family as rooted in Black culture, history, communal bonds, and continual movement toward freedom	Small farming community in rural South Carolina "a village, an enclave of people, traditions, and sometimes unbridled boldness" (p. 359) "a community dominated by five or six major families" (p. 359)	Open-ended life history interviews conducted over a 2-year time period. "I asked informants about their childhood, family and community life, schooling experiences, view of literacy, experiences with literacy, personal aspirations and goals for their children, and sources of inspiration" (p. 359)	Relationship to the "informants" is not indicated. Note that the community is generally suspicious of outsiders; does not address her access to the community. Connects data to "my childhood" indicating that she may have shared experiences with the participants (p. 361)
3. **Delgado-Gaitan (1992)**	"The study reported in this paper attempts to understand what education means to Mexican-American families within the household setting and to learn about the family's role in children's education." (p. 497)	"Demographic data and interviews revealed that the families in the study shared these characteristics: 1) membership in the Mexican working-class community; 2) Mexican immigrant status; 3) a common language (Spanish); and 4) a strong desire to have their	The study focused on six children and their parents. "Five of the families were 'nuclear families' in small one-bedroom apartments, occasionally having another family member reside with them on a temporary basis. The sixth family lived in a larger rented home,	"Carpinteria is a small city of approximately 12,000 residents adjacent to the larger city of Santa Barbara. Whites represent 67% of the population, Mexican Americans	Over the course of 9 months… "Data were collected through ethnographic observations and interviews." (p. 501) "Data were collected through ethnographic observations and interviews. Spontaneous parent–child interactions in the home were observed. During a 9-month period, all families were observed six times, in visits that lasted on the average of 2 hours each. Data were collected in the form of field notes, audiotapes, and videotapes." (p. 501)	Latina Researcher; Reflexivity section is not included: "The school's permission was obtained since the selection of the children was through the classroom. This quasi-official affiliation gave me a status that facilitated the families' acceptance of the study and agreement to participate. Trust between the researcher and the families was established within the first or second visit" (p. 502)

(*Continued*)

Cases	Research Question / Purpose	Participants	Definition of Family	Geographical Context	Research Design / Methodology	Reflexivity
		children succeed in school. Although their children were born in the United States, the parents had all emigrated from Mexico." (p. 500)	which is shared with another family" (p. 500) Families are connected across generations through culture, history, and language. Families in the present are linked through networks of mutuality and sharing. "Families in the study had relatives who lived nearby and their social life revolved around the extended family" (p. 504)	31%, Asians 1%, Blacks .5%, and others including American Indians, .55%.7" Agriculture and other low-paying jobs in the tourist industry drew population to settle in the area." (p. 499)		
4. **Li (2003)**	"Making the social realities of these children known to educators is the central theme of this article. My purpose is twofold. First, by providing an anthropological picture of one struggling Chinese Canadian	The Liu's family includes: Peter and Kathy (parents who immigrated from China to Canada in the 1970's); Erin (14), Gina (16), Fay (15), and Daniel (8). All of the children were born in Canada and are second generation Chinese Canadians.	Intergenerational list of the nuclear family includes children and adolescents. The findings, however, include members of their extended family – an uncle who owns a video store and takes in Gina who is struggling in school with English. We learn that Daniel was	Major city in Canada: The city the Lius resided in had a Chinese population of 4,000, comprising only 1.8% of the city's total population. The majority of the population	Data were collected over the course of 2 months; mainly in the family's business and in their home through observations recorded in fieldnotes, informal interviews, and document collection. Li used ethnographic methods to study the "family's home literacy practices" (p. 186) "During the visits to the family restaurant and home, my role as ethnographer varied from site to site; the types and intensity of participation with the family	Li (2003) positions herself using the classic 'insider-outsider' positionality. Li, herself is a Chinese immigrant who came to Canada in 1996 to work on her PhD. The Liu family are also Chinese immigrants who came to Canada for work opportunities. Li uses the metaphor of "researcher as advocate" (p. 187) She writes, "[c]oming from this

family, the Liu Family, I examine how different socioeconomic, linguistic, cultural, and political factors of cross-cultural living have contributed to their difficulties with schooling. Second, by unraveling the social realities of the Liu family, I aim to debunk the destructive myth of the 'model minority'" (p. 183)

They speak a combination of Chinese and English at home. The parents speak mainly Chinese and while they would like to learn English; their work schedule prohibits them from learning English. They place a high value on their children attending school, working hard, and learning English. The family lives in a neighborhood that is mainly Aborigine families and many of the residents live in poverty. The school the children attend was established in the 1980s by a provincial board of Education for Aboriginal children considered at-risk.

taken care of by his grandmother during a time when the parents were building their business.

were European Canadians and Aboriginal people (the latter represented 11.8% of the city's population and were primarily Indian and Metis; Statistics Canada 1996). Together with their extended family, the Liu family emigrated to Canada in 1978 from Canton, China.

members also varied greatly in different contexts....In the family home, I used a more direct observation method with children in their familiar settings....These observations entailed sustained involvement with [the children]... In other contexts I assumed a participant observer role and mingled with the children and the family as if I were one of them" (p. 186)

"I collected documents such as school newsletters, letters from the community, and menus. I wrote field notes and reflective notes after leaving the research setting" (p. 186)

critical perspective, my role as an ethnographer in this research has also taken on new meaning in that I was not just a researcher who was gathering information, but also an advocate for the children and family who were silenced within the discourse of power" (p. 187)

"I am an immigrant from China who came to Canada to pursue a PhD. in education in 1996. My cross-cultural background provided a unique position in this research. I was an insider in certain ways, but an outsider in others. My language and nationality created a common bond between my participating family and myself – I was one of them, an insider. However, as a researcher from a higher educational institution where the Liu family aspired their children to be, I was an outsider. In this sense, I functioned as a 'border crosser' of the boundaries of literacy, culture, and social

(Continued)

Cases	Research Question / Purpose	Participants	Definition of Family	Geographical Context	Research Design / Methodology	Reflexivity
		Interestingly, the Liu children may be considered "marginalized minorities" within this school community, in part, because of their developing control of English literacy and also because of the complex intersection of cultural exclusion, lack of opportunities for upward social mobility, and (unnamed) linguicism that the children and parents face at the school.				class. My experiences in China and Canada have influenced how I view literacy in the family. I look at the social reality of the Liu family as constructed through the uses of literacy within the sociocultural contexts of their home and their restaurant. Furthermore, I am able to look critically at the 'blaming the victim' approach, and focus not only on the responsibilities of the minority family, but more importantly, on the responsibilities of the schools and society that have marginalized the children and their families" (p. 187)
5. **Gonzalez et al. (1995)**	"We are particularly interested in how families develop social networks that interconnect them with their environments (most importantly with other households) and	Four teachers (two White and two Mexican-American). Each teacher recruited 3–4 families from their classes to participate in the study.	Families are extended and intergenerational within one household "I learned that the family was quite extensive. I met the middle school age son, two high school age daughters, a maternal	All of the schools are located within working-class predominantly Mexican neighborhoods in the Tucson, Arizona area.	In this article, we hear about the four teachers who were recruited (two White and two Mexican-American) and their household visits which were ethnographic in nature, their reflections in the study group "1", and four short case studies of parents with whom they learned about their household's funds of knowledge.	I do not think the main researcher/first author (Norman Gonzalez) revealed her background and positionality in the article. However, reflexivity is discussed a great deal as part of the inquiry process the teachers engaged in with the families. "The reflexive process involved in transcription

how these social relationships facilitate the development and exchange of resources, including the funds of knowledge" (p. 447)

grandfather, and a maternal uncle, all of whom shared the same household" (p. 459)

"Viewing households within a processual view of culture, rooted in the lived contexts and practices of their students and families, engendered a realization that culture is a dynamic concept, and not a static grab bag ..." (p. 456)

"Ethnography surfaced as more than techniques. It became the filter through which the households were conceptualized as multidimensional and vibrant entities" (p. 451)

The teachers used specific techniques such as "participant-observation, fieldnote writing, interviewing, and eliciting of life histories" (p. 451). They also interviewed the children in the household.

The households (2–3 from each teachers' classroom) were visited three times and the interviews lasted for an average of 2 hours each.

enabled the teachers to obtain elusive insights that could easily be overlooked. As they replayed the audiotapes and referred to notes, connections, and hunches began to emerge. The household began to take on a multidimensional reality that had taken root in the interview and reached its fruition in reflexive writing" (p. 454)

INDEX

academic databases, emergence of
188–190
Academic OneFile 209
Academic Search 103, 128, 189, 210
Academic Search Complete 37, 209
Academic Search Premier 209
Ackerman, J. M. 97
Adult Education Quarterly 57, 60
AEI *see* Australian Education Index (AEI)
African Journals Online (AJOL) 189, 210
Ahmed, S. 2
AJOL *see* African Journals Online (AJOL)
Al Ghanem, R. 30
Allington, R. L. 196
Al Manhal 210
Amanti, C. 171
Amazon 35, 103, 128
American Educational Research
Conference 113
analytical review template (ART) 20, 80,
84, 86, 90, 105, 106, 155–157, 160,
172, 181, 205–207; for integrative
critical literature reviews 108,
111–113, 238–239; inter-rater
reliability check 240–242; for
metasynthesis of family literacy
scholarship by BIPOC scholars
251–256
analytic memo 88
Annegarn-Gläß, M. 185
*Annotated Bibliography of Research in the
Teaching of English* 189

Anthropology and Education Quarterly 57
arguments with literature, making
63–66
ArticleFirst 80, 210
Art Index 210
ART *see* analytical review template
(ART)
Asad, T. 125
Asia Pacific Education 81
AT-EMP 84
Australian Educational Researcher 81
Australian Education Index (AEI)
189, 211
AUSTROM 211

Ba, H. 69
Bacon, C. K. 32–33
Baluch, A. 172
Bang, M. 151
Barroso, J. 5, 10, 32, 146, 203
Beach, R. 31, 97
Beck, C. T. 11, 146
Beck, I. L. 96
Becoming a Nation of Readers (BNR)
195, 196
Beile, P. 52
Beman, S. B. 187
Best Evidence Encyclopedia 212
Biancarosa, G. 98
bibliometrics 190–194; limits of 193–194;
mapping 191–193
Biological Abstracts 212

BIPOC (Black, Indigenous, People of Color) scholars 180, 181, 198; metasynthesis of scholarship by 144–173; analytical review template 251–256; counter-story, inviting 151–155; critical metasynthesis, designing 147; decolonizing 170–172; extracting and synthesizing findings 156–159; highly cited BIPOC scholars 148–150; limits of 172–173; possibilities of 172–173; publication 167–170; reading as a reviewer 155–156; reflections of 172–173; searching 147–148; synthesis representation 159–167

Blommaert, J. 82

BNR *see Becoming a Nation of Readers* (BNR)

bodies of scholarship, curating 177–183

Bomer, R. 98

Boote, D. 52

Bourdieu, P. 179

Braddock, R. 186

Brady, R. B. 99

Brantlinger, E. 96

Breed, F. 28

Brief History of Time: From the Big Bang to Black Holes, A (Hawking) 184

British Educational Research Journal 19

British Education Index 211

Brown, D. 186

Bruch, A. 185

Bulcaen, C. 82

Burnett, C. 30

Bus, A. G. 40

CADAAD *see* Critical Approaches to Discourse Analysis Across the Disciplines (CADAAD)

Carlisle, J. F. 97

Cazden, C. 64

CDA *see* critical discourse analysis (CDA)

CDS *see* Critical Discourse Studies (CDS)

CHAT theorists 145

Christie, J. 36, 96

citation coding scheme 106–107, 128

citation counting analysis 3, 108–110, 129, 145, 148, 181

CITE-ITEL 27, 40, 176, 182, 189, 212

CitNetExplorer 190

Cochrane Library, The 224

code book: from 2005 literature review 227–228; from 2016 literature review 229–231

coding 82–85; chart for spreadsheet 232–235

Comber, B. 36

ComDisDome 213

Commeyras, M. 97

Common Core State Standards 196

communicating with audiences 40

Comprehensive Dissertation Index 213

comprehensive edited volumes: analysis of 107; review of 111

Compton-Lilly, C. 84, 98, 100, 106

conceptual literature reviews 2, 201

conceptual mapping reviews 58, 59, 186

control groups 5, 148, 195

Cooper, H. M. 55–56, 148

counter-story, inviting 151–155

Creswell, J. W. 52, 55

Critical Approaches to Discourse Analysis Across the Disciplines (CADAAD) 75, 78

critical discourse analysis (CDA) 75, 77–83, 87, 90–92, 179

Critical Discourse Studies (CDS) 90

critical literacy research 190, 191

critical meta-ethnography 127

critical metasynthesis, designing 147

critical reviews 2

Critique of Anthropology 78

cross-case analytic process 39

C2-SPECTR 212

Cummings, K. D. 98

Cunningham Library, Australian Council for Educational Research 189

Current Contents on Disc 213

Daley, B. J. 187

Darwin, C. 184

data dumping 54

Dearborn, W. F. 19

decolonizing 182–183, 185; integrative critical literature reviews 116–117; meta-ethnography 141; metasynthesis by BIPOC scholars 170–172; traditional literature reviews 92

Delgado-Gaitan, C. 136, 141, 162–167, 259–260

DF-TCHED 84

dialectical interrogation 172, 187

Dickinson, D. K. 98, 201

digital literacy 26, 52, 53, 56–60, 62, 64, 66–69, 92, 145

266 Index

DiPardo, A. 95
Discourse Analysis Working
 Conference 113
Discourse & Society (Discurso & Sociedad)
 78, 81
disruptive interrogation 172
Dissertation Abstracts 214
Dissertation Abstracts International
 (currently ProQuest Dissertations and
 Theses database) 35, 37, 60, 103, 128,
 189, 190, 214
dissertation literature reviews 1, 7–8, 77,
 201; writing 51–70
distributing research syntheses 185
Docherty, S. 15
Dole, J. A. 40
Dorsey-Gaines, C. 126
Doyle, L. 128, 131, 138, 142
Dunlosky, J. 188
Dunsmore, K. 97, 111
Durst, R. K. 96
Dyson, A. H. 19

EBSCO 35, 37, 190
EconLit 214
Educational Abstracts 214
Educational Researcher 19
Education Full Text 103, 128, 189
Education Research Complete 214
Edwards, P. A. 136, 139, 141
Eisenhart, M. 30, 76–77, 125, 134
Elbow, P 68
Elementary School Journal 20
Emden, C. 15
ending a search: integrative
 critical literature reviews
 103–105; meta-ethnography
 128–130; traditional literature
 reviews 82
EndNote 60
epistemological orientation, identification
 of 33–34
ERIC (the *Educational Resources
 Information Center*, later the *Educational
 Research Information Center*) 37, 60, 80,
 176, 189, 215
Erickson, F 95
ESOL 80, 107
ESRC (ESRC Data Service, ESRD Data
 Store) 215
European Conference on Educational
 Research 113
Expanded Academic ASAP 215

Fabos, B. 62, 96
Fairclough, N. 92
family literacy 2, 6, 12, 31, 32, 34, 39, 53,
 56–60, 62, 64–69, 180, 181, 183, 198;
 citation counting analysis of 109;
 comprehensive edited volumes 107,
 111; included and rejected studies 105;
 integrative critical literature reviews 92,
 94, 99–102; meta-ethnography of 100,
 121, 122, 127–129, 134, 136–138, 141,
 142; metasyntheses of, by BIPOC
 scholars 145–173; primary studies of
 103–104; scholarship 103, 105, 108,
 109, 114–117, 121, 128; selection/
 rejection criteria 104
Feng, L. 187
Finfgeld-Connett, D. 62
Fisher, D. 111
Fisher, R. 4
Flores, T. T. 98, 156–157, 160–161
follow up review 77–80, 84, 87, 89,
 90, 177
Fowler-Amato, M. 99
Freedman, S. W. 95
Fuchs, E. 185
Fuente Académica 189, 216
Fuller, S. 64

Gadsden, V. L. 57, 61, 65, 67, 161–166,
 169, 259
Garan, E. M. 195–196
Gavelek, J. R. 97
Gee, J. 82, 92
generalizability 5–6, 19, 100, 125, 202
Genishi, C. 15
Gersten, R. 36, 40
Glass, G.V 18
Glesne, C. 52
González, N. 162–167, 171, 262–263
Google 60
Google Scholar 35, 37, 60, 102, 148–149,
 189, 216
Graduate Student Literacy Forum 62
Grant, C. A. 27
Graue, E. 27
Gray, W. S. 20, 25
Greene, S. 97
Green, J. 82
grounded formal theory 11, 201–202

Hadley, E. B. 98, 201
Hagerman, M. A. 152
Hammarfelt, B. 194

Handbook of Early Childhood Literacy 114
Handbooks of Reading Research 27
Handsfield, L. J. 27
Hare, R. D. 9, 10, 32, 100, 202
Hart, C. 3, 51, 55, 68, 82, 180
Harvard Educational Review 20
Hattie, J. A. C. 188
Hawking, S. 183
Heath, S. B. 106, 132, 133, 136, 137, 139
Hendrickson, J. S. 112
historical reviews 185–186
Hodges, T. S. 187
Hoffman, J.V. 99
Hoon, C. 147, 172, 173
Huey, E. B. 19
Hughes, S. 123, 135

identity studies 124
IMed 62
IMing 62
inclusive search 81
Indiana University 189
InfoTrac 216
Ingenta 217
inquiry team establishment 99–100
Institute of Education Sciences 176
integrative critical literature reviews 1, 2,
    8–9, 31, 94–117, 202; analytical review
    template analysis 108, 111–113,
    238–239; citation coding scheme
    106–107; citation counting analysis
    108–110; comprehensive edited
    volumes, analysis of 107;
    comprehensive edited volumes, review
    of 111; decolonizing 116–117;
    designing 100–103; early attempt at
    analysis 106; ending of search
    103–105; family literacy scholarship,
    searching and sampling 103; included
    and rejected studies 105; inquiry team
    establishment 99–100; limits of 117;
    literacy-related 95–99; possibilities of
    117; primary studies, locating
    103–105; publishing 113–116;
    purpose identification 99–100;
    reading as a reviewer 105–108;
    reflections of 117; response letter to
    editors 243–245; selection/rejection
    criteria 104; synthesis representation
    108–113
intergenerational literacy 57, 64–65
internal validity 5, 148
International Bibliography 80

International Political Science
    Abstracts 217
International Reading Association (now
    the International Literacy Association)
    20, 26, 189
international reviews 187
interpretive research synthesists 34
Inyega, H. N. 97

Jensen, L. 2, 146
Johnson, E. D. 62
journal editors 27, 40, 179
*Journal of Academy of Business and
    Economics* 57
Journal of Adolescent and Adult Literacy
    60, 187
*Journal of American Academy of Child and
    Adolescent Psychiatry* 57
Journal of Attention Disorders 57
*Journal of Educational Media, Memory,
    and Society* 185
Journal of Educational Research 20, 25
Journal of Literacy Research 20, 27, 60, 182
JSTOR: The Scholarly Journal Archive 7,
    60, 103, 105, 128, 189, 218
Juzwik, M. M. 98

Kalman, J. 159
Kearney, M. H. 2, 146
Kearns, D. M. 30
Kress, G. 92
Kucan, L. 96
Kucirkova, N. 98
Kuo, L. J. 187
Kyriacou, C. 187

Lammert, C. 98
Lancet Countdown, The 12
Land, C. L. 98
Language Arts 27, 60, 114, 182
Language in Society 81
LeeKeenan, K. 99
Lewis, C. 62
Lewis, T. 84, 98
Lexis Nexis Academic 37
Li, G. 132, 133, 141, 151, 161–166,
    260–262
Light, R. J. 5
Linguistics and Education 81, 139
Linguistics and Language Behavior
    Abstracts 218
Lipson, M.Y. 95

268 Index

literacy-related literature reviews 28–33; integrative critical 95–99
Literacy Research Association 27, 113
Literacy Research: Theory, Method, and Practice (formerly the NRC/LRA yearbook) 27
literature reviews 2; characteristics of 55–56; conceptual 2; decolonizing 92; definition of 51–70; dissertation 1, 7–8, 51–70; integrative 1, 2, 8–9, 31, 94–117; literacy-related 28–33; matrix 61; misconceptions about 53–56; thinking about 56–59; traditional 1, 6, 8, 15, 30, 57, 75–92, 204
literature search 59–62
Liu, Q. 186
Luke, A. 82
Luke, C. 152
Lysaker, J. T. 27

MacFarlane, L. 122, 123
Major, C. H. 4, 122
mapping analyses 2
Marin, A. 151
Marsh, E. J. 132, 133, 188
McCormick, J. 11–12, 146–147
McTigue, E. 187
McVee, M. B. 97
MEDline 219
Merriam, S. B. 52
meta-analyses 2, 127, 202; quantitative 5
meta-autoethnography 123–124
meta-ethnography 2, 9–10, 17, 31–32, 39, 121–142, 145; analytical review template for 205–207; critical 127; decolonizing 141; definition of 122; ending of search 128–130; family literacy scholarship, searching 128; limits of 138–139, 141–142; possibilities of 138–139, 141–142; publication of 139–141; reading as a reviewer 130–134; reflections of 138–139, 141–142; research, locating 128–130; response letter to editors 246–250; synthesis representation 134–137; team effort for 125–127
Meta-Ethnography: Synthesizing Qualitative Studies (Noblit and Hare) 127
metastudy 11, 202
metasyntheses 2, 5, 17, 202; definition of 145; goal of 178; qualitative 10–12, 32–33, 145–147, 203; of scholarship by BIPOC scholars 144–173

methodological syntheses 186–187
Mills, K. A. 36
misconceptions about literature reviews 53–56
MLA *see* Modern Language Association (MLA)
Modern Language Association (MLA) 80; International Bibliography 219
Möller, J. 30
Moll, L. C. 116, 130, 132, 133, 148, 162–165, 167, 171, 258
Morgan, S. 187
Mosenthal, P. 95
Multiliteracies (New London Group) 59

narrative review 203
Nash, B. L. 99
Nathan, M. J. 188
National Academy of Education 195
National Center for Family Literacy (NCFL) 60
National Council for the Teaching of English (NCTE) 189
National Reading Panel Report (2000) 27–28, 195, 197
NCFL *see* National Center for Family Literacy (NCFL)
NCTE *see* National Council for the Teaching of English (NCTE)
Neff, D. 171
Newell, G. E. 31, 96, 97
New Literacy Studies (NLS) 36, 58, 65
new research topic 56–59
NLS *see* New Literacy Studies (NLS)
Noblit, G. W. 2, 9, 10, 32, 100, 123, 124, 127, 128, 130, 135, 138, 139, 146, 202
No Child Left Behind 196
Norris, J. M. 15, 17, 18

Omolewa, M. 187
On the Origin of Species by Means of Natural Selection (Darwin) 184
Ortega, L. 15, 17, 18

Pahl, K. 132, 133, 135, 136
participatory research synthesists 34–35
Patton, M. Q. 52
peer-reviewed research syntheses 26–28
Petchauer, E. 97
Ph.D. Dissertation Handbook 68–69
Physiology and Psychology of Reading, The 25
Pielstick, C. D. 122, 123

Pillemer, D. B. 5
politics, and research syntheses 194–197
Prendergast, C. 151
primary studies: analysis/evaluation of 39,
85–87, 180; distilling evidence from
39; interpretation of 39; locating
103–105; sampling of 82; summarizing
180–181
Professional Development Collection 220
Project MUSE 220
ProQuest Research Library 220
PsycARTICLES 220
PsycCRITIQUES 220
Psychiatric News 57
PsychLIT 221
Psychological Abstracts 221
Psychology & Behavioral Sciences
Collection 221
PsycINFO 37, 80, 221
PubMed 222
Purcell-Gates, V. 126, 130, 132, 133, 139
purpose identification 34–35, 77–78;
integrative critical literature reviews
99–100; traditional literature reviews
77–78, 91–92

qualitative metasummaries 2, 203
qualitative metasyntheses 10–12, 32–33,
145–147, 203
qualitative research integration 11, 203
qualitative research syntheses 2, 3, 5;
designs 201–204; in literacy
studies: brief history of 19–28;
surveying 15–40; role in academic
fields 12
quantitative meta-analyses 5
quantitative research syntheses 3, 21–24
Quantz, J. O. 19

Race to the Top 196
Randolph, J. J. 8
Rawson, K. A. 188
reading as a reviewer: integrative critical
literature reviews 105–108; meta-
ethnography 130–134; metasynthesis by
BIPOC scholars 155–156; traditional
literature reviews 82–85
Reading First 196
Reading Recovery© 100
Reading Research Quarterly (RRQ) 20, 25,
60, 113, 114, 116, 121, 136, 140
Reading Teacher, The 20, 25
Reading Today 104

*Reclaiming Powerful Literacies: New Horizons
for Critical Discourse Analysis* 91
recursive processes, in writing dissertation
literature reviews 68–69
Redalyc 92, 190, 223
Reed, D. K. 98
reflexivity 4, 179
relevant literature, searching for 35
replicability 5, 28, 80, 148
researcher questions 83
Research in the Teaching of English (RTE) 20,
60, 189
research, locating: meta-ethnography
128–130; traditional literature
reviews 82
research syntheses 76, 203–204;
contribution of 17–19; designing 177,
184; general process for conducting
33–35; history of 5–6; peer-reviewed
26–28; politics and 194–197;
representing and distributing 181;
scholarship 15, 25, 52; scope of 5–6;
systematic 15; technology and
188–194; types of 1–3, 6–12; use of 40;
vast range of 183–188; writing 3; *see
also individual entries*
response letter to editors 236–237; for
critical integrative literature review
243–245; for meta-ethnography
246–250
response letter to reviewers 236–237
review designs 16, 17, 34, 79–80, 121,
129, 198
reviewing team, assembling 79–80
Review of Educational Research 8, 19, 20, 27,
52, 75, 79
Review of Research in Education 20
reviews designed to inform practice 188
Rice, E. H. 122, 123
Ridley, D. 7–8
Risko, V. 30
Robinson, H. M. 25
Rodney, P. 11, 146
Rogers, R. 8, 39, 84, 98
Rose Report 196
Roskos, K. 30, 36, 96
RRQ see Reading Research Quarterly (RRQ)
RTE *see Research in the Teaching of English*
(RTE)
Rubin, J. C. 98

SAGE 222
Samnani, S. S. 2

270 Index

sampling 31, 32, 34, 80–2, 89, 128, 141, 144, 158–159, 185; of collaborative analysis 126; family literacy scholarship 103; of grounded code definitions 160–161; memos 136–137; of metaphors 131, 134; of primary studies 82; scholarship 179–180; size of 5, 148; of sorted code definitions 162–165
Sandelowski, M. 2, 5, 10, 11, 15, 32, 146, 203
Sarroub, L. K. 160
saturation 54
Savin-Baden, J. 122, 123
Savin-Baden, M. 4, 122, 123, 127
Scammacca, N. K. 36
Schaffner, E. 30
Schaper, A. 98
Schiefele, U. 30
SciELO 92, 190
Science Direct 223
scoping reviews 2, 204
Scopus 37, 190, 191, 193
search(ing) 185; bias, overcoming 38–39; channels 36–38; database 36–38; memo 80, 81; scholarship 179–180; terms 35–40
Shanahan, T. 2, 28, 52
SIGLE 223
60th Yearbook of the Literacy Research Association 114
Smagorinsky, P. 64, 96
Smith, J. 31, 97
Social Sciences Citation Index, The (SSCI) 223
Sociological Abstracts 223
Sociology of Reading, The 25
South African Linguistics 84
Sperling, M. 96
SSCI *see* Social Sciences Citation Index, The (SSCI)
statistical research syntheses 2
Sulzby, E. 126
summarizing 54, 66–8, 180–181
Summary of Investigations Relating to Reading/Summary of Reading Investigations 20, 25–26, 189
Summers, E. G. 188–189
Summon 37
Sunday School 194
Suri, H. 1, 2, 18, 32–35, 38, 89, 91, 99, 124–125, 136, 155, 204
Swartz, D. 179

synthesis representation 185; BIPOC scholar 159–167; integrative critical literature reviews 108–113; meta-ethnography 134–137; traditional literature reviews 87–89
synthesists, as reflexive researchers 4
synthesizing 54, 66–68, 185; *see also* research syntheses; *individual entries*
systematic research syntheses 15
systematic reviews 2, 7–8, 204

Taylor, D. 126, 131–134
Teachers College Record 20, 182
Teaching Children to Read [the NRP report], 196
Teaching of Reading 25
Teale, W. H. 126
technology, and research syntheses 188–194
tertiary review 2
theoretical reviews 187
Theses A&I 224
Theses Full Text 224
Theses Global 224
Thompson, P. 132, 133
Thorne, S. 2, 10, 146, 203
timeframe of search 36
Toulmin, S. 63
traditional literature reviews 1, 6, 8, 15, 30, 57, 75–92, 94, 204; analysis of primary studies 85–87; audience 91–92; decolonizing literature reviews 92; ending of search 82; limits of 90–91; possibilities of 90–91; purpose identification 77–78; purposes of 91–92; reading, as a reviewer 82–85; reflections of 90–91; research, locating 82; review, designing 79–80; reviewing team, assembling 79–80; sampling of primary studies 82; searching and sampling 80–82; synthesis representation 87–89; uptake of 91–92
Turin, T. C. 2

Understanding Family Literacy: Conceptual Issues Facing the Field (Gadsden) 57
University of Cape Town 37
U.S. Department of Education 189

VanDerHeide, J. 31, 97
van Dijk, T. 92

Index **271**

Van Dike, L. M. 98
Varcoe, C. 11, 146
Vaska, M. 2
Vlach, S. K. 98
VOSViewer 190, 191, 193, 194
Vukelich, C. 30
Vygotsky, L. S. 64

Wade, S. E. 30
Wallin, J. A. 193–194
Warrington, A. 99
Wasik, B. H. 112
Web of Science 37, 80, 190, 217, 224
Weintraub, S. 25
Wetzel, M. 99
Wigfield, A. 30
Wiley InterScience (replaced by Wiley
    Online Library) 225
Willingham, D. T. 188
Wilson Select Plus 225

Wilson's Omni File (OmniFile Full Text
    Mega, or OmniFile Full Text Select)
    225
Winddance Twine, F. W. 152
Wixson, K. K. 95
Wolcott, H. F. 52, 67
WorldCat 226
writing dissertation literature reviews
    51–70; arguments with literature, making
    63–66; literature search 59–62;
    misconceptions about literature reviews
    53–56; new research topic 56–59;
    questions/recommendations 70; recursive
    processes in 68–69; summarizing *versus*
    synthesizing literature 66–68
Written Communication 20

Young, M. D. 96

Zimmer, M. 193

Printed in the United States
by Baker & Taylor Publisher Services